Women's Movements

Written by leading women's movement scholars, this book is the first systematically to apply the idea of social movement abeyance to differing national and international contexts. Its starting point is the idea that the women's movement is over, an idea promoted in the media and encouraged by scholarship that regards disruptive action as a defining element of social movements. It goes on to compare the trajectories over the past 40 years of women's movements in Australia, Canada, Japan, Korea, New Zealand, the United Kingdom and the United States. Finally, it looks at the extension of feminist activism into supranational and subnational institutions – the global and the local – and into cyberspace.

Comparing these diverse sites of political and social action illuminates some of the major opportunities and constraints affecting women's movements. It advances our understanding of the lifecycles of social movements by examining the differing ways in which women's movements operate and sustain themselves over time and space, ways that often differ from those of male-led movements. The book also engages with the question of whether there is an on-going women's movement – with sufficient continuity to warrant description as such – by presenting the voices of young activists East and West.

Filling an important gap in social movement research, this book will be of interest to sociologists, political scientists and gender studies scholars and researchers.

Sandra Grey is a Lecturer in Social Policy at Victoria University of Wellington, New Zealand. **Marian Sawer** is an Adjunct Professor in the School of Social Sciences, Australian National University, Australia.

Routledge research in comparative politics

Women's Movements

Flourishing or in abeyance?

**Edited by Sandra Grey and
Marian Sawer**

Routledge
Taylor & Francis Group

LONDON AND NEW YORK

First published 2008
by Routledge
2 Park Square, Milton Park, Abingdon, Oxofordshire OX14 4RN

Simultaneously published in the USA and Canada
by Routledge
270 Madison Ave, New York, NY 10016

Routledge is an imprint of the Taylor & Francis Group, an informa business

First issued in paperback 2010

Typeset in Times by Wearset Ltd, Boldon, Tyne and Wear

British Library Cataloguing in Publication Data
A catalogue record for this book is available from the British Library

Library of Congress Cataloging in Publication Data
Women's movements: flourishing or in abeyance?/edited by Sandra Grey
and Marian Sawer.
p. cm. – (Routledge research in comparative politics; 22)
Includes bibliographical references and index.
ISBN 978-0-415-46245-7 (hardback: alk. paper) – ISBN 978-0-203-
92739-7 (e-book: alk. paper) 1. Feminism–Cross-cultural studies. 2.
Women–Social conditions–21st century. I. Grey, Sandra. II. Sawer,
Marian. III. Title. IV. Series.
HQ1155.W68 2008
305.4209′051–dc22
2007046788

ISBN13: 978-0-415-46245-7 (hbk)
ISBN13: 978-0-415-66413-4 (pbk)
ISBN13: 978-0-203-92739-7 (ebk)

Contents

Contributors

Caroline Andrew is Professor of Political Studies and Director of the Centre on Governance at the University of Ottawa. She is co-author with Margaret Shaw of 'Engendering crime prevention: International developments and the Canadian experience' (*Canadian Journal of Criminology and Criminal Justice*, 2005) and with Fran Klodawsky of 'New voices: New politics' (*Women and Environments*, 2006). Her recent research interests are on the governance of diversity in Canadian cities and on the role of cities in immigration policies.

Joyce Gelb is Professor of Political Science at City College and the Graduate Center, City University of NY. She is Director of the Women's Studies Program at City College. She is author of *Feminism and Politics: A Comparative Perspective* (1989) and co-author with Marian Palley of *Women and Public Policies: Reassessing Gender Politics* (1987; 1996), and *Women of Japan and Korea* (1994). Her most recent book, *Gender Policies in Japan and the United States: Comparing Women's Movements, Rights and Politics* was published in 2003.

Gwendolyn Gray is an Adjunct Senior Lecturer in the School of Social Sciences, Australian National University. She is author of *The Politics of Medicare* (2004) and of a number of articles and book chapters on women's health and the politics of women's issues, including 'Women, federalism and women friendly policies' (*Australian Journal of Public Administration*, 2006). She is currently working on a book on the politics of women's health policy in Australia, which will be set in comparative perspective.

Sandra Grey is a Lecturer in Social Policy at Victoria University of Wellington. Her recent work has looked both at substantive representation of women in the New Zealand parliament and women's movements in Australasia. Publications include: 'New Zealand: The myth of egalitarianism' with Judith Davey (*International Social Policy*, forthcoming); 'Numbers and beyond: The relevance of critical mass in gender research' (*Politics & Gender*, 2006); and 'The 'new world'? Women and political representation in New Zealand' (*Representing Women in Parliament*, 2006). She is currently working on a comparative project examining activism by the New Zealand women's, union, and anti-poverty movements.

Kyungja Jung is Lecturer in the Social Inquiry Program at the University of Technology, Sydney. She has been conducting research on violence against women, North Korean women, sex trafficking, women's policy in South Korea and Australia and feminist activism in Australia and elsewhere. She has a PhD in Women's Studies and Social Policy from the University of New South Wales. As an activist, she founded the first rape crisis centre in South Korea in 1991 and worked for the Immigrant Women's Speakout Association of NSW.

Mona Lena Krook is Assistant Professor of Political Science and Women and Gender Studies at Washington University in St. Louis. Her research focuses on the adoption, implementation, and impact of candidate gender quotas worldwide. Recent publications appear in *Political Studies*, the *European Journal of Political Research*, and *Politics & Gender*. She is co-founder with Fiona Mackay of the Feminism and Institutionalism International Network, and co-editor with Sarah Childs of *Women, Gender, and Politics: A Reader* (Oxford University Press, forthcoming).

Fiona Mackay is Senior Lecturer in Politics at the University of Edinburgh. She is co-author of *Women, Politics and Constitutional Change* (2007), author of *Love and Politics: Women Politicians and the Ethics of Care* (2001), and co-editor of *The Changing Politics of Gender Equality in Britain* (2002), and *Women and Contemporary Scottish Politics* (2001). Current research interests include gender and constitutional change in the UK, and feminist institutionalist theory.

Sarah Maddison is Senior Associate Dean in the Faculty of Arts and Social Sciences at the University of New South Wales. She has published widely on young women and feminist activism and is co-author with Sean Scalmer of *Activist Wisdom* (2006) and co-editor with Clive Hamilton of *Silencing Dissent* (2007). She has also co-authored, with Emma Partridge, the recently published gender and sexuality audit reports for the Democratic Audit of Australia (2007). Her next book, on contemporary Indigenous politics, will be published in 2008.

CJ Rowe is the Policy Analyst/Researcher for the Canadian NGO Womenspace. Over the last nine years CJ has worked with national equality-seeking organisations conducting research, developing policy and lobbying on such issues as same sex marriage, transgender and transsexual human rights, women's access to internet communication technologies (ICTs), and violence against women. CJ holds a Masters of Arts in Legal Studies from Carleton University and has published many articles on violence against women and ICTs.

Marian Sawer is an Adjunct Professor in the School of Social Sciences at the Australian National University, where she leads the Democratic Audit of

Australia. Recent books include *The Ethical State?* (2003), *Us and Them* (co-edited with Barry Hindess, 2004), *Representing Women in Parliament* (co-edited with Manon Tremblay and Linda Trimble, 2006) and *Making Women Count* (forthcoming). From 2008 she will be leading, together with Sarah Maddison, a large project on the evolution of social movements.

Jacqui True is Senior Lecturer in International Relations at the University of Auckland. She is author of *Globalization, Gender and Postsocialism* (2003), a co-author of *Theories of International Relations* (2005), and co-editor with Brooke Ackerly and Maria Stern of *Feminist Methodologies for International Relations* (2006). Her current research examines gender-mainstreaming initiatives at the global level and comparatively in regional trade organisations.

Preface

Verta Taylor and Leila J Rupp

Reflecting on the persistence of women's movements

Since the late 1970s, media commentators and other observers have lamented or
celebrated the decline of feminism and women's movements and the arrival of a
post-feminist age. In the mid-1980s, when we were researching the US women's
rights movement in the 1950s for our book, *Survival in the Doldrums*, declara-
tions of the death of feminism were so prominent that feminist activists and
scholars were consumed by soul searching and debate over whether a vital
women's movement still existed and, if so, what its future might be.[1] The death
knells and obituaries of the 1980s did not make sense to us because we knew
first-hand that feminists were still marching by the hundreds of thousands, fighting for reproductive rights, taking back the night, and setting up battered
women's shelters. Feminists were also mobilising inside institutions, including
universities, the health care system, the military, churches, political parties, and
corporations. And a vibrant feminist oppositional culture was thriving in lesbian
feminist communities in most regions of the United States. It is in this context
that we, as newly minted assistant professors and feminists ourselves, set out to
recover the history of an earlier generation of feminists whose activism, like our
own, had been erased by the media and other public commentators after the
decline of the suffrage movement.

We searched for a metaphor that would capture what we saw happening in
the 1950s, when a small group of elite and aging activists from the suffrage
movement of the first decades of the century maintained their commitment in an
inhospitable environment and made connections with the resurgent movement of
the 1960s and 1970s. We considered 'hibernation', but the women we studied
were not asleep. We thought of 'chrysalis', but they were not protected by a
cocoon. We sought a word that would describe the process by which bulbs store
life and send new shoots through the earth in the spring, but never found one. If
we had known it, we might have gone with 'rhizome', a kind of plant that sends
its roots in all directions so that new shoots emerge far from the original growth.
Barbara Tomlinson,[2] who uses the metaphor to describe feminist arguments,
points out that the new plants that grow from the runners alter in response to the
environment, and, like crabgrass, are hard to eliminate. It is certainly a metaphor

that might describe women's movements as well as feminist arguments. But we ended up with 'doldrums', and then later Verta[3] developed the concept of 'abeyance' to describe the organisational and cultural processes that facilitated social movement survival in a hostile atmosphere.

There is a strong tenor of optimism in the concept of abeyance, even if the kind of women's movement we found during the 1950s was small, insular, and more politically conservative than the feminist movements of the 1960s and 1970s. The concept of abeyance called into question the prevailing view that the US women's movement mobilised through two intense waves of protest and virtually died in the interim. The flames of feminism, it turns out, are not that easy to put out. The abeyance formulation was also an optimistic way of framing a scaled-down period of women's movement activity because the theory assumed that, under the right conditions, feminism could re-emerge out of the doldrums as a movement full of passion, excitement, new ideas, and novel tactics, much like the feminism we had been part of in the 1960s.

The articles in *Women's Movements: Flourishing or in abeyance* report a remarkably similar trajectory of resurgence, retrenchment, transformation, and survival of women's movements in a wide range of developed democracies, including Australia, Canada, Japan, New Zealand, the United Kingdom, South Korea, Scotland, and the United States. In most of the countries (except South Korea, where democratisation occurred much later), women's movements peaked in two cycles of protest, but have persisted since the second wave of feminist protest in the 1970s. The cross-national and comparative approach offered by this collection of articles by leading scholars from around the globe provides a rare opportunity to examine similarities and differences in the way women's movements have developed over time. This allows a greater understanding of how the mobilisation, tactics, collective identities, and successes of women's movements are influenced by political, economic, and cultural opportunity structures at the local, national, and transnational levels.

In three sections, the volume contributes to ongoing conversations about the histories and trajectories of feminist activism, traditional and new spaces and tactics, and intergenerational relationships. Too often we have thought of women's movements in terms of 'white-hot mobilisation', the peaks of participation, success, and visible confrontational protest. The metaphor of 'waves' of the women's movement – generally divided into demands for basic civil rights such as property ownership and suffrage as the first, wide-ranging transformation and mass mobilisation as the second, and embrace of diversity and pleasure as the third – features the cresting waves but ignores the troughs between.

The articles in the first section tackle the question of what happens in the periods we have previously ignored, whether abeyance, institutionalisation and professionalisation, or outright death. Looking comparatively reminds us that no one model will do. As economically advanced democracies, these countries share certain similar characteristics, despite their very different histories. Political contexts, of course, have been critical in shaping women's movements and in facilitating or constraining success in moving towards feminist goals. In Western Europe and the United States, women's movements had the most success in changing policy where the left is either very strong, as in Sweden, or very weak, as in the United States.[4] In India, the domination of the communist party shaped the women's movement in Calcutta into a kind of political party, while political competition in Bombay facilitated more autonomous forms of organising.[5]

As a result of different histories and trajectories, women's movements grew outside the industrialised world precisely when we tend to think of the decline of feminism in the aftermath of the First World War. In places as different as China, Egypt, Cuba and Brazil women's movements took hold, while in the countries where women were newly enfranchised they went into abeyance. Such a comparative perspective raises a different kind of caution about the reliance on a wave model of women's movements, unless we imagine dramatically different nautical conditions in the different seas around the world.

A comparative approach also raises important questions about the 'new spaces' explored in the second section of the book. Once again, the dominance of 'white-hot mobilisation' makes us think of massive demonstrations in the streets and ignore other forms of activism. But the spaces and tactics of the periods between the peaks have often looked quite different. To take just one example, all-women organisations had come to seem old-fashioned and unappealing as the Euroamerican world became increasingly heterosocial in the first decades of the twentieth century. Likewise, where national interests or racial/ethnic solidarity unified women and men engaged in liberation struggles, gender separatism had little appeal. As a result, traditional forms of organising in women's groups declined. This reminds us that we need to look beyond established forms of organising at the national level, that we need to consider both the global and the local, and that cyberspace transcends all kinds of boundaries.

The final section of *Women's Movements* raises questions about our future. To return to our research for *Survival in the Doldrums*, we realised that one of the legacies of the 1960s and 1970s movements was the persistent image of feminists as young and militant. But in fact, in many times and places, and particularly in periods of abeyance, feminists who maintained a commitment to feminism born in an earlier phase grew grey in the process. As one British feminist told another in the mid-1860s, 'You will go up and vote upon crutches, and I shall come out of my grave and vote in my winding sheet'.[6] In this case, she had their fates reversed: her friend was long dead, but she walked to the polls at the age of 88.

As the often tense relations between self-proclaimed 'second wave' and 'third wave' feminists in the United States make clear, intergenerational relations in women's movements are not always smooth.[7] In our work on the 1950s, we found that aging feminists longed fervently for young blood but were ill-equipped to attract young or less elite women to their ranks. One member of the National Woman's Party complained that 'young women today don't want to have anything to do with any project which they think even hints of a "battle of the sexes"'.[8] The same complaints echoed in the transnational women's organisations between the wars. As one member grumbled, 'young people come into the work with the greatest lack of respect for the older people; they think we have made great blunders all these years and have kept the work back'.[9] From the other side, young women resented that too often older women who longed for new hands to lift the torch of feminism insisted that they change nothing about the way the struggle was waged. It is a lesson we older feminists must take to heart.

While carefully avoiding over-generalisation, the articles in this book advance social movement theory by rethinking the definition of social movements and testing existing theories of social movement continuity and life cycles. We realise now that underlying the abeyance model was an implied conceptualisation of what a thriving social movement ought to look like that was derived from the state-centred resource mobilisation and political process approaches that dominated social movement theory in the early 1980s. These approaches conceptually and empirically have tended to be restricted to understanding the role movements play in the political arena. Using the kind of protest event data traditionally used by the political process and contentious politics traditions to assess movement mobilisation, Van Dyke *et al.*[10] demonstrate that a state-centred conception of social movements misses a great deal of social movement activity, even during the 1960s cycle of protest. Analysing all of the protest events that occurred in the United States between 1968 and 1975, it is notable that three of the most influential movements over the past several decades – the women's, civil rights, and gay and lesbian movements – were less likely to direct protest actions at the state than at other institutions.

To understand the shifting organisational forms, tactical repertoires, collective identities, and venues of women's movements requires a broader, less state-centred conceptualisation of power that recognises that gender inequality has multiple sources, both symbolic and material. As the articles in this volume point out, women's movements both historically and in the present, and in many regions of the world, have combined tactics such as consciousness-raising, self-help, and discursive resistance oriented to cultural and social change, with mass demonstrations, civil disobedience, and conventional political actions aimed at bringing about changes in authority systems, both institutional and cultural. Drawing from the insights of new social movement theory,[11] the authors in this volume join other women's movement scholars[12] to argue that gender differences in the repertoires of women's movements require that we conceive of social movements more broadly as targeting not only political venues but also cultural norms, identities, and institutions.

The articles in this volume use this broader conception of social movements to address existing theories of social movement life cycles and continuity. Each of the chapters presents rich and compelling accounts of women's movements in developed democracies, revealing that important transformations have taken place in the scope, venues, and tactical repertoires of women's movements over time. The trajectory of most women's movements has been towards more

institutionalised, unobtrusive, cultural, and discursive collective action repertoires. The articles show that these changes have been the result of internal
movement processes, the transnational diffusion of feminism through civil
society networks, and the shifting political, economic, cultural, and institutional
environments that activists have confronted and targeted for change.

This volume presents rich and compelling evidence that, although social
protest tends to occur in waves, the retreat from protest and policy engagement,
the loss of mass support, and the emphasis on solidarity and feminist culture that
characterises contemporary women's movements in developed democracies is
consistent with predictions of existing theories of social movement cycles and
continuity.[13] The abeyance formulation has been widely used by scholars interested in a range of different movements as a way to understand continuity of
social movement activity between cycles of intense protest. This collection of
articles is the first, however, to use the abeyance concept to examine the state of
women's movements in different countries around the world. *Women's Move-*
ments: Flourishing or in abeyance contributes new theoretical insights by
showing that abeyance can take different forms and that social movements can
use a variety of strategies to nurture and sustain an oppositional collective identity during periods of quiescence. To overlook the more routine, institutionalised, and less public forms of collective action used by women's movements
to make claims and to sustain participants' commitment between peaks of intensive protest risks overlooking the powerful impact that women's movements
have had in shaping modern societies.

Notes

1 Rupp and Taylor, *Survival in the Doldrums: The American Women's Rights Move-*
   ment, 1945 to the 1960s.
2 Barbara Tomlinson (unpublished). 'Grammars of anger'.
3 Taylor, 'Sources of continuity in social movement: The Women's Movement in
   abeyance'.
4 Katzenstein and Mueller, *The Women's Movements of the United States and Western*
   Europe.
5 Ray, *Fields of Protest: Women's Movements in India.*
6 Anderson, *Joyous Greetings: The First International Women's Movement,*
   1830–1860, p. 206.
7 Reger, *Different Wavelengths: Studies of the Contemporary Women's Movement.*
8 Rupp and Taylor, *Survival in the Doldrums: The American Women's Rights Move-*
   ment, 1945 to the 1960s, p. 81.
9 Rupp, *Worlds of Women: The Making of an International Women's Movement,* p. 62.
10 Van Dyke *et al.,* 'The targets of social movements: Beyond a focus on the state'.
11 Melucci, *Challenging Codes: Collective Action in the Information Age.*
12 Staggenborg and Taylor, 'Whatever happened to the Women's Movement?'; Ferree
   and Mueller, 'Feminism and the Women's Movement: A global perspective'.
13 Taylor, 'Sources of continuity in social movement: The Women's Movement in
   abeyance'; Tarrow, *Power in Movement: Social Movements and Contentious Politics.*

Acknowledgements

This book had its origins in a comparative roundtable on women's movements held in association with the International Political Science Association Congress in Fukuoka, Japan, in July 2006. The roundtable was organised by Marian Sawer, as chair of the IPSA Research Committee on Gender, Politics and Policy. The papers were circulated in advance and leading social movement scholars contributed to the discussion, including Sylvia Bashevkin, Drude Dahlerup, Melissa Haussman and Jill Vickers.

When Sandra Grey had the idea of including the voices of young feminists in the final section of the book, those who helped locate activists included Linda Trimble, Kazuko Tanaka and Mary Hawkesworth. Our contributors have themselves played a central role in introducing and developing the concepts employed in the book, and we thank, in particular, Verta Taylor and Leila Rupp for their generous preface.

Catherine Strong's editorial assistance has been invaluable in the preparation of the manuscript – making her an important part of the editorial team. Finally, our editors at Routledge have at all times been helpful in answering our queries and supporting the project. We trust that it will be a worthy addition to their comparative studies list.

Abbreviations

ACT	Australian Capital Territory
APEC	Asia-Pacific Economic Cooperation
AWHN	Australian Women's Health Network
CEDAW	Convention for the Elimination of All forms of Discrimination against Women
CND	Campaign for Nuclear Disarmament
CWHN	Canadian Women's Health Network
EOC	Equal Opportunities Commission
EU	European Union
FCM	Federation of Canadian Municipalities
FDA	Food and Drug Administration
ICC	International Criminal Court
ICT	information and communication technologies
IULA	International Union of Local Authorities
KNCW	Korean National Council of Women
KSVRC	Korea Sexual Violence Relief Center
KWAU	Korean Women's Association United
LWCHC	Leichhardt Women's Community Health Centre
NDP	New Democratic Party
MAdGE	Mothers Against Genetic Engineering
METRAC	Metro Action Committee on Public Violence against Women and Children
MOGE	Ministry of Gender Equality
MSP	Member of the Scottish Parliament
NGO	non-government organisation
NOW	National Organization for Women
NWHP	National Women's Health Policy
OSCE	Organisation for Security and Cooperation in Europe
PFA	Beijing Platform for Action
PPT	political process theory
RCA	Reproductive Choice Australia
SC	Security Council
SCC	Scottish Constitutional Convention

UN	United Nations
UNIFEM	United Nations Development Fund for Women
UNMIK	United Nations Mission in Kosovo
US	United States
WAPC	Women Against Pit Closures
WCGJ	Women's Caucus for Gender Justice
WEL	Women's Electoral Lobby
WICI	Women in Cities International
WISE	Women's Initiatives for a Safer Environment
WSPU	Women's Social and Political Union
YWCA	Young Women's Christian Association

1 Introduction

Marian Sawer and Sandra Grey

The public face of the women's movement across developed democracies has changed profoundly over the past 40 years. The types and levels of activism found today bear only a minor resemblance to the consciousness raising and direct action of the late 1960s and early 1970s. This book explores the trajectories of 'second-wave' women's movements in a range of democracies to understand what has happened to these movements since they were making headlines.

We use the common term 'second-wave' to refer to the upsurge of activism by women in the 1960s and 1970s, while acknowledging that there may have been several waves in the long history of women's activism. Implicit in the wave metaphor is the notion that there has always been and always will be a women's movement, it is just its strength and visibility that varies.[1] Following Drude Dahlerup, we argue that there is sufficient continuity (or connection) between women's movements past and present to view them as part of an ongoing struggle for equality and autonomy.[2]

This was not necessarily how second-wave women's movements saw themselves when they burst upon the scene in the late 1960s. Women's liberation activists were often distancing themselves from the 'polite' methods of their mothers' generation when they adopted and adapted the repertoire of the antiwar and student movements. Consciousness raising and radical collectivism seemed to belong to a different world to the club rooms and deputations of the previous generation of feminist advocates. Continuities between women's movements over the last century are often more evident now, with the flourishing of feminist history, than they were when the second wave first arrived. An important part of this continuity is recognition of the work of earlier feminists, something acknowledged by the 'new voices' in this collection.

While continuities over time may be evident, as the name social movement suggests the subjects of this book are not static. We need to understand how the activism of groups seeking greater autonomy for women changes in terms of repertoires of action and modes of organising. Many of the chapters here review four decades of action by women's movements, enabling us to examine the commonalities and differences in the way movements in seven nations have evolved over time. The comparative case-study approach allows for grounded comparison of the seizing of political opportunities and the nature of discursive strategies, as well as external influences on movement trajectories. Relations with the state shift over this period, as do relations with political actors beyond the state. Political identities also change in response to the new configurations of politics and public discourse.

There have been a number of different approaches to explaining the changes occurring in women's movements. Verta Taylor has developed the concept of abeyance to indicate a shift into a holding pattern;[3] there is also the suggestion that women's movements have shifted into different arenas, for example, from the political to the cultural arena;[4] or that they have disappeared altogether in a 'post-feminist' era[5]. Unlike many scholars who lose interest when movements disappear from the streets, this book tracks the institutionalising of movements through the creation of professionalised or vocational advocacy groups and distinctive forms of service provision, through embedding within state and multilateral institutions, or outside in educational curriculum and the cultural sphere. This means not only examining movements when they are most visible, public and widespread, but also looking at continuing activity and lasting legacies, be they discursive or institutional. And while much focus in feminist and social movement literature is turning to the role of movements in transitional democracies, our authors feel there is still much to learn from examining the trajectories of women's movements in established democracies, particularly when they have been the subject of so many premature epitaphs.

Theorising social movements

The rise of new forms of political action in the 1960s as students and other middle-class radicals took to the streets led to social scientists' increasing interest in non-institutional politics and social mobilisation. Two major bodies of social movement literature emerged, that stemming primarily from Europe that focused on the creation of new collective meanings and identities, and that stemming primarily from North America that focused on resource mobilisation by new collective actors and the opportunity structures that enable this to take place.

Authors in this collection combine insights from both sides of the Atlantic to help understand the ever-changing and highly adaptive women's movements. For example, authors examine the impact of changing political opportunities, including conservative backlashes, on the repertoires of action used by women's movements; they look at the role of cultural activism and unobtrusive mobilisation in maintaining gendered claims; they use both cultural and institutional lenses to explain the trajectories of women's movements; and seek to understand how movements adapt as one of the core resources – members – falls away.

This is not a claim that authors in this collection are bridging the gap between the theories emanating from the United States and Europe, but that they utilise insights from both to examine women's movements. In typical feminist style, the authors pick and choose from the vast theoretical and methodological toolkit provided by social movement and feminist scholarship. But they do so critically.

In particular the authors in this collection are critical of the artificial divide between political process theory (resource mobilisation) and theories that centre on the construction of social meaning.[6] The chapters by Sarah Maddison and Kyunga Jung and by Fiona MacKay use both approaches to evaluate the trajectories of national women's movements. The desire to incorporate both the institutional and cultural lenses of social movement research is also taken into consideration here when defining the characteristics that distinguish social movements from other political and cultural actors. Any discussion of the trajectories and 'death' of women's movements, whether within nation-states or internationally, requires some boundaries to be drawn around the object of research.

The most common (and least contentious) assertion found in literature on mass mobilisations is that a social movement is not a single actor but made up of individuals and groups who are linked by a common identity, a shared set of values, or a collective grievance. A wide variety of actors may be involved, including individuals, groups, networks, and protest committees. These actors are brought together by a common message of, and desire for, social, cultural and political change. Movements introduce new ways of looking at the world[7] and challenge the rationale and operation of existing political and social systems. And while they may be 'relatively unified entities',[8] they are also fluid collectivities that move and change.

More controversial are propositions concerning the modes of operation that set social movements apart from other political actors. In much of the North American literature the primary conceptual difference between participation in traditional political institutions and protest movements is the contentious and disruptive nature of protests.[9] Sidney Tarrow acknowledges that movements engage in a variety of actions, but:

> [T]he most characteristic actions of social movements are collective challenges. This is not because movement leaders are psychologically prone to violence, but because, in seeking to appeal to new constituencies and assert their claim, they lack the stable resources – money, organisation, access to the state – that interest groups and political parties control.[10]

Collective challenges or 'dissent events' have been important for women's movements (as for other social movements) in attracting media attention and getting a message out to a broader public.[11] The demonstration against the Miss America beauty contest in 1968 and the 'freedom trash can' that gave rise to the ever-persistent myth of bra-burning, was one such event. However, disruptive protests are not the primary defining feature of women's movements. The examination of women's movements in Part I suggests that the definition of social movements should rest more on the mobilising of collective identity and the sustaining of challenging discourses than on the use of disruptive repertoires of action. In the case of women's movements the mobilisation of identity has involved both the institutionalising of women-centred discourses and their articulation in everyday life, as well as the more formal process of claims-making.[12]

Existing typologies of social movements, which emphasise the use of mass rallies, 'dissent events' and at times violence, have been based on movements led by men rather than on women's movements. Women's movement activists have used street protests as part of their repertoire of contention, but have also given evidence to inquiries and lobbied political elites. They have created feminist structures within government and other institutions and developed democratically delivered women's services as well as engaging in feminist cultural production and the politics of everyday life. Gender differences in repertoire are rarely noted in the social movement literature. One exception is Dieter Rucht, whose careful study of social movements in West Germany showed that the women's movement had the lowest proportion of protest events of five movements, despite the existence of large numbers of women's groups. His finding was that the women's movement focused on interaction in settings other than the streets and the media.[13]

The preoccupation of social movement research with disruptive protest has meant that relatively little attention is given to the periods in the life of social movements between the peaks of activism. What little research does exist on moments between the waves is often centred on the capacity of the state to accommodate social movement challenges. As has been noted, the women's movements that are central to this book engage in diverse forms of activism in a range of political venues. Even the most institutionally focused chapter, that by Sandra Grey, draws attention to the ways that activists have challenged the status quo through contentious action *and* unconventional organisations.

Women's movements have been distinctive for their creation of 'women-only' spaces in which women-centred perspectives are debated, developed, and maintained. In countries such as Australia, Canada and New Zealand, and even the United Kingdom (UK) up until 1905, the 'first wave' of the women's movement did not engage in disruptive collective action, although it was involved in separate institution-building. These institutions enabled women-centred discourses to develop free of male supervision, but they largely mimicked male institutions in the formality and hierarchy of their structure. This was most definitely the case with the Women's Social and Political Union (WSPU) in the UK, where disruptive action became part of the repertoire from 1905 but the organisational structure was hierarchical if not quasi-military. Nonetheless, few would deny that the WSPU played an important role in mobilising collective political identity. The historic memory of sisterhood and heroic actions that was carefully preserved through subsequent decades became an important resource for the second wave of the women's movement, sometimes in countries far away from the original sites of action.[14]

Unlike these earlier women's movements, recent movements have consciously striven to avoid the disempowering effects of male hierarchies, including those found in supposedly radical movements such as the anti-Vietnam War movement. The emphasis within women's movements was towards more empowering forms of organisation. This did not just mean structurelessness because, as American feminist Jo Freeman has said, structures are inevitable in group life and dominance within informal structures may be just as disempowering as within traditional hierarchies – the 'tyranny of structurelessness'.[15]

There is, however, organisational diversity within women's movements. Alternative women's spaces are not always based on non-hierarchical collectivist structures. To take but one example, rural women's groups may be more likely to adopt traditional hierarchical structures, even for seemingly radical purposes such as organising Reclaim the Night events.[16]

The eclectic approach to social movements represented by the contributors to this book can be summed up by defining movements as *sustained efforts to bring about social change by individuals and groups who share a collective identity developed on the basis of a common opposition to dominant norms, and who may use unconventional tactics and/or forms as part of their mode of operation.* This definition can be further particularised following American political scientist Karen Beckwith: women's movements are those where women mobilise around a collective identity as women, develop women-centred discourses and engage in gendered claims-making.[17] Hence women's movements include women-focused structures and claims-making, regardless of whether the actions involved are 'disruptive' in the sense social movement theorists frequently imply.

The definition is intentionally broad so as to encompass a whole variety of women's collective and individual actions, from organisations seeking political and civil rights for women, to feminist reformers in the interstices of national and transnational institutions, to cultural feminism and liberationist and separatist movements. It provides a base for comparison of movements despite their changing repertoires and modes of operation over the last four decades.

Indeed, diverse modes of organising, from pots and pans protests to parliamentary petitions, have generally been a feature of women's attempts to bring about social and political change. Different modes tend to be salient at different points in the life of movements but will also be found simultaneously. Even at times when 'routine' political activities are dominant, there might also be a cultural intervention such as writing a play to publicise an issue. The evidence of our book confirms the trend in the social movement literature to dethrone disruptive contention as the key defining element of social movements.[18] What is interesting is the timing and the circumstances in which activists have selected a particular repertoire of contention.

Adaptation and change in women's movement activism

Authors in Part I of this collection contest the idea that where there is less overt public policy contestation at the national level women's movements must be over, or at best in abeyance. They show that women's movements have increasingly relied on institutionalised activity from the mid-1970s. As a consequence of the UN Decade for Women (1976–85), as well as domestic pressure, new state agencies were created in many countries, including women's policy and equality agencies. Women's advocacy groups gained access to policy-making processes, often for the first time.

Public funding was also achieved for the women's services pioneered by second-wave women's movements, including women's information services, domestic violence refuges and women's health collectives (see Gwendolyn Gray in this collection). Public funding itself led to demands for more conventional forms of organisational accountability and, despite resistance, there was a drift towards more formal structures. As well as the drift of women's services towards hybrid structures, the shift to neo-liberalism in many countries has placed increasing constraints on women's advocacy. In place of operational grants from government to strengthen the representation of women in policy debate has come the micro-management of contracts to provide specified services tied to state objectives. In order to successfully tender for such contracts, organisations have to become corporatised and are heavily constrained in terms of political advocacy, an issue discussed here by Caroline Andrew, Sandra Grey, and Sarah Maddison and Kyungja Jung.

Although women during the 1970s and 1980s were creating space inside and outside the state for gendered claims-making, and generating state resources and access for once-marginalised groups of women, there was at the same time a decline in street protest and strong grassroots activism. This made it difficult to identify a recognisable 'women's movement', resulting in a loss of interest on the part of media, political parties and governments. It caused an erosion of the political base for interventions within the state and rendered women's policy agencies vulnerable to downgrading and disappearance, a pattern seen particularly clearly in the chapters on the Australasian women's movements.

Another outcome of the decline in 'public' activism examined in Part I is the 'deradicalisation' of the discourse of activists. In order to make themselves heard, activists spoke in the 'language of the day'. The discourse of liberation and the radical critique of patriarchy largely disappeared as policy claims were formulated in the language of equal opportunity. Moreover, activists themselves often disappeared into paid jobs as change agents, jobs often created by their unpaid work as community-based advocates of change. Even at the most pragmatic level, feminist policy advocates lamented the loss of a radical women's movement, which made femocrats sound so 'reasonable' to policy makers.[19]

While admitting the force of these critiques, it is important to acknowledge that women's movements also disappeared off the streets and lost visibility in countries where there were few opportunities for engagement with the state. The direct action phase of women's movements seemed only to last for about five years, regardless of whether feminists were becoming femocrats. Moreover, while those who took positions in government tended to have little time or energy left for extra-curricular activity, this did not necessarily mean the loss of women's movement networks. Attending women's movement events might be like irregular church attendance – an opportunity for reaffirmation of faith and values.

Why have women's movements changed?

The authors in Part I not only map the trajectories of women's movements, but also explore the internal and external factors impacting upon women's movement activism. These include the creation of alternative institutions that absorb members' energies, the achievement of participatory gains within the state, and the rise of neo-liberalism and conservative backlashes to women-centred claims. The responses to changes in the political environment, however, are not uniform. Changes may spark new activism, motivate groups to defend gains already made, or trigger a shift in modes of operation. In Australia, for example, the dismissal of a reforming Prime Minister in 1975 caused some feminist activists to give up on the possibilities of democratic reform.[20]

The paths taken by women's movements are never easy. Where feminists move into the state, there is the problem of staying true to feminist ideals. On the other hand, for movements that have retreated to personal networks and friendships, or to the practice of feminism in everyday life, there are the problems of policy and program losses at the political level – including those directly affecting women's equality such as childcare programs or income support for sole parents. Where the emphasis has shifted to cultural production, there are dangers of commodification of women's movement values. Where women have moved into international arenas there may be loss of connection with movements at home, while virtual communities of women in cyberspace may be a poor substitute for face-to-face communities.

The setting up of women's studies or, later, gender studies courses, is an example of how the institutional achievements of women's movements have themselves contributed to the changes observed over the past four decades. Institutionalisation is presented by some scholars as the inevitable outcome of social movement maturation. Certainly, social movements seek inclusion in existing institutions for those previously excluded.[21] However, social movements that succeed in achieving institutional goals are seen by many to change into 'something else' – for example opening up new opportunities in the power structure or in professional careers for those they have mobilised.[22] Evidence in this collection shows that this change impacts upon the public visibility and grassroots mobilisation of movements.

Finally, an internal factor impacting upon movement trajectory is the life course of members. In many cases, after a period of intense engagement, activists move on to other phases of their lives. New recruits are less numerous and, in the case of the movements studied here, often arrive via university women's studies courses rather than through previous forms of mobilisation, as is seen in the 'New Voices' section of this book.

The evolution of women's movements has not occurred in a vacuum. In this collection authors look at how distinctive political environments change in ways that bring more constraints than opportunities. For example, historically women's movements looked to the public sector for protection and support against exploitation and abuse, but this strategy provided diminishing returns in the 1990s. The increased influence of neo-liberalism has fuelled hostility towards movements seeking to expand the role of the public sector – whether in relation to labour market regulation, environmental or consumer protection or income redistribution. Neo-liberal think tanks and advocates within government ranks have targeted the kind of centralised industrial relations systems on which feminists have relied for progress towards equal pay and family-friendly employment provisions, while also excoriating the 'welfare state dependency' supposedly encouraged by providing adequate support for sole parents and other vulnerable people. Women have been closely associated with the welfare state from the beginning, both as social reformers and as beneficiaries.

In addition to this neo-liberal hostility to the 'nanny state', with all its gender connotations, there have also been other forms of conservative backlash impacting on the women's movement internationally. In the nations examined it is clear that hostility towards gendered claims-making has caused women's movements to adopt a more defensive posture. While in the 1970s women's movement activists 'set' an international agenda for social and political change, by the late 1990s movements in many developed democracies were struggling to halt the erosion of earlier policy gains and to maintain 'women-only' institutional space.

In some nations, discursive shifts and the rise of neo-liberal individualism has been so marked that collective action to achieve social goals hardly appears a real option, collective identities become fragmented and social movements delegitimised. For example, neo-liberalism reframes social movement advocates as simply 'special interests' – seeking to maximise their own returns rather than to make a better world. Neo-liberal discourse places stress on individual market choices and cultural consumption over the value of collective action to achieve shared goals.[23] The significance of social movement identities is displaced by a construct of the individual as author of their own choices, unconstrained by inequalities of power or expectations.

While neo-liberalism casts doubt on the authenticity of collective values or interpersonal utilities, collective identities have also been problematised from another source, that of academic gender studies and postmodern philosophy. 'Speaking for' shared identities and values is called into question on the grounds that it is problematic to speak for more than one, and that identity is necessarily fragmented and contingent. This concerted challenge, coming from different sources, was faced by movements across the seven nations examined in this collection.

Another challenge presenting both threats and opportunities for social movements is that of globalisation. While women's movements have long used transnational action and institutions to bring pressure on domestic governments, the increased significance of international institutions has created new opportunities, explored in Part II of this book. Our authors show that learning has taken place both between different 'waves' of national women's movements, and between movements in different nations. Learning across national borders has always played a significant role for women's movements.[24] New communication technologies have made such sharing easier and have sped up both the dissemination of information through transnational networks and the instigation of action in transnational arenas. But while there are new transnational spaces for women's activism, globalisation also creates problems for the traditional state-focused activism of women's movements.[25]

While a range of both internal and external factors have impacted on the trajectories of the movements studied in this collection, authors in Part I confirm findings elsewhere[26] that women's movement goals are most likely to be achieved when feminists are working both inside and outside the state, with a strong movement and alliances outside and political support and well-designed policy structures inside. Karen Beckwith argues that this 'double militancy' of activists, participating in different political venues, and with identities and commitments relating to both, may be a distinctive characteristic of women's movements.[27] The need for coalition-building of varying kinds as well as action in different arenas is also emphasised in Part III by the 'new voices' looking to the future.

Most of the authors in this collection identify an erosion of the kind of collective identity earlier women's movements expressed. And while cautious about seeing disruptive protest events as the key definer of social movements, they acknowledge that without disruptive protests movements are less visible. Gwendolyn Gray, Sandra Grey, Sarah Maddison and Kyungja Jung all examine the loss of visibility of women's movements and agree it has weakened the ability of those inside political institutions to act on behalf of women. Political leaders become convinced that they can save money by winding back women's policy gains without fear of political pain.

Theorising social movement change

This book introduces a range of theories to see if they help interpret the changes witnessed in women's movements over the last four decades. Such patterns of change have often been explained by life-cycle models of activism, or by wave analogies. Our evidence in part confirms that protests come in waves or cycles. Within the literature on movement evolution, it is claimed that intense social movement activism and engagement has a naturally short life span. This hypothesis has received an influential form in Sidney Tarrow's life-cycle model of social movements.[28] It is argued that social movements become possible within certain historical conjunctures and by their nature, as non-institutionalised mass movements, cannot be sustained long-term. Their adoption of more institutional forms, incorporation into existing institutions, or their collapse altogether is seen as inevitable. It is also argued that the limited life of movements relates to their inability to maintain the emotions that fuel them, including rage at injustice.[29] This view of social movement life cycles lends itself to proclamations of a movement's death when the activities of movement activists are no longer visible.

Authors in this collection also examine the view that the retreat from disruptive protests is the sign of a movement in 'abeyance'. As already noted, the term abeyance was introduced by Verta Taylor to depict a holding process by which movements sustain themselves in non-receptive political environments and provide continuity between different waves of mobilisation. Important here are the emotional cultures of social movements that may sustain a core nucleus of activists after the receding of broader mobilisation – in other words, social movement organisations may be sustained by close friendships based on shared values.[30]

Social movement abeyance may itself take a number of forms, from the commemorative activities that form a reservoir of values and identity, to the institutional deposits left behind as movements recede. Paul Bagguley, for example, suggests that unobtrusive mobilisation within mainstream institutions and the institutionalising of women's services is the repertoire of contention of a social movement in abeyance.[31] The key concept is that abeyance periods are characterised by a retreat from contentious political action and policy engagement.

The pattern of hibernation described by Leila Rupp and Verta Taylor[32] in the United States is not the only thing that may occur between 'the waves' of women's movement activism. While small but enduring organisations held onto women's movement values between the first and second waves of the women's movement, our collection shows that there is now a broader range of strategies available to preserve collective memory. While some of the strategies are eerily familiar, like archiving women's movement knowledge and affirming feminist values through awards, scholarships and named lectures, others derive from the institutional inroads made by feminism into government, trade unions, political parties, universities, professional bodies and civil society organisations of all kinds.

While some see the role of personal and submerged networks as places of retreat in hostile political environments, there are also those that argue that such networks form the core of all movements. European social movement theorists such as Alberto Melucci emphasise the way that social movement identities both manifest themselves and are sustained within submerged networks. As a result it is argued that research needs to be refocused into new areas of society in order to gauge the activism and challenges of social movements.

Evidence from the women's movements analysed in this collection suggests that both abeyance and life-cycle models of social movement evolution need some revision. This collection challenges the view that institutionalisation is a 'natural maturation', as it is not the only route women's movement activists have taken. Neither does institutionalisation guarantee ongoing and unfettered attention to gendered claims-making. There is no guarantee that structures created within, and alongside, the state will continue to serve as spaces for women's empowerment. Joyce Gelb highlights the backlash and hostility women's agencies faced during the 1990s and more recently. This backlash is also discussed by a number of the 'new voices' in Part III. As institutional gains are threatened, activists look for new spaces where women's movement activism can take flight.

Models of social movement change must not only allow for ebbs and flows in levels of activism, but also incorporate the way that movements find new venues

and less contentious forms of claims-making. Some of the new spaces and innovative collective actions being promoted by women are to be found at the local
and the supranational levels and, of course, in cyberspace. Activists are not just
roosting in these spaces but pushing forward new policy initiatives and cultural
challenges. Part II of this book explores the opportunities created by the changing architecture of international and local governance, whether women's movements can flourish in these new spaces, and the implications for the
conceptualising of social movements. As decision-making moves upwards and
outwards to global and regional forums and downwards or sideways to local
partnerships or networked governance models, women's movements have been
reorganising and reorienting themselves to these new political venues.

Looking to the future

The picture presented in this book appears bleak for those seeking to hold on to
idealised recollections of women's liberation movements or the repertoires of
contention associated with the 1960s and 1970s. However, looking at the long
history of the women's movement, we should not despair of another upsurge of
claims-making, whatever form it might take. It is unlikely to take the form of
1970s radicalism, with more women locked into the paid workforce than ever
before in order to pay the costs of education, housing, and childcare. Neither are
existing state structures in developed democracies likely to provide a forum for
the type of radicalism that flourished in the 1970s, even where hybrid services
continue to model democratic service provision. A new repertoire of contention,
new modes of organising, and new spaces are needed to both maintain and
regenerate women's movement activism.

   Three distinct patterns have appeared in developed democracies to counteract
the loss of alliances inside the state and to fend off hostility from both political
elites and countermovements. All of these options, it seems, are informed by
transnational learning between women's movement organisations. The first,
described by Jacqui True and Mona Lena Krook in this collection, is looking to
supranational organisations and their capacity to promote norms of gender
equality, rather than directly to the nation state. The narrowing of domestic
political opportunities has led to a renewed global focus. However, as with
domestic action, this global focus is not without difficulties in part because of
the complications of ensuring 'double militancy' in a globalising world.

   As well as looking upward towards the international and regional levels,
women's movement actors have also been looking downward to sub-national
levels for change. This is mirrored in other social movements such as environmental movements. Caroline Andrew assesses both the opportunities and risks
presented at the sub-national level by network models of governance involving
collaborations and partnerships between government and non-government
bodies. Just as with the 1970s women-centred institutions which provided
alternative spaces and models of operation, sub-national action on issues such as
community safety provide the possibility of 'bottom-up' decision-making which

fits squarely into social movement theorising on submerged networks. Andrew sees current sub-national groups in Canada as 'teetering between being new spaces for the women's movement and being new spaces for government co-option'.

The final chapter in Part II discusses women's movement activists' use of cyberspace. New ways of operating and connecting are continuing to evolve in cyberspace and CJ Rowe examines how this space can be used to the advantage of feminists. While providing clear evidence of lively and innovative uses of cyberspace, Rowe examines some of the problems of cyberspace for activism and activists – including the digital divide, which she says is continuing to limit the potential of this 'new frontier'.

The mapping of women's movements over the past four decades shows them to have been a dynamic force that both alters and is altered by the social and political contexts within which they operate. As was noted in the opening, social movements are not static and it important to understand how activism directed to achieving greater autonomy for women has changed and continues to change. Women's movement activism has encompassed the street protests of the 1960s and 1970s, the policies achieved by femocrats in the 1980s, the women-friendly social services pioneered by feminist groups, and the daily life-changes sought by cultural activists. The very successes of these movements have changed the terrain on which activists now work.

The changes in opportunity structures over the last four decades may require renegotiation not only of the repertoires of contention but also of the very identity of women's movements and feminist activists in ways that may make them unrecognisable to their 'foremothers'. While abeyance implies continuity between waves of movements, a clear part of social movements is the ongoing process of collective identity formation, and this often involves internal conflict. Some authors in this collection call for renewed debate about the core ideals at the heart of women's movements as part of this ongoing identity formation. So the final word in this collection is given over to wisdom from young women activists who all self identify as feminists and participate in a range of social movements and interest groups. How do young feminists in seven nations – Australia, Canada, Japan, Korea, New Zealand, Scotland, and the United States – conceive of their 'movement' and its relationship to the past? What trajectory do they see for feminist activism in the future?

Notes

1 Dahlerup, 'Continuity and waves in the feminist movement'.
2 Dahlerup, 'Continuity and waves in the feminist movement'.
3 Taylor, 'Social movement continuity'.
4 Staggenborg, 'Beyond culture versus politics'.
5 Epstein, 'What happened to the Women's Movement?'.
6 Oliver *et al.*, 'Emerging trends in the study of protest and social movements'.
7 Eyerman and Jamison, *Social Movements*; Melucci, 'The symbolic challenge of contemporary movements'.

8 Melucci, *Nomads of the Present*, p. 25.
9 McVeigh and Sikkink, 'God, politics, and protest', p. 1426.
10 Tarrow, *Power in Movement*, p. 4.
11 Scalmer, *Dissent Events*.
12 Staggenborg and Taylor, 'Whatever happened to the women's movement?'; Mansbridge, *Everyday Feminism*; Kriesi, 'The organizational structure of new social movements in a political context', p. 153.
13 Rucht, 'Interactions between social movements and state in comparative perspective'.
14 Sawer, 'Wearing your politics on your sleeve'.
15 Freeman, 'The Tyranny of Structurelessness'.
16 'Getting started: Reclaim the night info kit' www.isis/aust.com/rtn/started.htm. Accessed 30 January 2007. See also Sawer, *Out from the Gilded Cage*.
17 Beckwith, 'The comparative politics of Women's Movements'.
18 McAdam *et al.*, '"There will be fighting in the streets"'; Meyer and Tarrow, *The Social Movement Society*.
19 Sawer, *Making Women Count*.
20 Sawer, *Making Women Count*.
21 Tilly, *Big Structures, Large Processes, Huge Comparisons*, p. 306.
22 Katzenstein, 'Feminism within American Institutions', pp. 27–54.
23 Sawer, 'From women's interests to special interests'.
24 Dahlerup, 'Continuity and waves in the feminist movement'.
25 Burgmann, *Power, Profit, and Protest*, pp. 35–42.
26 Weldon, *Protest, Policy, and the Problem of Violence Against Women*; Lovenduski, *State Feminism and Political Representation*.
27 Beckwith, 'Beyond compare', p. 442.
28 Tarrow, 'Cycles of collective action'.
29 Goodwin *et al.*, *Passionate Politics*.
30 Taylor, 'Social movement continuity'.
31 Bagguley, 'Contemporary British Feminism'; Mary Katzenstein in 'Feminism within American institutions' coined the term 'unobtrusive mobilisation' to refer to the ways feminists organised within male-dominated institutions.
32 Rupp and Taylor, *Survival in the Doldrums*.

Part I
In abeyance?

2 The state of women's movement/s in Britain

Ambiguity, complexity and challenges from the periphery

Fiona Mackay

What is the state of the women's movement in Britain in the early twenty-first century? Standard accounts have tended to present a uniform picture of its trajectory: after an initial flourishing in the 1960s and 1970s the movement fragmented, dissipated and de-radicalised, stymied by the cold climate of neo-liberal Thatcherism and the unravelling of simple notions of universal sisterhood. Feminist activism continued but largely by means of unobtrusive mobilisation within institutions and through distinctive service delivery. Paradoxically, the apparent decline of the movement has coincided with the growth of women's involvement in, and feminist impact on, the mainstream politics and political agenda of political parties, trade unions, and governments at different levels.

There have also been significant changes in political opportunity structures since the late 1970s. In common with many other advanced industrial democracies, the British state has undergone considerable restructuring and reconfiguration, accompanied by globalised neo-liberal discourses about the need to reduce the scope and social spending of welfare states. These trends include 'uploading' of power and responsibility to supra-state bodies such as the European Union; the 'lateral loading' of state functions to non-elected state bodies, for example QUANGOs and Executive agencies; the 'downloading' of administrative and legislative power to new devolved institutions; and the 'offloading' of state power to non-state actors, such as businesses, charities and families.[1] Although these trends have continued under successive administrations, the return of New Labour to power in 1997 after 18 years in opposition provided another important change in political environment. Taken together, these developments suggest the need to revisit and reappraise the role and impact of organised women and their interactions with conventional power politics.

Overall there has been surprisingly little research into the state of the women's movement in Britain, with the last comprehensive account in the early 1990s.[2] Most works rely upon secondary sources and there has been little empirical study of contemporary women's organising at central British or English level. I draw upon recent accounts which reappraise and update the story of feminist activism – particularly those that utilise a social movement framework

– in order to evaluate the extent to which the women's movement is flourishing, in abeyance, or defunct.

However, I argue that these assessments provide only a partial picture: the 'British' in British women's movement does not withstand close scrutiny. Much of what is passed off as British feminism might more accurately be characterised as English feminism. Scant attention has been paid to the territorial diversity of the women's movement/s in Britain. The low profile of movement activism in England stands in sharp contrast to the evident and strategic mobilisations of organised women in Scotland, Wales and Northern Ireland. This adds a layer of complexity to the task of assessing whether the British women's movement is in 'abeyance'. All this suggests that territory and level are significant in understanding the form and trajectory of contemporary women's movements, their identities and their strategic engagement with conventional power politics.

Definitions and standard accounts

Women's movements are notoriously difficult to define. The patterns of women's activism do not fit neatly into models of social movements, particularly those that focus upon particular organisational forms or repertoires of action. The women's movement in Britain is no exception. As elsewhere, there are definitional disagreements and confusion over what constitutes a movement. In addition, Somerville notes that much of the British literature is under-theorised, comprising personal testimony, historical accounts and prescriptive analyses. Often written by activists, the aims of such accounts are to bear witness to what has happened and to inform future strategy, rather than contribute to systematic evaluation.[3]

There are two broad paradigms used by scholars of social movement activism: 'political process', a tradition arising mainly in North America, and 'cultural', arising mainly in Europe (as was noted in the Introduction). The first, a 'political process' model, has 'contentious politics' at its core. It takes as its primary focus that of state/movement interactions and is concerned with social movements as collective mobilisations which visibly, publicly and actively challenge the state and the status quo, and which employ unconventional protest tactics at least some of the time. The goal is political and policy change. The second, a 'cultural' model, is concerned with identity and non-instrumental goals; with challenging meanings, creating and expressing new or marginalised subjectivities, bearing witness and building solidarity. A 'challenging codes' model, its principal goals are around personal, group and cultural change. It may be less visible than 'contentious politics' models require, operating through informal and 'submerged networks' in between critical events. Neither model fully captures the character and form of second-wave feminism in Britain, although elements of each help us to understand particular aspects and its twin goals of political and cultural change.[4]

The women's movement in Britain has been conventionally characterised as comparatively decentred or polycentric, comprising myriad localised and non-hierarchical groups and informal networks, coming together for relatively few national-level events and protests. Unlike counterparts in the US, no single national co-ordinating body – or peak organisation – such as the National Organization for Women has emerged in the UK.[5] Joyce Gelb's oft-cited comparative evaluation of second-wave feminism in the US and Britain criticises the British women's movement of the time for being ideologically state-averse and organisationally ineffectual, failing to organise and co-ordinate in order to take advantage of the political opportunities of the 1960s and 1970s. She characterised British feminism as 'politics without power', albeit in the relatively difficult context of the closed, secretive, centralised and partisan character of British governance and politics. Gelb undoubtedly privileged the 'political process' model in her analysis, however she also judged the cultural impact of the British movement to be negligible.[6]

Reappraisals of 1970s activism suggest there has been a tendency to exaggerate the anti-state orientation of the movement and that institutionalised feminist politics was already in play in the 1970s, coinciding and interacting with unconventional protest politics.[7] This supports the findings of other chapters in this book (see Gwendolyn Gray, Sandra Grey, and Sarah Maddison and Kyungja Jung). For example, second-wave British activists joined with older equal rights feminist networks and feminist activists in trade unions and political parties, in order to monitor the implementation of the Sex Discrimination and Equal Pay Acts. Women's Aid groups provide an example of the radical flank of the movement engaging early and consistently with the state at UK, English, Welsh, Scottish, Northern Irish and local levels, in order to challenge state policy and claim state funding for their activities. Contrariwise, there is evidence of the continuity of contentious politics in the 1980s and 1990s as well as of at least partial success in terms of feminist institutional politics and cultural change.

Questions of scale

Earlier comparative accounts of women's movement activism in Britain tended to over-emphasise the British state level with a consequent neglect of activities and partial successes at local and European level.[8] More recent work has highlighted the importance of supra-state and sub-state dynamics – as structures of political opportunity – leading to a reappraisal of the 'success' of women's movement activism in Britain in the 1980s and 1990s, especially in comparison to the US.[9]

In response to the reconfiguration of the British state and the 'uploading' of power and competences to the European level, feminist activism reoriented to engage at the supra-state level. This activism took the form of feminists strategically mobilising through a re-energised Equal Opportunities Commission (EOC)[10] to seek redress for gender grievances through European institutions. British feminists also began to play an active role in campaigning and lobbying to 'mainstream' feminist perspectives in European treaties and agreements, legislation and programmes through their participation in the European Women's

Lobby.[11] The European Commission and the European Court of Justice provided crucial alternative arenas for feminists to press gender equality claims during the inhospitable decades of Conservative administrations.[12] As Sylvia Bashevkin demonstrates, in the areas of women's rights and equal opportunities and pay in employment, more than 40 per cent of the decisions that promoted gender equality came from either the European Commission or the European Court of Justice, rather than the Thatcher and Major governments.[13] From the 1990s onwards, the European Commission has been an important actor in promoting the adoption of gender mainstreaming by the British government and other public bodies in the UK.[14]

Attention to scale has also brought into focus the international dimension and the mobilising opportunities provided by UN feminist initiatives such as CEDAW and the women's conferences. The run up to the 1995 Beijing Conference and subsequent Platform for Action provided leverage for women's groups to press claims with the Conservative government of the day, including commitments to gender impact assessment and the creation of some limited policy machinery within government.

A national/British level focus also tended to underplay the significance of the interactions between local women's movements and local authorities in the 1980s and 1990s. Local government women's committees, established in left-wing Labour councils in England, Scotland and, to a lesser extent, Wales, provided important space and resources for women's groups and feminist ideas in the wider context of oppositional politics. Women's committees and their support units pioneered radical policies such as workplace crèches and job shares, and championed equal opportunities in employment and service delivery. They developed analyses of the practical consequences of women's differences, including distinctive service needs, and introduced monitoring of service delivery in health, social services, education and transport – the precursor of gender mainstreaming. They also supported a flourishing of local women's groups and projects in the 1980s, through grant aid. However, the existence of women's committees was relatively short lived; most of these initiatives had been abolished or neutralised by the early 1990s, apart from some exceptions, mostly in Scotland.[15]

Questions of trajectory and repertoire

There is an implicit consensus in the UK literature on women's movements about the types of activities that organised women undertake in pursuit of reform and transformational change to politics and society; however, in the absence of clear working definitions, there is a diversity of opinion as to whether or not these 'add up' to a movement.[16] For the feminist academic and activist Lynn Segal, writing in the late 1990s, the women's movement no longer exists in Britain, having grown 'rapidly as a mass movement ... peaking in the 1970s before dissolving as a coherent organisation'.[17] A co-ordinating structure and unity of organisation appear paramount to her implicit definition of a movement.

In contrast Natasha Walter argues that 'something that looks very much like a women's movement does still exist in Britain [and rightly so]. It is not a mass movement ... but a large collection of single-issue organisations that press for feminist aims in many different accents'.[18] For others, this plethora of organisations represents the 'residue' of a now-defunct movement, with legacies in terms of women's civil society, the wide reach of feminist ideas and analyses, legislative and social change, more diverse gender roles and relationships, and feminist institutional politics.

The 1980s and following decades have not conformed to a neat typology or trajectory. An acrimonious split after the last national women's liberation movement conference in 1978 did not signal the end of contentious politics, nor did it herald the end of struggles over diverse identities, which continued into the 1980s and beyond.[19] Contentious politics co-existed with institutionalised politics and 'unobtrusive mobilisation'[20] within political parties and public organisations. In particular, the 1980s witnessed two mass mobilisations of women: the Greenham Common peace movement; and Women Against Pit Closures. At the height of the Greenham demonstrations in the early 1980s, tens of thousands of women turned out to protest at the planned siting of Cruise nuclear weapons at the airbase at Greenham Common in Berkshire, England. For example, in December 1982, the Embrace the Base action involved 30 000 women linking hands around the nine-mile perimeter fence. Greenham women used a repertoire that combined instrumental direct action (such as blocking roads and sabotage) with expressive and symbolic actions aimed at challenging dominant codes (for example, personalising the impersonal by pinning keepsakes and photographs on the perimeter fence, bringing home the costs of 'peace'). Although the protestors failed to prevent the arrival of the missiles in 1983, the camp – and symbolic protest actions – continued until the closure of the base in 1992.[21]

The second galvanising event was the miners' strike against pit closures in 1984–85. The dispute sparked unprecedented organisation and mobilisation of women in English, Welsh and Scottish coal-fields, with far reaching and long lasting consequences. In a 'rare instance of working-class women participating in high profile political action', women went beyond their traditional role running soup kitchens and welfare, taking a more proactive and public role including picketing, pithead occupations, organising rallies, public speaking and fund-raising. The Women Against Pit Closures (WAPC) action 'did not begin as feminist intervention, nor did ever become a wholeheartedly feminist movement', however it was influenced by feminist ideas and the 'role model effect' of Greenham Common. Many local WAPC support groups came to have close connections with Greenham women as well as with women's groups within the Labour Party and Campaign for Nuclear Disarmament. Many individual women were radicalised as a result of their experiences, going on to other forms of feminist activism, self-organisation and self-expression.[22]

As well as oppositional politics and mass mobilisation, the 1980s saw the production and distribution of feminist ideas through the self-expression – and unprecedented visibility – of diverse women involved in feminist publishing, theatre, art and film making ventures. Feminism also entered education and academia, through the development of Women's Studies and the insertion of feminist perspectives into Arts and Humanities. By the 2000s, however, many of these activities were in decline and less visible: with the demise of feminist theatre groups and long running publications, such as *Spare Rib*. Many Women's Studies programmes have closed or reoriented to Gender Studies, and the radical edge has been knocked off feminist pedagogy under pressure to standardise and conform to academic norms.[23]

In terms of a feminist civil society – or sector – although many women's movement groups and projects have been short-lived, there continues to be a large and diverse range of women's organisations, including self-help groups, support networks and service delivery organisations. Several, such as the long-established Women's Aid networks in England, Scotland, Northern Ireland and Wales continue to combine service delivery with radical campaigning work and lobbying for legislative and policy change with respect to domestic violence. Associations and networks operate at national, regional and local levels and are characterised as overlapping and interconnected, 'generating an integrity and robustness greater than the sum of their parts'.[24] However, in the absence of recent research to map the state and size of the women's sector across the UK, it is hard to draw firm conclusions about its relative strength and any change over time.

During the 1980s and 1990s feminists also entered conventional institutions such as political parties, trade unions, voluntary and public sector bodies, local government and state bureaucracies. The result of this was the transformation of the public face of the women's movement into one of 'respectable feminism' by the 1990s. This trajectory is similar to that in New Zealand and Australia (see Gwendolyn Gray and Sandra Grey in this book). The visibility of women – including many feminists – in mainstream political organisations is taken by some commentators as the primary sign of the continued existence of a women's movement and its impact on mainstream politics. On the other hand, the same developments can be read as signs 'of cooption into mainstream politics and a neutralisation of the radical demands of the women's movement'.[25]

There are examples of institutional success in elected and non-elected political positions. The wilderness years for the Labour Party and Labour movement made them more receptive to feminism and provided opportunities for feminists to enter and influence structures and policies. The twin processes of party modernisation and feminisation of the Labour Party are well documented and took place over a decade or more. Internal campaigns resulted in the introduction of controversial gender quotas and, subsequently, record numbers of women MPs entered the House of Commons with the incoming New Labour government in 1997. More than a hundred women sit on the Labour benches, comprising a quarter of the parliamentary party. An unprecedented number of appointments of women, some feminist, have been made to ministerial positions. In addition, new women's policy machinery was established in the administration, under the control of a Minister for Women.[26]

Abeyance or beyond movement?

According to Paul Bagguley, preoccupation with the conditions facilitating the emergence and mobilisation of the movement has meant less focus on questions of if and how the movement has declined. As he notes, demobilisation and decline are 'taken for granted' in most accounts and therefore are not subjected to considered analysis.[27] In contrast to more pessimistic opinions, he argues that although the contemporary women's movement in Britain is in apparent decline, it is not a spent force but rather a social movement in abeyance. In other words, it is in a mode of existence where it is not actively confronting the social system, but is instead preoccupied with self-maintenance (through, for example, service providing voluntary organisations, educational activities, incorporation into elite politics and so on). He is one of the few writers on women's movement in the British context that explicitly uses the 'abeyance' concept developed to explain patterns of activism in the US.[28]

Bagguley expands the concept of abeyance to take more account of 'partial success', the impact of changes in political opportunity structures, and of political incorporation. These factors have led to the 'abeyance' of feminism and 'this abeyance has been accompanied by a change in the dominant repertoire of contentions from public protest to working within the male establishment'.[29] In particular, he integrates Katzenstein's idea of 'unobtrusive mobilisation' into the abeyance model, arguing that unobtrusive mobilisation is *the* dominant mode of contentious politics during periods of abeyance.[30] He contrasts this with the dominant repertoires of contention during periods of insurgence or resurgence, such as direct action and protest.

Unobtrusive mobilisation – even with an explicit feminist agenda – is double-edged. On the one hand, it provides opportunity for influence and change. On the other, it is inevitably limited in scope and vulnerable to dilution and cooption, the price paid for the sustenance of feminist ideas, activities and structures in times of subdued activism. These trends are similar to the findings of Sandra Grey, and Sarah Maddison and Kyungja Jung in this collection. Furthermore, the carrying structures and tactics that maintain feminism in difficult times also bring inherent problems in the sense of 'deflecting, incorporating and demobilising the movement even further'.[31]

Nevertheless, according to Bagguley, it is abeyance rather than decline or backlash which most adequately describes the current state. This is because decline overlooks and underplays the continuities that persist in terms of networks and legacies; in turn, backlash is inappropriate to the UK context, where countermovements are not significant forces as compared with other nations such as the US and Japan (see Joyce Gelb, this collection).

Taking an alternative approach, Kate Nash measures current signs of activity against core criteria derived from the two contrasting models of social movements. She argues that, according to the political process or contentious politics model, there can be no social movement without extra-parliamentary activity such as direct action and protest. There are organisations and groups, and there are feminist institutionalised politics, but they do not add up to a movement. She suggests they could possibly amount to a new movement in the making, especially if the occasion arose for defensive protest, such as the need to defend abortion legislation.

Turning to the submerged networks or challenging codes model, there are grounds for suggesting a women's movement still exists in so far as there are self-identified feminists engaged in cultural activities, women's studies centres, and in women's refuges. However such a movement is small-scale and likely to remain so, given the centrality of solidarity to a movement and the problematic simplifications needed in order to produce movement solidarity. Furthermore, the more complex reality of social and political life and our more complex understandings of it have meant that the movement has lost a common adversary. The early movement mobilised around the common adversary of the patriarchal-capitalist system at abstract level and, at concrete level, men.

Nash suggests that the women's movement has never fitted neatly into either model but that in its current state it does not meet the core requirement of either: it has little in the way of unconventional political action, and is without a common adversary or a simple solidarity. She argues that instead, post-movement 'micro politics' (the politics of everyday life, involving small acts of disruption and resistance) might best describe the current state of play. The legacy of social and economic change and feminism is that contemporary women are insistent on the 'redistribution of agency' through the everyday renegotiation of concrete relationships at work and in their personal lives.[32] Feminism has been successful in challenging dominant codes in so far as there is 'widespread receptivity to feminist ideas' even though most women do not self-identify with a movement.[33] This is accompanied by formal political activity 'and the potential for occasional, if defensive, mass mobilisation'.[34]

The missing territorial dimension

Nuanced though these contemporary assessments are, they fail to present the whole picture. Few appraisals have taken into account the significance of sub-state national identity in the British context.[35] This is particularly puzzling given the significance of institutional and constitutional restructuring in the UK, which has resulted in political devolution and the creation of new institutions and inter-relationships between the different nations of the union; and between state and citizens. It is all the more surprising, given the very visible gains for women in terms of high levels of female representatives in the Scottish Parliament (34.1 per cent in 2007) and the National Assembly for Wales (46.7 per cent in 2007), greatly in excess of the historically high rate of 20 per cent female representation in the British House of Commons (2005).[36]

The conflation of Britishness and Englishness by activist organisations and women's movement scholars alike has meant scant attention has been paid to patterns of activism in Scotland, Wales and Northern Ireland. There are similarities in the origins, ideas, repertoires of action and campaigning goals of women's movements in the four sub-state territories of the United Kingdom. However, there are contrasts stemming from distinctive territorial identities, national histories, specific institutions and different political opportunities. Whilst some work on British feminism notes territorial dimensions of diversity,[37] more usually, where differences are noted, they are not addressed nor do they impact upon the conclusions of their 'British' analysis. In other – equally rare – cases, commentators modify their terminology and make explicit they are concerned solely with the English experience.[38] It remains commonplace for the 'British' chapters in international edited collections to present arguments and accounts that only consider England.[39] To counter this trend, I briefly outline the trajectory of the women's movement in Scotland, which differs from the English experience in several important ways.[40]

The women's movement in Scotland and state restructuring

Although women's movement activists in Scotland participated in national/British conferences and activities of the second wave and were concerned with similar issues, they primarily organised on a Scottish scale. In part this was because of the need to engage with distinctive Scottish institutions, such as the legal system, education, local government and the distinctive policy networks of administrative devolution. In addition, the women's movement became more distinctively Scottish in the 1980s in the context of the resurgence of devolution campaigns after the failed referendum of 1979, the growing politicisation of national identity and Scottish opposition to neo-liberal welfare state reform – seen as disproportionately impacting upon Scotland, and Scottish women in particular.[41]

In the 1980s and 1990s in Scotland, a broad and strategic coalition of women activists mobilised to place feminist concerns on the home rule agenda. There were vigorous debates within the women's movement on devolution and the shape that a reformed and regendered politics might assume. Discussions took place through conferences and rallies, reports, newsletters, pamphlets, articles and manifestos such as the *Woman's Claim of Right in Scotland* (1989), and women's groups' submissions to the Scottish Constitutional Convention (see below). This culminated in the '50/50' campaign: a set of demands for equal representation in any new parliament, increased access and voice for women's organisations in the policy process, and new inclusive forms of politics.[42]

The women's movement in Scotland can be characterised by dense linkages. Groups were able to build upon long traditions of working together in co-ordinated action at an all-Scotland and local level around multiple issues including women's poverty, violence against women, gender-sensitive public services and women's representation. They had also responded together to the mobilising opportunities provided by the European Union and the UN.[43] Municipal feminism survived for longer in Scotland than in England, with local government women's committees flourishing until the mid-1990s.[44] This generally enabling environment provided further opportunities for networking and joint campaigning, of which the radical Zero Tolerance Campaign to tackle violence against women was an exemplar. This campaign provided a shorthand symbol for the radical possibilities of coalitions between the women's movement and the local state in the context of oppositional politics.[45]

Activists in the women's movement in Scotland can be also characterised as displaying double or multiple militancy (see the Introduction for fuller attribution of this term). In other words, many women were active in autonomous women's organisations, women's sections within political parties and trade unions as well as in the mainstream of political and civic organisations, including devolution campaign groups. To illustrate the point we could take the example of one individual, Alice Brown, simultaneously a leading feminist academic and activist, a key 'insider' in the Labour party and the Scottish Constitutional Convention (serving on the working group considering electoral systems and on the Convention's Constitutional Commission), and an 'architect' of the Scottish Parliament through her role in the Consultative Steering Group on the Scottish Parliament. An embodiment of both the dual and multiple militancy strategies, she argues that without the persistence of women campaigners, the issue could have been 'traded' or downgraded at various points.[46]

These dual strategies enhanced the ability of campaigners to exert leverage, maintain momentum, broker deals and build coalitions. With respect to the issue of women's political representation, the Labour Party proved to be the key 'carrying agent' for the 50/50 campaign as a result of the congruence of feminist demands with wider Labour party priorities and modernisation processes in Scotland and at UK-central levels.[47] A loose, time-limited coalition, the Scottish Women's Co-ordination Group, used both insider and outsider tactics to press political parties for improvements in women's political representation, through reforms in candidate recruitment procedures including the introduction of gender quotas. Whilst the Labour Party was the only party to implement quota measures that guaranteed 50/50, other parties responded with formal and informal measures. The overall outcome was that, in the first elections to the new Scottish Parliament 37.2 per cent of members of the Scottish Parliament (MSPs) were female, including 50 per cent of Labour MSPs.

In addition, the movement was operating in the context of a strong, politically-focussed civil society. Institutional expression of a strong civil society can be seen in the creation and work of the Scottish Constitutional Convention (SCC), an unofficial body established by key groups in civil society together with some political parties, which debated and considered potential blueprints for a Scottish Parliament during the 1980s and 1990s. Many of the body's recommendations were adopted by the incoming Labour government in 1997, in its White Paper *Scotland's Parliament*. From its inception, women members of the SCC and their activist networks ensured that gender equality and feminist concerns were debated and taken into consideration at each stage of the design process.

In addition to gains in women's representation, the institutional 'blueprints' of the parliament contained important mechanisms for promoting the participation and influence of women in policy development and more accessible working practices and political cultures. Among the gains were the inclusion of equal opportunities as one of the four key principles of the Scottish Parliament, alongside power-sharing, accountability, and access and participation. There was the adoption of 'family friendly' sitting hours in the parliament and the observation of school holidays, the establishment of a visitors crèche in the parliament building; the creation of a parliamentary Equal Opportunities Committee and an Equality Unit in the Scottish Executive. Both parliament and government are committed to 'mainstreaming' equality – including gender equality – across all their areas of work including legislation and policy-making. The parliament has the power to impose duties on public bodies to ensure they have due regard to equality legislation and memoranda accompanying executive bills must include an equal opportunities impact statement.

What difference does adding Scotland make?

Incorporating Scottish experience presents a challenge to accounts of the decline or abeyance of the women's movement in Britain. It also highlights the importance of territorially specific political opportunity structures – or interactive contexts – in understanding different trajectories and differential impacts. Being located on the periphery appears important in terms of oppositional mobilisation and alliances. Widespread perceptions that Thatcherite neo-liberal reform hit Scotland and Wales hard, and Scottish and Welsh women the hardest, fuelled a powerful sense of grievance and facilitated mobilisation in these countries.[48] In contrast, women in London and the Home Counties of England were more insulated from the 'hard times' of welfare retrenchment and economic restructuring. According to Dobrowolsky, these differential locations map onto strategic repertoires: 'the closer to the English hub ... the more limited and conventional' are the strategies and action undertaken by feminist activists, and the weaker the links between elite women and grassroots women's organisations.[49]

There are important legacies of this more insurgent movement activism for feminist institutionalised politics and feminist civil society. At least in the short term, devolution has opened up mainstream politics and the policy process to a greater extent than is apparent at UK/English level.

Early studies of gender dynamics in the Scottish Parliament have suggested that there has been some re-gendering of politics, particularly through the 'normalisation' of women politicians and at least some reconsideration of the masculine norms, values and behaviours traditionally played out in power politics.[50] Interviews with MSPs presented a picture of men and women 'equally at home' in the Scottish Parliament in contrast to the marginalisation experienced by many female members of the UK parliament (MPs).[51] The Women and Equality Unit, based at Whitehall, is regarded as less outward facing than the Equality Unit in Scotland, and much less concerned or connected with grassroots women's organisations. Similarly, equality mainstreaming has been given greater political and organisational priority by government in Scotland (and Wales and Northern Ireland) than in London.[52]

The opening up of the policy process in post-devolution Scotland is considered to be one of the key outcomes of devolution and a clear break with the past and with London.[53] As a result of the influence of civil society on the process and form of devolution, access has improved noticeably for women's organisations in the post-devolution period as it has for other civic groups. In the absence of empirical research on the access and influence of women's organisations after 1997 at UK or English level (and it is difficult to unpick the two, given both target Westminster and Whitehall), it is hard to make definitive judgements and comparisons. However, I will take action on domestic violence as a proxy measure of comparative feminist influence. Action on domestic violence is a policy priority of feminists in both Scotland and England, particularly for those in the refuge movement and the wider violence-against-women coalitions.

Action against domestic violence or domestic abuse has been recognised as an achievement of the first Scottish Parliament and Scottish Executive. A strategic approach was adopted from the start through the *National Strategy to Address Domestic Abuse in Scotland* in 2000.[54] Through membership of the Scottish Partnership on Domestic Abuse, Scottish Women's Aid exerted significant influence over the shape and content of the final National Strategy including the feminist definition of domestic abuse, its links with other forms of violence against women, and the insistence on detailed work-plans and reporting mechanisms. They maintained the momentum through their position on the national implementation group and sub-groups and through a dense network of personal contacts with influential ministers and parliamentarians. The urgency with which domestic abuse was tackled in Scotland in comparison with Westminster is indicative of the difference devolution has made to women's substantive representation and citizenship in this respect. Scotland tackled the issue in a 'joined up' way early and first. It had a head start of at least three years on England in terms of a national strategy, national refuge building programme and ring-fenced funding to tackle domestic abuse.[55]

Expenditure patterns provide another measure. The Scottish Executive committed around £32 million to support work in this area for the period 2000–06. While comparisons between Scotland and England are difficult to make, if we take the respective populations as a guide (5m: 50m), then, crudely speaking, English spending would need to be in the region of £320 million (2000–06) to be proportionate with Scotland. The most optimistic reading of the figures provided[56] suggests spending in the region of £50 million in England, less than a sixth of Scottish expenditure in proportionate terms.

Conclusions: 'Only Contradictions on Offer'

Lynne Segal concluded her review of British feminism at the millennium under the apt heading of 'Only Contradictions on Offer'.[57] I take this insight as my starting point.

By seeking to establish the significance of territory and the need to recognise distinctive movements in Britain, I do not want to suggest that the Scottish movement has not also experienced the trends of fragmentation, institutionalisation and de-radicalisation experienced in England and other Western industrialised democracies. Whilst the Scottish women's movement has had a more recognisably 'contentious politics' mode than its counterpart in England, it is important to recognise that protest tactics have been only a minor part of movement repertoire and that much work has been unobtrusive mobilising within political parties, trade unions and mainstream nationalist movements. Nor do I want to suggest that the Scottish movement is undifferentiated and unified; it shares with other movements the problems of finding solidarity across differences. However, territorial identities and nationalist movements have provided powerful carrying structures for feminist politics in the 1980s and 1990s.

The inclusion of the Scottish case – and, had space permitted, of Wales and Northern Ireland – challenges and complicates linear and uni-directional accounts of movement life cycles. It suggests multiple trajectories in a single state, and underscores the observations made elsewhere of both continuity and variety. And it adds a layer of complexity to the task of assessing whether British women's movement is in 'abeyance' or over.

One answer to the latter question has been that there is no women's movement without a clear 'adversary' and without a common identity mobilised around the category 'woman'. It seems to me that this approach, adopted by Kate Nash, over-privileges one definitional criterion. Bagguley's more optimistic assessment is that the British women's movement is not in decline but in abeyance. The costs of abeyance explain the ambiguities when attempting to evaluate success. However, does the term abeyance obscure more than it illuminates?

The concept of abeyance presents problems in presenting a wide range of outward as well as inward-facing activities as 'holding' actions in preparation for a return to an original 'real' movement mode. The 'pure' core implicit in the abeyance model also stands in contrast to characterisations of women's movements as interactive, adaptable and adapting. Women's movements are not only shaped by their environments but also shape and create opportunities. This is amply demonstrated by the Scottish case, where women successfully inserted gender claims into broader oppositional politics in the 1980s and 1990s. The idea of movement 'clusters' – put forward by Banaszak and her colleagues – is a more useful way of conceptualising the current landscape of activities and groups in the UK than the concept of abeyance. Movement clusters comprise of groups and networks differentiated by identities and ideologies, varying degrees of institutionalisation, different organisation forms and repertoires of action. Movements as sets of clusters evolve and adapt in response to previous and current engagements with the state, in interaction with changing political opportunity structures, and in response to changing identities, solidarities and social relations.[58]

Demobilisation and decline are generally 'taken for granted' in the case of the UK women's movement, which explains why there has been little empirical study of contemporary women's organising beyond Scotland, Wales and

Northern Ireland. In England, most attention has been on the performance of New Labour governments in terms of policy agenda and policy developments, and the impact of new Labour policies on women, rather than on the activities and lobbying of organised groups.[59] At the very least, the analysis presented here suggests that territory and level are significant in understanding the form and trajectory of contemporary women's movements in Britain, their identities, and their strategic engagement with conventional power politics. The new architecture of British politics has created new sites and opportunities for feminist interventions and has also been shaped by them. The interconnections between feminists in different jurisdictions and the implications of those interactions have yet to be fully documented and analysed. Women's movements continue to challenge not only gender norms but also the constraints imposed by social movement theorists.

Notes

1 Framework taken from Banaszak, Beckwith and Rucht, 'When power relocates', p. 7.
2 Lovenduski and Randall, *Contemporary Feminist Politics*.
3 See for example, Somerville, 'Social movement theory, women and the question of interests'; Wandor (ed.), *Once A Feminist*.
4 See Introduction to this volume; also discussions in Bagguley, 'Contemporary British Feminism'; Byrne, 'The politics of the Women's Movement'; Nash, 'A movement moves'.
5 The Women's National Commission was established in 1969 by the UK government as a formal consultative women's umbrella organisation. However for most of its existence it has failed to engage fully with, or represent, the diversity of women's organisations. See Stokes 'The UK Women's National Commission'.
6 Gelb, 'Feminism in Britain'; Gelb, *Feminism and Politics*.
7 Nash, 'A movement moves'.
8 See, for example, Gelb, *Feminism and Politics*.
9 Bashevkin, *Women on the Defensive*; Bagguley, 'Contemporary British Feminism'; Gelb and Hart, 'Feminist politics in a hostile environment'; Walby, *Gender Transformations*.
10 The EOC is the arms-length public authority charged with monitoring the implementation of sex equality legislation. See Lovenduski, 'An emerging advocate'.
11 Hart, 'Redesigning the polity'.
12 Hart, 'Redesigning the polity'; Gelb and Hart, 'Feminist politics in a hostile environment'; Meehan and Collins, 'Women, the European Union and Britain'.
13 Bashevkin, *Women on the Defensive*.
14 Rees, *Mainstreaming Equality in the European Union*.
15 Edwards, *Local Government Women's Committees*; Lovenduski and Randall, *Contemporary Feminist Politics*; Breitenbach *et al.*, *The Changing Politics of Gender Equality in Britain*.
16 Nash, 'A movement moves'.
17 Segal, *Why Feminism?*, p. 9.
18 Walter, *The New Feminism*, p. 44.
19 Lovenduski and Randall, *Contemporary Feminist Politics*.
20 See Introduction to this volume.
21 Roseneil, *Disarming Patriarchy*; Lovenduski and Randall, *Contemporary Feminist Politics*, pp. 113–122.
22 Lovenduski and Randall, *Contemporary Feminist Politics*, pp. 122–125.

23 Warwick and Auchmuty, 'Women's studies as feminist activism', p. 185.
24 Bagguley, 'Contemporary British Feminism', p. 182.
25 Nash, 'A movement moves', p. 313; Byrne, 'The politics of the Women's Movement', p. 56.
26 Lovenduski and Randall, *Contemporary Feminist Politics*; Lovenduski, *Feminizing Politics*; Childs, *New Labour's Women MPs*; Squires and Wickham-Jones, 'New Labour, gender mainstreaming and the Women and Equality Unit'.
27 Bagguley, 'Contemporary British Feminism', p. 170.
28 See Introduction to this volume for a fuller definition of the term 'abeyance'.
29 Bagguley, 'Contemporary British Feminism', pp. 172 and 180.
30 Katzenstein, 'Feminism within American institutions'.
31 Bagguley, 'Contemporary British Feminism', p. 182.
32 Mann, 'Musing as a feminist in a postfeminist era'.
33 Katzenstein, 'Comparing women's movements of the United States and Western Europe', p. 8.
34 Nash, 'A movement moves', p. 325.
35 A rare exception is Dobrowolsky, 'Shifting states: Women's constitutional organising across time and space'.
36 Bagguley notes the high levels of representation in Scotland and Wales but assumes it to be a simple by-product of wider Labour party modernisation processes.
37 Lovenduski and Randall, *Contemporary Feminist Politics*; Lister, *Citizenship*.
38 See, for example, Nash, 'A movement moves'.
39 Breitenbach *et al.*, 'Understanding women in Scotland'.
40 Unfortunately space constraints mean I can only examine the Scottish case. For Wales, see Beddoe, *Out of the Shadows*; Chaney *et al.*, *Women, Politics and Constitutional Change*. For Northern Ireland, see Brown *et al.*, 'Women and constitutional change' and Yvonne Galligan, 'Women in Northern Ireland's politics: Feminising the armed patriarchy'.
41 Breitenbach, 'The Impact of Thatcherism on women in Scotland'; Brown, 'Thatcher's legacy for women in Scotland'; Breitenbach and Mackay (eds), *Women and Contemporary Scottish Politics*.
42 See Breitenbach and Mackay, *Women and Contemporary Scottish Politics*.
43 Breitenbach, 'The Women's Movement in Scotland in the 1990s', pp. 77–89.
44 Breitenbach and Mackay, 'Keeping gender on the agenda – the role of women's and equal opportunities initiatives in local government in Scotland'; Edwards, *Local Government Women's Committees*.
45 Cosgrove, 'No man has the right'; Gillan and Samson, 'The zero tolerance campaign'; Mackay, 'The case of zero tolerance'.
46 Brown, 'Deepening democracy'.
47 See Russell *et al.* 'Women's representation in the Scottish Parliament and the National Assembly for Wales'.
48 Breitenbach, 'The Impact of Thatcherism on women in Scotland'; Brown, 'Thatcher's legacy for women in Scotland'; Breitenbach and Mackay 'Introduction', *Women and Contemporary Scottish Politics*.
49 Dobrowolsky, 'Shifting states: Women's constitutional organising across time and space', p. 134.
50 Mackay *et al.*, 'Towards a new politics?', p. 97.
51 Childs, *New Labour's Women MPs*.
52 Beveridge *et al.*, 'Mainstreaming and the engendering of policy-making'; Squires and Wickham-Jones, 'New Labour, gender mainstreaming and the Women and Equality Unit'; Mackay and Bilton, *Learning from Experience*.
53 Keating, *The Government of Scotland*.
54 Scottish Partnership on Domestic Abuse.
55 Mackay, 'The impact of devolution on women's citizenship in Scotland'.

56 Mackay, 'The impact of devolution on women's citizenship in Scotland'. Information gathered from Women and Equality Unit, Home Office Domestic Violence Team, and various departments February-March 2004, supplementary information posted late March 2004 at www.womenandequalityunit.gov.uk/domestic_violence/index.htm. Accessed April 25, 2004.
57 Segal, *Why Feminism?*
58 Banaszak *et al.*, *Women's Movements Facing the Reconfigured State*, p. 19.
59 See for example Annesley *et al. Women and New Labour*.

3 Autonomy and engagement

Women's movements in Australia and South Korea

Sarah Maddison and Kyungja Jung

The Korean and Australian women's movements have both been vigorous in pursuing relationships with the state. These strategies have produced significant advances in gender equality in both countries, and have seen a partial institution-alisation of feminist perspectives within state policy-making processes. However, a triumphalist view of the gains of liberal feminism does not tell the whole story in either country. Both women's movements have experienced risks and disadvantages by maintaining a strong state focus, not least in terms of the implications for a continuing autonomous movement. A significant challenge has been the ability to adapt to changing political contexts.

This chapter explores the ways in which women's movements in both countries have changed and adapted to new environments. The analysis is developed through our suggestion that there are two lenses through which to view the trajectories of social movements. The first lens, which we are calling the institutional lens, directs our analysis towards changes in political opportunity structure, context and institutions, such as the process of democratisation, in the Korean case, or in the Australian case, the rise of neo-liberalism, the introduction of the new managerialism and the dominance of public choice theory within government. The second lens, which we are calling the cultural lens, instead points to the cultural consequences of state engagement, including, in Australia, the decline of liberationist discourse and the hegemony of liberal feminism and in Korea, the institutionalisation of the movement. Further, this lens suggests that the dominant state focus of Korean and Australian feminism has neglected a broader feminist political culture, evident in Korea through the decline in autonomous feminist organising, and in Australia, through the loss of a radical feminist focus on women's personal experiences of oppression. These lenses mirror the two major strands in social movement theory discussed below.

Variants of social movement theorising

As outlined in the Introduction to this book, there have been competing para-digms in the literature on social movements, each asserting their explanatory power in making sense of social movement activity. Scholars working in the political process theory strand (PPT) link the development of social movements to 'a broader "political process" ',[1] which enables those groups that have been excluded from political influence to attempt to gain access to state power. Sidney Tarrow suggests that making these links enables scholars to 'embed the study of movements within a larger universe of contentious politics and thence to politics in general'. PPT encourages analyses of the relationships between social movements and the state with the view that 'activists do not choose goals, strategies and tactics in a vacuum' and that actors' agency can only be properly understood within a structural context.[2]

Other scholars, however, claim that the external political focus of PPT does not allow factors such as culture or emotion[3] to be seen as crucial to the development and maintenance of movements and movement organisations. Some, such as Stacey Young, are critical of the limited definition that PPT provides for a movement's success, that is, the extent to which social movement organisations are accepted by political elites.[4] Young contends that this view is consistent with the dominance of liberalism in much analysis of collective action that consequently neglects movements' radical and cultural politics.

In contrast, the so-called 'new' social movements approach provides a significant 'culturalist challenge'[5] to the political process paradigm through its emphasis on the signs and codes that are produced and contested at all levels of society and that reveal the potential of the symbolic challenge of contemporary social movements.[6] In the case of feminist activism, for example, it is clear that changing culturally inscribed codes that govern existing gender relations can have significant material effects in women's lives. By producing alternative frameworks of knowledge and meaning, and allowing for new ways of living that confront the 'rationality of the system'[7] contemporary social movements offer a deep challenge to the existing order that goes beyond instrumental politics. In contrast with more traditional understandings of social change that concentrate on political parties, pressure groups and institutional politics, the 'new' social movements approach provides greater acknowledgement of the role that movement actors play in transforming cultural patterns.[8]

The Australian women's movement: reviewing femocracy, relocating the movement

Beginning in the 1970s, the Australian women's movement forged a unique relationship with the state that was notable for the high levels of 'interconnectedness' between activists outside the state and those within the bureaucracy.[9] In the intervening decades there has been much justified praise for the innovative 'wheel' model of women's policy machinery developed through this relationship. This 'internationally remarkable' model gave the rest of the world the 'femocrat', the name for feminists appointed to positions in the bureaucracy with a specific directive to improve policy outcomes for women.[10] However the recent decline of Commonwealth and State femocratic structures and processes, which has been met with barely a whimper from the broader women's movement, has led many to question the sustainability of the model. As the struggle for gender equality – once considered a 'permanent priority' in the national capital – began to be wound back, some directed their anger to the current federal government while others renewed their questioning of what may have been lost through the 'hegemony of liberal feminism' in Australia.[11]

The handful of published histories of the Australian women's movement recount a familiar story.[12] Women's Liberation arrived in Australia in 1969 and developed rapidly. In 1972 a reformist organisation, the Women's Electoral Lobby (WEL) was formed by women wanting to move beyond talk of women's liberation to focus on political reform. WEL wanted to reach out to suburban and rural women perhaps uncomfortable with the radicalism of Women's Liberation and to influence the 1972 federal election. With the election of the reforming social democrat Labor government in 1972 feminists successfully entered the state, an innovative model of women's policy machinery was developed and a period of rapid policy advancement ensued. Over the following years the mainstream movement appeared to enter a period of abeyance, resulting in the loss of many gains from the previous period. What is less frequently explored is what was lost along with the radical, liberationist discourse of the early Women's Liberation movement. The following two sections of this chapter revisit this history through the institutional and cultural lenses.

The institutional view

Much in the literature concerning the second wave of the Australian women's movement points to the fortunate coincidence of a resurgent women's movement and a reforming federal Labor government (the story presented in Gwendolyn Gray's chapter). It is often concluded that the women's movement in Australia would not have pursued such a close relationship with the state, nor would feminists have been so successful in institutionalising their goals, were it not for this fact.[13] Aside from this particular political circumstance, however, it is also acknowledged that the women's movement had little option but to engage with the state as a means of contesting the gender-blind way that policy problems were being constructed.[14] For those feminists who chose this path, the state was not conceived of as a monolithic or unified entity, but rather as providing complex 'arenas of discursive conflict' in which feminists could intervene with transformative intent despite the compromises that this would inevitably entail.[15]

As already noted, this state focus did produce some notable outcomes, not the least of which was an acceptance (that lasted several decades) that feminist-informed gender analysis had a legitimate place at the heart of government policy making. However, even in the 1970s there were concerns that the movement was rushing to take advantage of a favourable political opportunity structure despite the sort of organisational immaturity that would make it difficult to withstand the pressures that came with this relationship.[16]

Certainly the model of policy machinery developed by feminists in the 1970s was a model specifically for the times, characterised as it was by 'an interest in bureaucratic innovation, less hierarchy, more street level administration and more openness to the community'.[17] With the benefit of hindsight that is not clouded by the emotions of the time, however, perhaps the construction of a model that relied, at least in part, on a broad social democratic consensus and on external pressure from the women's movement, was somewhat misguided.[18] The pressure required under this model needed to come from a visible, united, and highly mobilised movement; the sort of movement that history shows is only ever in episodic existence over longer cycles of movement continuity.[19]

Since the 1970s, the political opportunity structure has changed dramatically. Although the blame for current circumstances is often laid at the feet of long serving Prime Minister, John Howard (who held office between 1996 and 2007), many of the external problems that have contributed to the downturn in feminist influence and visibility are rooted in the broader political and economic context. A restructured economy has shifted the political focus from social justice considerations to a neo-liberal market-driven focus on individualism and a winding back of the welfare state.[20] As in the case of New Zealand, discussed by Sandra Grey in this collection, women's non-government organisations began to be framed as 'special interest groups', further reducing the pressure on government to listen to feminist policy advice.[21] The introduction of new public management techniques to reform and reduce the size of government led to a reduction of 'in-house policy expertise' including gender analysis expertise.[22] Inside government, as women's units became less 'risky' in career terms, more nominally 'femocrat' positions were being filled by women with no background in the women's movement.[23] Meanwhile, feminists in government continued to grapple with their dual sense of accountability both to government and to an increasingly diversified women's movement. Over time, and by necessity, feminists became focussed on 'defensive politics'[24] as they tried to hold on to their gains and resist both a neo-liberal onslaught and a neo-conservative backlash against feminism itself.

The result has been the almost total demise of a feminist presence in government. Although Marian Sawer points out quite rightly that the decline cannot be entirely attributed to the movement's 'entrist', state-focussed strategy,[25] it is also probable that the dominant state focus did contribute to a certain invisibility for the broader movement, particularly as movement organisations were partially 'regularised' and 'harnessed' by their funding relationship with government.[26] The paradox for feminists was that the price of policy success inside government was an increasing lack of influence and access for activists outside the bureaucracy.[27] This in turn meant that the women's machinery itself would be unable to function in an increasingly hostile political context.

At least this is the conclusion that can be drawn from an analysis through the institutional lens: that the observable 'fall of the femocrat' is the inevitable outcome of a decline in political opportunities and a changing political context. This ' "period" perspective' would be the standard assessment offered by political process scholars.[28] However, as Mary Katzenstein suggests, this perspective misses things that may be better explained with a look through the cultural lens.[29]

The cultural view

Along with the story of liberal feminist dominance described above, histories of Australian feminism also record the radical feminist critique of the reformist, state focus that emerged in the Australian women's movement in the 1970s. A more ambitious and revolutionary understanding of social change animated these liberationists, who scorned full citizenship, equality and reform as meaningful goals. Socialist and radical feminists, who dominated the Women's Liberation groups, articulated a far broader social critique than could be accommodated by even a reformed state. There was fear that liberal feminists, and in particular the newly christened femocrats, would be co-opted and serve merely to legitimise the 'irredeemably patriarchal' state without fundamentally changing it.[30] Hester Eisenstein summarises the view that:

> [U]ltimately the interests of feminists and of the state diverged radically: the state worked for capitalism and patriarchy, whereas the women's movement worked to dismantle both systems.[31]

The focus for radical feminists was on both 'self-emancipation' and on doing away with the hierarchical structures of many existing social movement organisations.

Despite these critiques, however, with the success of the WEL intervention in the 1972 election a new path seemed set and, in some senses, the divisions between feminists expanded. While in many ways organisations such as WEL found it useful to have groups expressing the more radical discourse that made reformist demands seem reasonable, eventually the movement as a whole began to be constituted by its relations with the state.[32] The 'ascendency' of a 'hegemony of liberal feminism' meant that the reformist strand of the movement came to dominate the discourse of the women's movement as a whole, over time virtually silencing the more revolutionary liberationists.[33] Jean Curthoys has controversially argued that liberation theory and ideas were repressed in the movement, not as a conscious move, but because it became an unconscious requirement that they not be expressed in a way that undermined the movement's developing relationship with the state. She suggests that this resulted in a 'compulsory dissociation' that prevented any recognition of the more positive aspect of women's liberation.[34] In turn, a more muted radical voice contributed to the organisational disappearance of women's liberation groups themselves, although some persisted into the 1990s.

A decline in more radical liberation discourse is common to many movements, producing a type of 'amnesia' that is 'socially produced, packaged, promulgated, and perpetuated'.[35] As Nancy Whittier has argued, 'cultural hegemony triumphs by making non-dominant points of view invisible or unthinkable'.[36] This results in the complexities of radical ideology and struggle disappearing from the 'public imagination' reducing political, and in this case, feminist critiques to their liberal version, 'easily graspable within the dominant "grammar" or paradigm'.[37] It is possible to surmise that one outcome of the decline in liberationist discourse within the Australian women's movement is that the state was able to not only respond on its own terms,[38] but was also able to *remake the movement* on its own terms.[39] As movement veteran Joan Bielski recently assessed:

> With hindsight, the women's movement underestimated the strength of the dominant culture and the countervailing forces, and showed a naive faith in the state, the political system and legislation to deliver them justice.[40]

There is nothing here to suggest that radical movements by themselves will always be vigorous, nor will they always make gains. But they are an essential component of a broader movement that can apply both internal and external pressure on states. The decline in liberationist discourse in the Australia women's movement created losses for the broader movement, for example the loss of emphasis on discursive politics, in both speech and print, that were part of the more direct attempts by the early movement to 'change fundamentally the way people think'.[41] The roneoed copies of Annie Koedt's *The Myth of the Vaginal Orgasm* from the 1970s were replaced with glossy brochures that promoted government achievements for women. Also lost was the radical women's movement focus on the private and the personal, the emphasis on consciousness raising, the transforming of individuals through personal renewal, the unveiling of previously 'taboo subjects' and the capacity to make connections between these personal and cultural issues and the broader economic and political context.[42]

The entry into government also profoundly challenged the feminist commitment to non-hierarchical organisational forms and the sort of connections and group processes that were possible (although not without problems of their own) in these contexts. The loss of these personal connections may account for the subsequent loss of visibility for the movement as personal commitments to organising and attending public protests waned. And along with the public protests have gone many of the important feminist cultural events that promoted movement visibility and were essential to defining an ongoing collectivity. The net effect is the inevitable 'dilution' of feminism, particularly in its more radical forms, through the process of negotiation and compromise that a state-focussed feminism necessitates.[43] Or, as Elizabeth Wilson suggests, when one half of a political continuum, such as radical feminism, disappears or is repressed, what is left is a 'peculiar kind of vacuum' that is challenging to the survival of the political whole.[44]

None of this is to in any way glorify or reify radical feminism over the liberal variant. The false promise of sisterhood among women, along with the problems of 'structurelessness' and disorganisation are too well known for that. Indeed it has been argued that it was the very disorganisation of Women's Liberation that created the space in which Australian liberal feminism could flourish.[45] Nor is it to suggest that radical deinstitutionalisation alone will be effective. However, it does seem that through the cultural lens there is a different view of the factors that may have helped sustain the movement through a difficult political period, and which may have enabled the sort of continued pressure on government that could have ensured the survival of the femocrat. And perhaps this view does still offer a slightly more hopeful vision. The cultural lens provides for recognition of movements as persisting in culture, through dispersed networks and organisations submerged in daily life. While there is no denying the net reduction in the size and influence of the Australian women's movement, nor the current absence of feminist activism from the visible mainstream of state-focussed institutional politics, it must also be noted that there *are* groups and organisations, including groups of younger women, still at work in a broadly conceived movement. In many cases these groups – in communities or in coalition with other movements – are invisible to the institutionally trained eye.[46]

Korea: democratisation and institutionalisation

The recent history of the Korean women's movement has been dramatically different from the situation in Australia. For two decades the Korean movement was focused on the struggle for democratisation rather than on advancing women's rights per se. It is only in recent years that a 'gender perspective' has begun to be institutionalised within the Korean state. The rapid pace of this institutionalisation, however, has left many feminist activists concerned with the weakened critical nature of the women's movement, and for the future autonomy of their movement.

Despite these concerns, it is clear that at present the Korean women's movement is active, visible and influential. There is a mass grassroots base and substantial funding from its own membership and fundraising activities that allows a degree of independence from government funding. Overall, Korean women's organisations have more resources, are larger in membership and have a greater number of full-time workers than Australian organisations.

While the contemporary Korean and Australian women's movements diverge, there are similarities between the contemporary Korean women's movement and the Australian movement of an earlier period. Much like the Australian women's movement in the 1970s, the Korean women's movement initiates and organises a wide range of activities including the production of feminist newspapers and journals, a feminist food co-op, an alternative cultural group, a singing group, rape crisis centres, domestic violence services, women's refuges and so on. Despite a 20-year time lag, the Korean women's movement and the Australian movement have also taken similar steps with regard to the significant role of women's studies graduates and feminist scholars in the development of women's policy and policy machinery, the emergence of femocrats, and both movements' engagement with the state. Given these similarities there are questions to be asked about how the Korean movement can avoid some of the problems that have befallen Australian feminism during the last ten years.

The institutional view

This section reviews the development of the women's movement in South Korea and discusses the nature of the movement in the process of a political transition. The analysis sees the development as progressing from a traditional Confucian structure under authoritarian military rule, through democratic struggle to the achievement and consolidation of democracy. Throughout these transitions, the Korean women's movement has demonstrated a remarkable adaptability.

In the early 1970s, women's groups were not particularly concerned with issues regarding women's rights and equality, although there were some women's groups concerned with promoting and implementing government policies. For example, the Korean National Council of Women (KNCW), an umbrella organisation founded in 1959 by middle-class women, served as an agency to promote government policies and played a critical role in implementing the family planning program. The nature of the KNCW was shown in their slogans: 'National Development by Women's Power' (1964), 'Women's Duty in Modernisation' (1966) and 'The 1970s and the Population Problem' (1970).[47] In the 1970s, the struggle to reform family law and occasional labour strikes by female factory workers were the major activities of the women's movement.

Feminist issues were also being raised in the universities. In 1977, the first women's studies course was established at the Ewha Women's University, which has become a major site of feminist theory and activism. Although there was criticism that an uncritical acceptance of western feminism would increase confusion between feminists, feminist academics helped to promote the recognition of women's issues as a major social question.

As a consequence of international pressure and national activities, the government agreed to amend various discriminatory laws relating to women. The Equal Employment Act of 1987 was the first action taken by the government after the ratification of CEDAW, although this legislation was seen by progressive feminist activists as insufficient to bring substantial equality in employment. The setting up of the Basic Plan on Women's Development in 1985, and the amendment of the Mother and Child Health Act in 1986, brought women's issues to the level of policy discourse under the agenda of women's development. However, the 'women in development' policy framework in the 1980s failed to address the causes and consequences of gender inequality.[48]

For Korea, 1987 was a momentous year in its transition to democracy, with university students, intellectuals, workers and middle-class people forming an alliance in opposition to the Noh Tae Woo regime, and demanding democratisation and constitutional reform of Korean politics and government. These protests culminated in the People's Peaceful March on June 26, 1987, involving 1.3 million demonstrators in 37 cities. As a result President Noh Tae Woo drafted a conciliatory declaration, which accepted a direct presidential election system under a substantially amended new constitution.

After the 1987 reforms, political freedom, characterised by free elections and the consequent strengthening of civil society, transformed both the democratisation movement and the women's movement. The women's movement gave priority in the 1980s to the issues of democracy and nationalism rather than emphasising its own autonomy and independence. The women's movement tried to mobilise women into the democracy movement. After democratisation, however, the progressive women's movement, which had been part of the movement for democratisation, kept a distance from the national social movement and began to organise its own activities related to women's issues. Gender-specific issues finally became the main agenda of the women's movement in the late 1980s and early 1990s, including Equal Opportunities and Equal Employment (1988–89); rape and trafficking in women (1990), sex slavery during the Second World War and sexual violence (1992).

After the establishment of a civilian government in 1993, the question of legitimacy became critical to the social forces that had previously operated outside institutional politics. In particular, through the globalisation drive of Kim Young-sam (1993–97), Korea directed its attention towards the international arena. State and civil society actors, including the women's movement, drew on international standards to press for social change.

In 1994, Korea was elected as a member state of the UN Commission on the Status of Women. The elections for the National Assembly and local councils, as well as the 1995 World Conference on Women in Beijing, constituted the political backdrop against which the women's movement adopted a gender perspective. The movement no longer saw the state as an antagonist, but as an arena where women's problems could be tackled. This change in perception facilitated a 'politics of engagement with the state' in the 1990s.[49]

During this time progressive women's movement organisations also began to receive financial support from the government. Organisations formally incorporated themselves in order to secure legitimacy and gain access to state funds, as happened in other nations such as New Zealand, Canada, and Australia (see Gwendolyn Gray and Sandra Grey, this collection). The women's movement worked to bring women's issues onto the mainstream policy agenda, campaigning for legislation for women's policies. The women's movement also actively participated in conventional political processes such as elections.[50] The efforts inside the government and by the women's movement brought considerable policy gains in the area of sexual violence, domestic violence, sexual harassment and sex trafficking. Some activists have described this period as 'the renaissance era of the women's movement in Korea'.[51]

The election of President, Kim Dae-jung, in 1997 (the first successful opposition candidate) was viewed as 'another major step towards democratic consolidation'.[52] The DJ administration, the so-called 'People's Government', highlighted a partnership with civil society and gained historical support from labour and civic groups. In 2003, former human rights lawyer Roh Moo-hyun took office with anti-American rhetoric and populist promises: democracy with the people, a society of balanced development, and an era of peace and prosperity.

Under the governments of Kim Dae-jung (1998–2002) and Roh Moo-hyun (2003–07), there has been a strong alliance between government and the women's movement, with gender mainstreaming being adopted as the main strategy to achieve gender equality in all areas of policy. There has also been a dramatic increase in female participation in the legislature. In the 2004 general election, women won 39 out of 299 seats (13 per cent), a two-fold increase over the outgoing Assembly, where there were only 16 female law-makers (5.9 per cent). Four female ministers were appointed and, surprisingly, Kang Keum-sil was appointed as the first female Minister of Justice in Korea. In 2006, Han Myung-suk, a well-known feminist activist, was appointed as Korea's first woman prime minister.

Under the DJ administration in particular, a firm organisational base for major women's policies in the state and local governments was established, culminating in the establishment of the Ministry of Gender Equality (MOGE). Support for feminist organisations was dramatically increased. Moreover, a number of feminist activists were appointed as senior government officers and they became the first femocrats in Korea. Korean femocrats were recruited from diverse backgrounds such as former women's movement activists, political parties and women's studies graduates. It is too early to evaluate their achievements and limitations. All policy areas were to be scrutinised to address and rectify both persistent and emerging disparities between men and women. Accordingly, the term *gender* instead of the term *women* was first introduced to women's policy discourses in Korea.

Despite its limited budget and staff, the MOGE made a significant contribution to expanding policy discourse. It launched initiatives to accelerate gender mainstreaming such as the introduction of a gendered perspective into the national budget planning process. One of the most important accomplishments was its contribution to the passage of the Maternity Law Reform Bill in 2001, which guarantees three months paid maternity leave and one year of partially paid parental and family nursing leave.[53] MOGE, along with women's movement organisations and other civic organisations, has also been running a campaign against Hoju-je, a family register system that has upheld a patriarchal structure of Korean society by granting priority to men over women in heading a family. In 2005, a majority of law-makers voted in favour of revising the Civil Law to replace the hoju system. This victory has resulted from the vigorous efforts of women for more than 30 years.

The cultural view: achievements and reflections

Viewed through the institutional lens, the achievements of the women's movement are seen by Koreans and outsiders as a success story. But there are a number of issues revealed by the cultural lens that need also to be considered in evaluating the trajectory of the Korean movement. In particular, this lens suggests that the movement has not been successful in developing a broader gender consciousness in Korean society and culture. With an eye to the trajectory of the Australian movement this lack of deeper cultural change may have negative consequences for feminist autonomy.

As feminists have assumed a more significant role in state institutions and processes, there has been growing criticism about the institutionalisation of the women's movement in Korea.[54] From a women's movement point of view, institutionalisation was viewed as a strategy rather than the ultimate goal. Some feel institutionalisation has weakened the role of movement organisations and the activities of organisations in the autonomous women's movement have transformed into government-funded projects or services, rather than activities oriented to social and cultural change.[55]

In particular, the progressive Korean Women's Association United (KWAU), a nationwide umbrella organisation with 30 000 members and 28 women's organisations, has been one of the major targets of criticism. No one denies the leading role the KWAU has played in engaging with the state through involvement in the policy making process. Nicola Jones has even pointed out that a hybrid women's movement, represented by two umbrella organisations (the progressive KWAU and the conservative Council of Korean Women's Organisations), enabled feminist activists to maximise political opportunities and gain respect as legitimate actors in formal political negotiations. However, this institutional success needs to be balanced with a broader consideration of the factors contributing to strength and effectiveness of the women's movement in Korea. Questions need to be asked about whether absorbing the energies of organisations such as the KWAU into governmental activities will diminish the factors that made it significant in the first place. The efforts of well-qualified and trained activists, their success in mobilising the general public, and their ability to use such diverse strategies as lobbying, petitioning, street demonstrations and single-issue campaigning are potentially at great risk through institutionalisation.

Further, some research suggests that feminist involvement in state machinery or political parties could fragment and weaken the women's movement more broadly.[56] The representatives of some women's movement organisations have already been criticised for being eager to enter into government positions or political parties at any cost. Some organisations have even revised their constitutions to enable this integration into government. In this context there developed a saying that NGO means 'Next Government Officials'. The close connection between government officers and the women's movement, in particular the KWAU, has been seen as co-option of the movement. Where women's organisations rely on funding from the government, it has become more difficult to criticise government policies, and funding has also been seen as leading to a privileged voice for some feminists. Because of KWAU's now overpowering influence, the voices from minority organisations such as new organisations, or organisations that are not members of the KWAU, tend to be excluded from agenda setting, resource allocation and participation in the policy process. There are even signs of conflict between 'old feminists' (established, institutionalised) and 'young feminists' (independent and autonomous feminist groups) – a tension that is mirrored in Australia's and other women's movements explored in this collection.

Apart from these questions about the consequences of a loss of movement autonomy, there are also questions about whether feminist entry into the state has been effective in terms of real policy gains. Critics say that the most developed women's policies are those that attract attention but do not require much in the way of financial allocation and that the development of women's policies has been used as a tool to attract female voters. It is argued that women's policy is mere electoral rhetoric and that the true nature of the policy commitment to women's issues is demonstrated in the General Budget, which shows that only 0.29 per cent of the total government budget (2002) is spent on women-related programs and policies. In addition, there is often a discrepancy between laws and policies and the reality of implementation,[57] possibly as a result of the speed of the development of women's policy.

Policy development in Korea has relied, perhaps too extensively, on international policy discourse and programs. For instance, the concept of gender mainstreaming, as introduced in Beijing in 1995, has been widely used among academics, activists and policy experts in Korea. However there seems to be widespread confusion over the meaning of gender mainstreaming and related concepts among low-level government officers. While international policy borrowing is common, including from Australia, specifically Korean issues have been less well addressed by the policy community. For instance, policies for women who have escaped from North Korea and for female migrant workers need to be tackled, as does the feminisation of poverty and informalisation of the female workforce.

Although there has been a huge change in the perception of women's status and role in Korean society in the last ten years, there remains a significant gap between femocrat-influenced policy statements and the culture of Korea. For example, when MOGE was first set up, those who objected to the establishment of the department left numerous complaint messages on its home page, leading to a brief closure of the ministry's website. Even today, the consciousness of gender equality in the policy community, or among the people as a whole, has not caught up with feminist-influenced policy statements. Greater cultural change is needed in order to enhance people's awareness of, and commitment to, gender equality in Korea. As is seen in the case of Australia, this sort of cultural change is essential for protecting institutional reforms and policy developments.

Conclusion

What can the view through these two lenses tell us about the long-term autonomy and survival of the Australian and Korean women's movements?

In the case of Australia, we hope they redirect attention from the much-discussed generational schism in the movement brought about by suggestions from older women that young women were not 'reach[ing] out for the torch' in the way that they had hoped.[58] Although it is clear that young women are still engaging in feminist activism on university campuses, in the community and in coalition with other movements,[59] it would be useful to reconsider – without blame – why it is that young women are not engaging with a more 'mainstream' feminism.[60] Perhaps the answer is, in part, revealed through the questions suggested by the cultural lens. What is interesting for young women, as a political generation coming of age over the last ten or 20 years? Where is the personal connection? What is relevant about contemporary feminism to the sorts of oppression young women are dealing with in their own lives? Similar questions may be asked in Korea over the next few years if young women there begin to perceive institutionalised feminism as irrelevant in their own lives.

In the case of Australia, the institutional lens shows us that a decline in the political opportunity structure necessitates a revisiting of favoured strategies.[61] As the femocracy crumbles perhaps it is time to turn away from the state, and to develop a renewed focus on networks and organisations. The cultural lens supports this view and suggests that although the movement is certainly constrained by context, that context includes the movement itself.[62] Feminist activists are not entirely dependent on the political opportunity structure, including the government of the day, for their connections to one another, nor to their grassroots. If it now appears that a liberal feminist focus and the decline of a more radical feminism have not served the movement well over time, perhaps a revival of the more radical, cultural, personal and autonomous elements of the movement may help revive an earlier dynamism.

The Korean case shows that the role of the women's movement is also changing because of its relationship with the state and women's policy machinery. Many studies have indicated that the strength and independence of the women's movement is vital in the development of women's policy and effective implementation.[63] It is suggested that femocrats are better able to enhance state responsiveness to woman's issues when working alongside autonomous women's movements.[64] More significantly, it needs to be remembered that the success of the femocrat strategy depends upon the simultaneous existence of a strong and autonomous women's movement[65] – the insider/outsider strategy discussed in the Introduction to this collection.

In her doctoral research on Korean women's politics, Nicola Jones argues that the timing of movement emergence as well as the choice of alliance and discursive strategies significantly impact upon movement groups' abilities to realise their political goals.[66] In South Korea, unlike Latin America and Eastern Europe, democratisation did not necessarily lead to a decline in women's political influence. The key factors in avoiding marginalisation included establishing umbrella organisations to coordinate the representation of women's gendered demands, forging alliances with progressive civic movements, engaging with the state both from outside and within state institutions and framing interests in culturally resonant ways. However, as the Australian case highlights, the risks of femocratic strategies also need to be considered. The women's movement in South Korea has now reached a point where critical reflection is needed in order to maintain the movement's autonomy and independence.[67]

Much research indicates that despite the presence of more women in the policy-making process and women's policy machinery, it will be impossible to make further progress in Korean women's policy without the presence of a strong, autonomous women's movement.[68] Weldon argues that 'it is not just the existence, but also the autonomy of women's groups that is important for their success in influencing policy'.[69] An autonomous women's movement is an essential voice in the critique of government policies, improving the 'substantive' representation of women in the policy-making process.

Suzanne Franzway *et al.* once argued that, for the sake of its own ongoing legitimacy, the state will always need to deal with feminism and the women's movement to some extent.[70] However, time has shown that state agencies and funded women's organisations are, to varying degrees, controlled by government and therefore are easier to manipulate and silence. In Australia, the last decade has demonstrated nothing more clearly than the extent of the entrenched opposition to women in Australian politics[71] and the ease with which seemingly permanent achievements can be done away with in a hostile political climate. For Korea, which has long looked to other countries for ideas and inspiration in their struggle for gender equality, the Australian women's movement offers some sobering lessons. Perhaps the focus for contemporary movements should not be on presenting a more coordinated national organisational response in order to demand an adequate state response, as the institutional lens might suggest. Perhaps the first step is to attend to the grassroots, to a feminist culture that attends to local issues and which may revive a broader belief in the radically transformative potential of women themselves.

Notes

1 Diani, 'The concept of social movement', p. 158.
2 Tarrow, 'Paradigm warriors', p. 76.
3 For a discussion of their importance see for example Polletta and Amenta, 'Second that emotion?'; Goodwin and Jasper, 'Caught in a winding, snarling vine'.
4 Young, *Changing the Wor(l)d*, p. 20.
5 Buechler, *Social Movements in Advanced Capitalism*, p. 52.
6 Melucci, *Challenging Codes*.
7 Masson, 'Language, power and politics', p. 59.
8 Jennett and Stewart (eds), *Politics of the Future*, p. 1.
9 Magarey, 'The Sex Discrimination Act 1984', p. 127.
10 The 'wheel' model was designed by feminists in the movement and entailed a centre or 'hub' located in the 'major policy co-ordinating agency of government, and spokes in line departments and agencies'. Twenty years later this 'distinctive institutional design' became the benchmark adopted by the United Nations for women's machinery of government. Sawer, *The Ethical State?*, pp. 111 and 114.
11 Summers, *The End of Equality*, p. 122; Magarey, 'The Sex Discrimination Act 1984', p. 128.
12 See for example Kaplan, *The Meagre Harvest*; Lake, *Getting Equal*.
13 Yeatman, *Bureaucrats, Technocrats, Femocrats*, p. 89; Sawer, 'Australia: The fall of the femocrat'.
14 Bacchi, 'Rolling back the state?', p. 65.
15 Sawer, *The Ethical State?*, pp. 112–113.
16 See for example Ryan, *Catching the Waves*, p. 125; Reid, 'The child of our movement', pp. 12–13.

17 Sawer, *Sisters in Suits*, p. 37.
18 Franzway *et al.*, *Staking a Claim*, p. 134; Segal, *Why Feminism?*, pp. 24–25, Lake, *Getting Equal*, p. 260; Burgmann, *Power, Profit and Protest*, p. 155.
19 Rupp and Taylor, *Survival in the doldrums*.
20 Wilson, 'Feminism today'; Segal, *Why Feminism?*, p. 25; Bacchi, 'Rolling back the state?, p. 55; Sawer, *The Ethical State?*, p. 115.
21 Maddison and Denniss, 'Democratic constraint and embrace'; Sawer, 'Australia: The fall of the femocrat'.
22 Sawer, 'Australia: The fall of the femocrat'.
23 Sawer, *Sisters in Suits*, p. 32.
24 Wilson, 'Feminism today', p. 214.
25 Sawer, 'Feminism and the state', p. 101.
26 Kaplan, *The Meagre Harvest*, p. 35.
27 Eisenstein, *Inside Agitators*, p. 19.
28 Whittier, *Feminist Generations*, p. 83.
29 Katzenstein, *Faithful and Fearless*, p. 32.
30 Sawer, *The Ethical State?* p. 112.
31 Eisenstein, *Inside Agitators*, pp. xv–xx.
32 Burgmann, *Power, Profit and Protest*, p. 153.
33 Magarey, 'The Sex Discrimination Act 1984', p. 127.
34 Curthoys, *Feminist Amnesia*, pp. 5–6.
35 Du Plessis and Snitow quoted in Segal, *Why Feminism?* p. 11.
36 Whittier, *Feminist Generations*, p. 53.
37 Young, *Changing the Wor(l)d*, p. 2.
38 Franzway *et al.*, *Staking a Claim*, p. 158.
39 Young, *Changing the Wor(l)d*, p. 2.
40 Bielski, 'Australian feminism 2004', p. 7.
41 Young, *Changing the Wor(l)d*, p. 3; Katzenstein, *Faithful and Fearless*, pp. 17–18; Campo, '"Having it all" or "had enough"?', p. 65.
42 Lake, *Getting Equal*, pp. 232–233; Kaplan, *The Meagre Harvest*, p. 78; Segal, *Why Feminism?*, p. 5.
43 Sawer, *Sisters in Suits*, p. 252.
44 Wilson, 'Feminism today', p. 215.
45 Lake, *Getting Equal*, p. 238.
46 For a discussion of the work of young women in the contemporary Australian women's movement see Maddison, 'Young women in the Australian women's movement: Collective identity and discursive politics', pp. 234–256; Maddison, '"A part of living feminism"'.
47 Chin, 'Self-Governance, political participation, and the feminist movement in South Korea', p. 96.
48 Kim *et al.*, *A Feasibility Study for Building Korean Gender Management System*.
49 Kim, 'A frame analysis of women's policies of Korean government and women's movement in the 1980s and 1990s'.
50 Chin, 'Reflections on women's empowerment through local representation in South Korea', p. 295.
51 Jung, *Constitution and Maintenance of Feminist Practice*.
52 Jones, *Mainstreaming Gender*, p. 92.
53 Jones, *Mainstreaming Gender*, p. 316.
54 Korean Women's Association United, *Workshop for Evaluation of Women's Policy in the Kim Dae Jung Government and Policy Suggestion*; Kim, 'A frame analysis of women's policies'; Cho, 'Consequences of the entry of the representatives of women's movement organizations into political institutions'; Jung, 'The institutionalization of the Women's Movement'.
55 Jung, 'The institutionalization of the Women's Movement'.

56 Hassim, 'The gender pact and democratic consolidation: Institutionalizing gender equality in the South African State'; Jones, *Mainstreaming Gender*, p. 131.
57 Kim *et al.*, *A Feasibility Study*.
58 Summers, 'Letter to the next generation', p. 197.
59 Maddison, 'Young women in the Australian women's movement'.
60 Bielski, 'Australian feminism 2004', p. 9.
61 Franzway *et al.*, *Staking a Claim*, p. 168.
62 Gelb and Hart, 'Feminist politics in a hostile environment', p. 181.
63 Alvarez, *Engendering Democracy in Brazil*; Weldon, *Protest, Policy and the Problem of Violence Against Women*.
64 Weldon, *Protest, Policy and the Problem of Violence Against Women*; Hassim, 'The gender pact and democratic consolidation'.
65 Jung, 'The institutionalization of the Women's Movement'.
66 Jones, *Mainstreaming Gender*, p. 5.
67 Cho, 'Yet unsolved problems: Discussion on the 17th general election and evaluation of the KWAU's response'; Yoon, 'Exploring changes in progressive women's movement'.
68 Weldon, *Protest, Policy and the Problem of Violence Against Women*; Hassim, 'The gender pact and democratic consolidation'.
69 Weldon, 'Beyond bodies', p. 1161.
70 Franzway *et al.*, *Staking a Claim*, p. 54.
71 Summers, *The End of Equality*; Chappell, 'Winding back Australian women's rights', pp. 475–488.

4   Institutional, incremental and enduring

Women's health action in Canada and Australia

Gwendolyn Gray

For at least 25 years, analysts have written about the decline of the women's movement and the advent of a 'post-feminist' era. It is said that the mass mobilisations and innovative collective actions of the 1960s and 1970s have given way to complacency (or maybe exhaustion and despondency). Other writers, however, have argued what is being witnessed is the process of movements developing 'abeyance' structures which allow them to scale down, maintain a core of supporters and hibernate during unfavourable periods. A state of readiness is preserved, giving movements the capacity to contribute to later waves of protest.[1]

This chapter examines theories of decline or abeyance by examining four decades of activism by the Australian and Canadian women's health movements. As with other sections of the women's movement, direct action has become less common than it was in the 1960s and 1970s, when women called for radical transformation of the conditions of women's lives. Although direct action has declined and demands have been moderated, neither the Australian nor the Canadian women's health movements can be said to be in 'abeyance', in the sense of merely presiding over a 'holding process', the meaning of abeyance adopted in this collection. Rather than marking time, groups of various kinds in the two countries are engaging regularly in policy-oriented action, although this is truer of Canada. The focus is on incremental advance, the production and dissemination of information, and the maintenance of existing state-funded infrastructures.

Further, these case studies do not support the depiction of social movement trajectories as necessarily moving from an early period of direct politics to later periods of institutionalisation and/or 'unobtrusive mobilisation'. Closer inspection of the activities of the two movements reveals that a variety of tactics and strategies, some conforming to the conflictual model and some having an institutional flavour, were used from the beginning.

Two insights of the literature are strongly corroborated. First, both cases demonstrate the central importance of political opportunity structure. According to this perspective, political action depends not only on the resources that a group can muster but also on the context in which action occurs. Second, both movements fit comfortably into a characterisation of the early twenty-first century women's movement as rich, complex and diversified, both in composition and modes of action. This portrayal, developed recently by prominent feminist theorists[2] rejects the idea that adaptation and changes necessarily denote decline.

Early political opportunities and catalysts for mobilisation

Women's health movements have been an important strand of the women's movements in Australia and Canada since the mobilisations of the 1960s and 1970s, although strong organisation developed a little earlier in Australia. The promotion of women's health as a legitimate political issue became a priority for feminists who viewed the subordinate status of women as a major factor contributing to ill health. Although diverse, women's health advocates have been united by agreement on a number of problems. Both movements developed a strong critique of conventional medical care systems which they saw as both reflecting and perpetuating women's unequal status. As well as contributing directly to women's lack of control over their bodies and their lives, it is argued that these systems over-medicalise normal processes, such as pregnancy and childbirth, and trivialise many issues of crucial concern to women. Social and emotional problems are frequently treated with inappropriate medical solutions such as tranquillisers. Moreover, conventional medical care systems fail to provide a range of services which women see as vitally important.

On the basis of this critique, Australian women moved into action in the first half of the 1970s. At the grassroots level in every State groups were formed with the aims of information sharing, skill development and the promotion of radical change. New services were set up, including telephone helplines, refuges, abortion counselling services, helplines for lesbians, women's health centres and abortion, rape crisis, sexual assault and domestic violence centres. The political opportunity structure was ripe for achievement, with the election of a reforming Labor government at the national level in 1972.

Under the Whitlam government, the first Australian grassroots-initiated women's health centre received public funding in 1974. Before that government lost office at the end of 1975, seven other grassroots women's health centres, 11 refuges and numerous other services, such as helplines, were funded.[3] The first National Women's Health Conference was held in 1975, organised by the Australian Department of Health as the Commonwealth's special contribution to International Women's Year. It was opened by the Prime Minister.

The Canadian women's health movement was not as strong as its Australian counterpart in the early years. When organisation took place, it tended to be around particular issues, such as reproductive health, DES (diethylstilbestrol), women and pharmaceuticals, violence against women and breast cancer. Canadian women were concerned with changing the conditions of women's lives but the initial radicalism characteristic of the Australian women's movement seems to have been weaker.[4] Boscoe *et al.* describe the early years as follows:

Women came together to share experiences and knowledge. We looked at
our cervixes, fitted diaphragms, helped each other get off mood-altering
drugs ... we shared stories about our interactions with the medical system ..
. We came to recognise the impact of issues such as violence and racism on
our health ... we understood that women's health is a political, social and
economic matter...[5]

They go on to describe the networks that were formed and the myriad activist
and self-help groups that were set up. However, in the absence of radical reforming governments such as Australia had at the national level in the early 1970s,
the Canadian network of publicly funded institutions established in the early
period was small.

Major strategies over four decades

In attempting to promote change that would improve women's health, feminists in Australia and Canada have undertaken a variety of activities in a
number of arenas, from the community level to the highest levels of national
policy-making. This diversity has been maintained and there has been a steady
proliferation of groups in the two women's health movements. In the 1970s
and 1980s in Australia, women's health networks in each State and Territory
were the main organisational face of the movement. In 2008, while some of
the old formal networks still operate, there are hundreds of additional groups
across the country.

Since the 1970s in Australia, those working in women's health services
(both government and non-government) have constituted a core network of
women's health advocates. Surrounded by a constellation of other groups –
some tiny – coalitions are formed for particular purposes. In Canada many
specialised groups active from early days still operate. The establishment of
the Women's Health Contribution Program in 1996 promoted a network of
individuals, organisations and groups who work and collaborate around
women's health research and the impact of gender. Broad participation is fos-
tered by the work of the Canadian Women's Health Network, which was
funded as part of the programme.

A major difference between the two movements is that there has always been
a strong focus on service provision in Australia, whereas the production and dissemination of information has been a higher priority in Canada. Otherwise, there
is a striking similarity in the orientation and modes of operation chosen by the
two movements. A strong critique of the biomedical model of health is founda-
tional to both movements and both aim to bring about social change by influencing policy and practice 'at all levels in government, in health services and in
communities'.[6]

In the 1960s and 1970s, many of the challenges to the social, cultural, economic and political systems were visible, noisy and direct. Marches, demonstrations and 'sit ins' were common forms of action and radical reform was

demanded. Some groups participated in public policy processes from the beginning. As 'policy-oriented mobilisation' gave rise to policy gains, more recruits were attracted to the women's health movements. This in turn, shaped the broader political opportunity structure.[7]

Towards the end of the 1970s, the political context began to change in English-speaking democracies as neo-liberalism gained ground.[8] According to Taylor, when successful social movements are confronted with 'a nonreceptive political and social environment', 'abeyance' structures are developed. In some versions of the abeyance story, the advent of this organisational mode results in lost opportunities[9] while in others, the strategy may achieve partial successes.[10]

Women's health action, however, did not move in a linear fashion from radicalism and direct protest action to abeyance or institutionalisation. A mix of tactics and strategies were used from the beginning. Grassroots activism resulted in consciousness-raising meetings, self-help groups, women's health publications and the establishment of women's health centres, shelters, rape crisis services, telephone help lines and counselling services, to name just a few.[11] Direct action was common, especially around reproductive health issues. However, in Australia in particular, direct action took place alongside more conventional forms of activism, such as the establishment of services and lobbying governments.[12] A 'double agenda' or 'double militancy' was developed: separate women's health services were created to help fill the vast unmet need that women identified. At the same time practice in and around the centres was intended to change 'the fundamental values and structures of society'.[13] In one notable case of combined direct and conventional action, a pair of Sydney buildings was illegally occupied to set up the Elsie Women's Refuge at the same time that a funding submission to government was being written.[14]

Serious disagreement over the question of cooperation with the state, partly explained by the fact that radical feminists were a particularly strong force in women's health, pervaded the movement.[15] While for some members the aim was to 'smash patriarchy ... by Christmas',[16] others envisaged a longer term project and sought to work through more institutionalised channels. Stevens describes this situation in her history of Leichhardt Women's Community Health Centre (LWCHC), Australia's first grassroots women's health centre, as follows:

> [S]ome thought that they should take advantage of the more favourable situation to try to build some permanent outposts for women, such as women's services controlled by women. Others thought that the movement needed to maintain its radical and oppositional stance without the support of government funding or interference. The tensions between these positions were not resolved and they often coexisted in a type of unhappy marriage within projects, including LWCHC, where defiance and acquiescence were twin progeny.[17]

While tensions persisted, a majority of feminists regarded the state 'as sufficiently neutral to accommodate women and women's interests'.[18] Government funding was sought and accepted by a wide range of service providers, including women's health centres, rape crisis and sexual assault centres, refuges, helplines and information lines.

In more recent years, there have been fewer instances of direct action, but the women's health movement of Australia continues to operate through multiple avenues and organisations. Major national and sub-national conferences, festivals, workshops and forums are held regularly. Incredibly diverse programmes and projects operate out of the network of feminist centres including community development, information dissemination and support projects. There is regular contact through the channels of modern technology in the form of online discussions and information sharing, videoconferencing and teleconferences. Submission writing, lobbying and direct action take place on an 'as needs' basis. For example, women across the country sprang into action in 1990 when a case was brought against the Canberra Women's Health Centre under the *Sex Discrimination Act 1984*. A complainant claimed that the Centre was discriminatory and should be closed because similar services were not provided for men. Women (and some men) marched in the streets in the ACT in the early 1990s calling for a change in the law to allow the establishment of an out-of-hospital community-run abortion service. Later in the decade, when a private members bill seeking to impose severe restrictions on the provision of abortion was introduced into the local legislature, women again geared for action. They staged among other things, a well-attended rally outside the Assembly. And the removal of most references to abortion from the criminal code of Western Australia was surrounded by an intense direct and indirect action campaign in 1998. In 2002, both direct and indirect action preceded legislation which removed abortion from the criminal code of the ACT, the first Australian jurisdiction to take this step. Direct action included operating information stalls at major shopping centres across the Territory in the weeks prior to the passage of the legislation.

Some of the changes in organisational mode have occurred due to technological advances. Teleconferencing and e-mail, the cost of which has fallen dramatically, enable network members to communicate frequently and effectively. Major national conferences and campaigns can be organised by women in different corners of the continent with very few (expensive) face-to-face meetings. In 2004, for example, members of the Australian Women's Health Network (AWHN) found out that the draft funding agreements between the Commonwealth and the States and Territories for 2004–09 had deleted reference to women's health. These agreements are the channels through which services established under the National Women's Health Program are jointly funded. Indeed, the draft agreements stated explicitly that no money was to be spent on programs other than communicable diseases, cancer screening and health risks. Members of the AWHN Committee, drawn from each State and Territory, gathered hastily in Melbourne to devise a strategy. A media release was written, a background paper put together and a letter sent to all relevant Parliamentarians. A lobbying strategy, involving Commonwealth, State and Territory governments, each of which would have to sign the new agreements, was devised.

Women outside government worked with women inside government. When the agreements were eventually signed a few months later, they retained reference to all existing programs. A national campaign, of some months duration, had been conducted by women from all jurisdictions with only one face-to-face meeting.

Other campaigns may be noisier and involve more segments of the broader women's health network. The 2005–06 campaign to remove legislative roadblocks in the way of the importation of RU-486 was highly publicised and involved action on many fronts. Some 20 non-government organisations came together in a new coalition called Reproductive Choice Australia (RCA), including Sexual Health and Family Planning Australia, Australian Reproductive Health Alliance, AWHN, Women's Health New South Wales, the Women's Electoral Lobby and the Public Health Association of Australia. RCA worked intensively to support a private members bill, introduced into Parliament by the Australian Democrats and subsequently co-sponsored by women senators from four different parties.

Heated public discussion was fuelled by the Health Minister's very public opposition to the RU-486 Bill and the Prime Minister's indication that he did not support it either. In particular, RCA set out to inform debate through media, web, public forums, fact sheets, letters and information sessions. It monitored the media, writing responses to all significant published opinions: there were over 1000 media articles in the 12 month period prior to the passage of the legislation. It systematically lobbied members of the National Parliament after the Prime Minister announced that a 'conscience vote' would be allowed on the matter; developed briefing and key message materials; sought funding from patrons; developed and managed an active web site; and co-operated on a petition with new on-line campaigning organisation, GetUp!. Pro-choice members of the Senate supported an enquiry into the Bill by the Social Affairs Committee, which took evidence in different parts of the country. After months of controversy the Bill passed through Parliament in February 2006.

Likewise in Canada, multiple forms of action were utilised from the beginning of the women's health movements. Strong mobilisation around abortion took place early. For example, an Abortion Caravan was created in 1970, which was supported by feminists all over the country. The Caravan began in Vancouver and eventually reached Ottawa where 35 feminists chained themselves to the public gallery of the House of Commons, closing down the Parliament.[19] Pro-choice rallies and marches were still being organised in 2004.[20] Other early initiatives included the establishment of the Montréal Health Press in 1968, founded when a group of McGill University students produced the first Birth Control Handbook in Canada at a time when providing such information was illegal.[21]

One of the most effective Canadian strategies was the production of a play, *Side Effects*. Women's health advocates worked with the Great Canadian Theatre Company to develop a play based on the problems women experienced with prescription drugs. The play toured successfully from coast to coast, while a French language version toured in Quebec. Women's health issues gained a higher profile and many new action groups were formed as a result.[22] As in Australia, health centres were established, although they were fewer in number. The Vancouver Women's Health Collective was established in 1972, the *Centre de Sante des Femmes du Quartier* of Montréal in 1978, along with several other Quebec centres, the Winnipeg Women's Health Clinic in 1981 and *Health Sharing: A Canadian Women's Health Quarterly* was first published in 1979.

Efforts in the 1980s to organise a Canadian women's health network floundered due to a lack of resources but took off in 1993 when seed money was made available by Health Canada. Since then, the network has moved from strength to strength as a trusted source of women's health information and as a means of linking community-based women's health groups, research centres and service providers. It is described further below.

In summary, then, there is no clear evidence of movements in abeyance, in part because multiple forms of action have been used from the beginning. However, there have been shifts and fluctuations in modes of action in both countries and these variations are closely related to changes in political opportunity structure, especially in Australia.

Changes in organisation, participation and opportunity structure

Favourable political opportunity structure stands out as the major factor assisting women's health groups to achieve some of their aims and influencing the tactics and strategies chosen. Political opportunity structure is conceptualised differently by different theorists.[23] In Tarrow's definition it comprises those 'dimensions of the political environment that provide incentives for people to undertake collective action by affecting their expectations for success or failure'.[24] Opportunity structure, theorists argue, can account for the rise, fall and transformation of movements and can help to explain differences between sister movements in different nations.[25]

Following Meyer,[26] political opportunity structure is used here to mean simply the political context in which social movements operate, leaving aside the question of which came first, the movement or the opportunity. A central feature of opportunity structure is the degree to which governments are open to the claims being made by a movement. For example, Rankin and Vickers argue that institutional arrangements and ideological climate help define 'the limitations and opportunities that confront movements which attempt change through state-directed action'.[27]

The election of a conservative Liberal Party government at the national level in Australia in 1975 changed the political opportunity structure. The period between 1975 and 1983 saw the progressive defunding of the community health program under which most of the women's health initiatives were funded. No new services were funded by the Commonwealth during this 'five-year drought',[28] except for an additional 75 refuges which happened to be supported by the Prime Minister and one of the party's most senior women.[29] Without the support of Commonwealth policy, the health centres became 'much more vulnerable to those who had opposed them from the beginning'.[30] At the same time Labor governments elected at the sub-national level were persuaded to support women's health initiatives. The exception was in Queensland, where a National Party government, in power between 1957 and 1989, remained overtly hostile to women's health initiatives.[31]

While not all senior Labor party members were sympathetic to feminism, women in the party found enough support to make progress, particularly at the sub-national level. The Wran government of New South Wales set up an inquiry into women's health in 1984 which led to the establishment of ten new women's health centres, a women's unit in the Health Department and the employment of women's health nurses, coordinators and education officers at the service provision level.[32] In the same year, a supportive Labor government in South Australia appointed a well-known feminist as Women's Health Adviser and set up three new women's health centres. In a clear example of Australian-style shifts in political opportunity structure, one of the new centres was approved in 1979 but abandoned when Labor lost office later the same year.[33] In Victoria, the Cain Labor government (1982–90), under pressure from grassroots activism and party women, authorised an extensive women's health consultation, followed by the development of a Women's Health Policy. A Program Unit was added to the Health Department and a new information centre, Healthsharing Women, was set up, along with eight new regional women's health centres. Western Australian Labor governments appointed a women's health working party, established a Women's Health Unit and funded four women's health centres in the 1980s. Similarly, initiatives were undertaken by Labor in Tasmania and the ACT in the late 1980s and early 1990s. An opportunity for action finally came to Queensland in 1989 when Labor regained office.

Had it not been for Labor dominance at the subnational level in the late 1970s and early 1980s, many of the women's health initiatives may not have survived. The Commonwealth systematically withdrew funding from the community health program after 1975 and handed responsibility back to the States and Territories completely in 1981, along with responsibility for centres, refuges and rape crisis services which had been funded through it. State governments, under pressure from the women's movement, eventually agreed to step into the vacuum and fund centres and services from their own treasuries.[34]

Although 'the radical, tumultuous, optimistic' atmosphere of the 1970s had subsided and some women's health services had moved 'closer to the bureaucracy',[35] the re-election of a Commonwealth Labor government in 1983 (when Labor still held office in four States) opened another important political opportunity. Recognising the possibilities, a group of South Australian women intent on getting women's health back onto the national agenda organised a second national women's health conference in Adelaide in 1985. The conference called for a national policy on women's health, along with a national program, to be consistent with the principles of the World Health Organisation's 'Health for All' strategy. After three years of policy development, the National

Women's Health Policy (NWHP) and Program were endorsed by Commonwealth, State and Territory Health Ministers in 1989.

The National Women's Health Program, funded jointly for two four-year
periods, spawned an extraordinary array of initiatives, including refashioned
mainstream services, more separate women's health centres, information and
referral services and all manner of special projects. During the same period, a
women's health unit was established in the Commonwealth bureaucracy.
Although many in the women's health movement felt that progress was too
slow, by 1994 there were 55 publicly-funded, women-run health centres, most of
which provided medical services as well as a full range of education, counselling, support and information services. By then, 262 publicly funded services
for women escaping violence had been established and attitudinal changes had
been promoted through programs for professionals, such as police, judges and
doctors.[36] In addition, a large Commonwealth-funded longitudinal, study,
Women's Health Australia, was set up in 1995.

Ironically, while the Commonwealth was supporting women's health innovations, New South Wales centres came under threat when non-Labor governments were elected between 1988 and 1995.[37] Political opportunities, therefore,
waxed and waned at both levels of government according to the party in power.
After the late 1980s, women's policy machinery was progressively dismantled
in much of the country. The non-Labor Commonwealth government, elected in
1996, completely withdrew from a policy leadership role and handed responsibility for women's health programs over to the States and Territories in 1997.

The hostility of the Commonwealth to women's health initiatives since 1996
has not precluded modest advances in sub-national jurisdictions where Labor
governments predominate.[38] Experience in the State of Victoria serves as an
example. As discussed above, a network of urban and regional women's health
services was established in 1987. In 2002, a four-year Women's Health and
Well-Being Strategy was launched, focussing on disadvantaged women and the
areas of safety and security, mental and emotional health and participation. On
the expiry of the Strategy, a group of women's health providers collaborated to
write a new policy proposal to influence policy over the years 2006–10.[39] The
plan, *Women's Health Matters*, was endorsed by 36 key community and
women's health groups. The Labor Government responded positively to pressure for removal of abortion from the State's criminal code and, in 2007, sought
advice from the Victorian Law Reform Commission on options for abortion law
reform to be considered the following year.

Federalism, by arranging a nation into a number of political jurisdictions,
creates the possibility of sub-national innovation. Some equality-seeking groups
support these arrangements, which they argue create spaces for innovation and
experimentation. Others are concerned that people in different jurisdictions do
not have access to a uniform set of policies and services. Australian women's
health has certainly benefited at times from having sympathetic governments at
the sub-national level. However, major expansion is unlikely to be initiated by -
cash-strapped States and Territories. Moreover, before we rush to make

generalisations about the potential advantages of divided jurisdiction, we should remember that political conditions can also vary from one part of a unitary country to another, when local government is strong and has a large role in policy and program development.

Not unexpectedly, given the high level of convergence between the major political parties in Canada,[40] political opportunity structures did not fluctuate as dramatically according to the party in government. Nevertheless, party difference played a role and political opportunities did vary. Early moves to organise a formal Canadian Women's Health Network (CWHN) lost momentum when no resources could be found, but the project took off in 1989 when Health Canada approved seed funding. In terms of a national policy response, advances were made during periods of both Progressive Conservative and Liberal governments. The Trudeau Liberal government provided funds for *Healthsharing* in 1981. A national symposium in 1988 was the stimulus for the establishment of a Federal/Provincial/Territorial Working Group on Women's Health. The first national policy document, *Working Together for Women's Health: A Framework for the Development of Policies and Programmes (WTWH)*[41] was released in 1990. Along with the establishment that year of the Women's Health Bureau at Health Canada, these developments took place under the Mulroney Progressive Conservative government. The Hon Mary Collins, Mulroney government Minister responsible for the Status of Women (1990–93) and Minister for Health and Welfare (1993) was influenced by Australian developments and is reported to have owned a copy of the Australian NWHP.

It was the endorsement of women's health as an important issue by the Liberal Party of Canada in 1993, an election year, which led to a major expansion of activity. Party political competition appears to have played a role in this development: women were strongly mobilised in groups across the country and supporters occupied positions of influence within political parties and the bureaucracy.[42] According to a senior female Liberal Party policymaker, women's health was too important to be left to one side. The challenges were to work out ways to use the limited policy levers available to the national government and to devise an effective policy within the financial exigencies of the time. Research centres, rather than special service provision (for which the Government of Canada lacks constitutional authority), became the answer. Thus, a combination of forces – strong support amongst party women and femocrats, a mobilised movement at the community level and the forces of electoral competition – created a major political opportunity.

In power, the Liberal government set up the Women's Health Contribution Program in 1996. Under the program, five regional research Centres of Excellence for Women's Health were established. The centres operate as partnerships between academics, community-based organisations and policymakers. At the same time, the Canadian Women's Health Network was funded to disseminate information, especially the information generated by the research centres, and to foster critical debate. Shortly afterwards, Health Canada moved to ensure that drug companies included women in clinical trials in appropriate numbers.

Health Canada's *Women's Health Strategy* was released in 1999, a response, the Minister said, to growing recognition of the importance of a social view of health, to the Beijing *Platform for Action* and to the recommendations of the National Forum on Health.[43] When the movement called for revision and update of the Strategy in 2005, the federal government responded positively.[44] In 2000, gender-based analysis was introduced and a Women's Health Indicators Project was launched in 2002.[45]

At the provincial level innovations were made during periods of positive political opportunity but, again, were not as closely linked to party differences as in Australia. The Ontario Women's Health Council, which advises the Minister of Health, was set up by a Progressive Conservative government in 1998. The incoming McGinty Liberal government announced the establishment of a Women's Health Institute in 2005. In Manitoba, where the left-of-centre New Democratic Party (NDP) was in power after 1999, a Women's Health Unit was established and a Women's Health Strategy endorsed. The Manitoba government and the NDP governments of Saskatchewan and British Columbia have collaborated with the Prairie Women's Health Centre of Excellence to promote the development of gender-based analysis, to incorporate gender into health planning and to create awareness about women's health issues across the different stages of women's lives. In contrast, in Alberta, where the Klein Progressive Conservative government has held office since 1992, there has been no attempt to develop a specific women's health policy. The four provinces of Atlantic Canada are relatively poor and in recent years have been dominated by Progressive Conservative governments.

The political opportunity structure that perhaps most closely resembles Australia is that in British Columbia. In 1994, an NDP government established a Women's Health Bureau and set up an Advisory Council on Women's Health. A range of women's health projects were developed and pursued. In 2001, however, a Liberal government was returned to office. The new government's philosophical approach 'differed markedly' from that of its predecessor. The Women's Health Bureau was absorbed into a new unit and funding was eliminated for the Women's Community Health Grants Program.[46]

Thus, changes in political opportunity structure in both countries influenced the timing of innovations and the shape of policies and programmes. It is also one of factors that influenced the tactics and organisational modes of movements themselves. For example, the Australian Women's Health Network, after several very negative responses early in the period, has made only limited attempts to influence and communicate with an unsympathetic Commonwealth government since 1996. Moreover, repeated and inconclusive discussions about how best to move forward have had a negative impact on both morale and membership. Nevertheless, the women's health movement has survived. It continues to work on a number of fronts, maintaining past achievements when it can and attempting to move forward whenever possible.

Abeyance or 'measured adaptation'?

Early conceptualisations of 'abeyance' had negative connotations, with the notion evoking suggestions of 'decline, failure and demobilisation'.[47] Taylor acknowledges long-term positives but nevertheless describes abeyance as a state of contraction and hibernation.[48] Some analysts, however, have argued that change does not necessarily mean hibernation and that a distinctive feminist culture has been created which is nurtured in networked activities. Women continue to challenge public policy, as well as to work for changes in 'the realms of culture, identity, and everyday life'.[49] According to this view, a changed but nevertheless rich, versatile and vigorous twenty-first century women's movement has materialised.[50]

The present women's health movements are diverse but use more institutionalised strategies than previously. In Australia, a mosaic of non-government, women-controlled health centres and projects forms a backbone for the movement alongside a network of special government services. Service providers work together with a multitude of women's health associations and organisations, many of them tiny, as needs arise. A typical women-run centre works within a feminist framework, acknowledging the diversity of women, and is concerned with all aspects of well-being. It provides information and referrals, liaises with other health services, conducts needs analyses and runs information sessions, workshops, and seminars. It engages in consultancy and advocacy and collaborates with other agencies, often using a community development focus. It encourages and supports women's self help groups and provides training and consultancy for service providers, workers and volunteers. At the local level, feminist culture is employed as a form of resistance.[51]

AWHN (completely unfunded except for an operational grant in 1993–94) has staged well attended national conferences every five years since 1995. It runs a web site, an e-mail discussion list and produces an electronic newsletter. The management committee confers regularly by teleconference and organised a national forum to profile women's health in the election year of 2007. Collaboration takes place with other organisations and advocacy and lobbying is pursued where possible. Overall, however, activities are restricted because all workers are volunteers and the financial base is insecure. It is a pale image of its funded Canadian counterpart.

A very different set of dynamics operates in Canada. Instead of being found in service provision, the strongest networks of women's health activists are to be found in research and information dissemination. The organisations set up under Health Canada's Women's Health Contribution Program have continued to receive funding since 1996. The CWHN, publicly funded and therefore relatively strong, provides access to health information, builds links between groups, disseminates research findings, promotes the involvement of diverse groups in health related action, arranges forums for critical debate and promotes women's involvement in research, health service planning and policy development.[52]

The CWHN operates an extensive web site providing links to resources and databases, produces a monthly e-bulletin, publishes a biannual magazine, *Network*, and responds to the media. It participates in the work of the Canadian Health Network, a partnership of 25 health promoting organisations and works with Health Canada, the Centres of Excellence for Women's Health and other organisations as appropriate. In 2005 it hosted a high profile event – the First National Women's Health Roundtable and Reception, on Parliament Hill, Ottawa – attended by women's health advocates, researchers, professionals and parliamentarians from all parties, suggesting that working alliances are a major asset.[53]

The federally funded Centres of Excellence are producing research that places them at the cutting edge of current health policy debates and places Canada as a world leader in women's health research. In the first decade, over 300 research reports were produced. The projects are diverse and include work on tobacco use and marketing, the mental health needs of rural communities, the experiences of groups of Aboriginal women, and race and ethnicity as determinants of health. The centres also collaborate with other groups and with governments on special research projects.

Health Canada funds a National Coordinating Group on Health Care Reform and Women whose role is to coordinate research and to translate the research results into policies and practices. For example, in 2002, it published a major exposition of the impact that privatisation in the health sphere is having on women, with contributions from nine Canadian jurisdictions.[54] Another funded working group, Women and Health Protection, composed of researchers, health providers, educators, and consumers, works to draw attention to problems for women in relation to pharmaceutical products and medical devices.

A major achievement is the establishment of the Institute of Gender and Health. When new Institutes for Health Research were announced in 2000, a group of activists from across Canada formed a working group to campaign for an Institute dedicated to women's health research. The Institute of Gender and Health, established in 2001, is part of Canada's premier health research agency, and is the first of its kind in the world.[55]

Canada's central, publicly funded women's health research and information dissemination organisations form part of a loosely connected national network, which includes grassroots women's health centres, provincial networks and myriad groups organised around issues such as breast cancer and midwifery. Thus, although direct politics is not a dominant feature of the movement's activities, it can in no way be said to be in hibernation. Rather, it is active in a range of sites, is vocal and visible and has an influential voice in policy debates.[56] The recent political context of women's health action in Canada is thus very different from that in Australia, where a delegation (of mature women) from AWHN to the Minister for the Status of Women early in the life of the Howard government was welcomed with the question, 'Well girls, is there anything left to achieve in women's health?'

Conclusion

Early in the twenty-first century members of the Australian and Canadian women's health movements are more likely to be found writing submissions, disseminating information, facilitating service provision, undertaking research and promoting community development than marching on the streets. However, it is clear that neither movement is in hibernation. 'Invisible action', a term carrying negative connotations, can mean positive action involving behind-the-scenes policy-oriented action, consciousness-raising and feminist practice in everyday activities. While current activism may be less visible to the public or the media than the activism of the 1970s, it is certainly not obvious that it is less effective. In Australia at least, many activists in the early period had no idea how government worked. Women who had to call on expert help to write a funding submission in the 1970s can now write one blindfolded. There were few women-focused institutions through which to work, so the choice of tactics and strategies was extremely limited. It is not surprising, then, that as activists found themselves in different circumstances, they chose somewhat different, more 'institutionalised' ways of working. It may be true that it is less easy for governments and bureaucracies to ignore social movements during periods of mass mobilisation but, in Australia, at least, national governments bent upon sidelining women's health successfully did so, even in the early days.

Women's health movement activity in Australia and Canada shows that institutionalisation does not necessarily mean absence of fundamental challenges to the state and its institutions. There is, as Dorothy Broom has emphasised, a fundamental irony in 'using the state to change the state',[57] bringing with it the twin dangers of co-option and retribution. To a large extent, the question of whether co-option has taken place depends on how it is defined. Institutionalised politics is a normal part of the activities of some movements and is not necessarily evidence of contraction. The extent of co-option also depends upon the timeframe in which change is expected. The project of western women's health movements includes the aim of moving thinking and practice towards a social view of health. Radical change is required, therefore, in the economic, social and cultural spheres, change that can only be expected over a very long time. Despite the magnitude of the project, the Canadian and Australian women's health movements are both currently working slowly towards this goal in different ways. In Canada, the main arena of action is the world of ideas. In Australia, activity is more concentrated at the level of service provision, among a range of agencies, operating on culture and local politics.

It should be said that women's health has never been an issue with a huge political profile or a large budget in either country. The Australian Women's Health Program, for example, was funded at about half the level that was initially envisaged and Canada invested in research partly because it is cheaper than service provision. While women's health services are extremely popular in the communities in which they are provided, the 'engaged' movement, like the women's movement as a whole, has always been small. And it has enemies. Persuading governments to take the radical action necessary to achieve major change is extremely difficult; slow incremental reform is probably the most that can be hoped for, especially in view of the ascendancy of neo-liberalism in both countries with its deleterious impact on women's economic security and therefore on health. Nevertheless, the Canadian and Australian women's health movements have both developed a strong sense of collective identity and purpose, both are in the game of influencing culture and both are making use of the resources available to them even when political environments are hostile. Both movements continue to challenge aspects of social, cultural and political arrangements and both are in a position to influence public policy as political opportunities emerge.

Notes

1 Bagguley, 'Contemporary British feminism: A social movement in abeyance?'; Taylor, 'Social movement continuity'; Sawyers and Meyer, 'Missed opportunities'.
2 Reger and Taylor, 'Women's movement research and social movement theory'.
3 Gray, 'How Australia came to have a National Women's Health Policy'.
4 Brown, *The Challenge of Caring*; Winnipeg Consultation Organising Committee, *The Strength of Links*.
5 Boscoe *et al.*, 'The Women's Health Movement in Canada', p. 7.
6 Sawyers and Meyer, 'Missed opportunities', pp. 192–193.
7 Cullen and Sinding, 'Changing concepts of women's health – advocating for change', p. 11.
8 Bashevkin, *Women on the Defensive*.
9 Sawyers and Meyer, 'Missed opportunities'.
10 Bagguley, 'Contemporary British feminism'.
11 Broom, *Damned If We Do*; Cullen and Sinding, 'Changing concepts of women's health – advocating for change'; Gray, 'How Australia came to have a National Women's Health Policy', pp. 109–110; Boscoe *et al.*, 'The Women's Health Movement in Canada'.
12 Stevens, *Healing Women – A History of Leichhardt Women's Community Health Centre*.
13 Broom, *Damned If We Do*, p. 34.
14 Summers, *Ducks on the Pond*, pp. 315–336.
15 Gray, 'Women's health in a restructuring state', p. 207.
16 Broom, *Damned If We Do*, p. xviii.
17 Stevens, *Healing Women*, p. 17.
18 Kenway, 'Feminist theories of the state', p. 112.
19 Brodie *et al.*, *The Politics of Abortion*, p. 44.
20 Vancouver Women's Health Collective, 'Outreach and activism' at www.womenshealthcollective.ca/whats_new.htm, p. 5.
21 Canadian Women's Health Network, 'Montréal Health Press may have to stop the presses'.
22 Winnipeg Consultation Organising Committee, *The Strength of Links*, pp. 7–8.
23 Meyer, 'Protest and political opportunities'.
24 Tarrow, *Power in Movement*, p. 85.
25 Tarrow, *Power in Movement*, pp. 81–99; Meyer, 'Protest and political opportunities', pp. 125–131.
26 Meyer, 'Protest and political opportunities', p. 126.
27 Rankin and Vickers, *Women's Movements and State Feminism*, p. 10.

28 Broom, *Damned If We Do*, p. 82.
29 Sawer, *Sisters in Suits*, pp. 37–54.
30 Broom, *Damned If We Do*, p. 76.
31 Stevens, *Healing Women*, pp. 99–100.
32 Broom, *Damned If We Do*, p. 77; Stevens, *Healing Women*, pp. 98–102.
33 Broom, *Damned If We Do*, p. 77.
34 Broom, *Damned If We Do*, pp. 76–81; Stevens, *Healing Women*, p. 98; Gray, 'How Australia came to have a National Women's Health Policy', p. 122.
35 Broom, *Damned If We Do*, p xvii.
36 Gray, 'How Australia came to have a National Women's Health Policy', p. 111.
37 Stevens, *Healing Women*, p. 104.
38 However, because financial arrangements in Australia are so highly centralised, expensive innovations at the State and Territory level are unlikely.
39 Women's Health Victoria, *Womenshealthmatters: From Policy to Practice, 10 Point Plan for Victorian Women's Health, 2006–2010*.
40 Gray, *Federalism and Health Policy*, pp. 184–187.
41 Working Together for Women's Health: A Framework for the Development of Policies and Programs, Federal/Provincial/Territorial Working Group on Women's Health, April 1990.
42 Working Together for Women's Health, pp. 75–76.
43 Health Canada, *Health Canada's Women's Health Strategy*, pp. 1–4.
44 Hankivsky, *Women's Health in Canada: Beijing and Beyond*; Canadian Women's Health Network, 'Gearing up for a review of Canada's Women's Health Strategy'.
45 Canadian Women's Health Network, 'The Women's Health Bureau'.
46 Donner, *Producing a Profile of the Health of Manitoba Women*, p. 5.
47 Bagguley, 'Contemporary British feminism', p. 170.
48 Taylor, 'Social movement continuity', p. 772.
49 Reger and Taylor, 'Women's movement research and social movement theory'.
50 Staggenborg and Taylor, 'Whatever happened to the Women's Movement?'; Reger and Taylor, 'Women's movement research and social movement theory'.
51 Reger and Taylor, 'Women's movement research and social movement theory', p. 112.
52 Canadian Women's Health Network, 'Background', at www.cwhn.ca/about.html.
53 Canadian Women's Health Network, 'First National women's health roundtable and reception on Parliament Hill'.
54 Armstrong *et al.*, *Exposing Privatisation*.
55 Canadian Women's Health Network, 'Institute of Gender and Health: A year in review'.
56 Boscoe *et al.*, 'The Women's Health Movement in Canada', p. 12.
57 Broom, *Damned If We Do*.

5 Out of sight, out of mind

The New Zealand women's movement

Sandra Grey

From a vibrant, colourful, and theatrical movement in the 1970s, to an institutionalised set of actors in the early twenty-first century, the New Zealand women's movement has experienced major changes in both the way it operates and the way it is perceived. These changes have led to varying claims about the state of the movement. In the 1990s feminist Sandra Coney stated: 'The movement was silent because there is no movement – only isolated groups working on specific issues'.[1] By contrast, feminist economist Prue Hyman claims there is still a feminist movement in New Zealand and elsewhere:

> Many areas of work ... continue, and many young women are active recruits. Some may not use the word feminist of themselves, with the backlash and other negatives ... giving the word a bad name in some circles – but ask what they believe, and the concepts are there.[2]

And there are those who claim that while the women's movement does exist in New Zealand, in the early twenty-first century it is in a 'trough'. 'The women's movement is ongoing. Yes, there are waves and troughs and activities take many faces changing with historical context. Who knows when the next crest of the wave will occur?'[3]

Given the contradictory views from feminists about the movement to which they belong(ed), it seems timely to carry out a systematic 'audit' of the state of the women's movement in New Zealand. Has the movement gone into what Verta Taylor calls abeyance – a holding pattern on which to build a new mobilisation? Has the movement 'matured' and as a result institutionalised? Or is Coney accurate in her assertions that the women's movement she was a part of is finished?

This chapter analyses protest event coverage in three metropolitan newspapers and the publications of women's organisations in order to examine the state of the New Zealand women's movement after 1995.[4] I will compare activism by women's groups after 1995 with existing historical accounts of the activities of feminists during the 1970s, the heyday of the women's liberation movement. While it is always contentious to claim a broad consensus exists in academic and feminist writing, there is general agreement that New Zealand saw a burgeoning of women's movement activity during the 1970s.[5]

Using the definition set out in the introduction, this chapter explores the trajectory of the New Zealand women's movement by looking for individuals and groups challenging existing norms, and who may use unconventional structures and/or tactics in their gendered claims-making. The approach is institutionalist, as it focuses on the interaction of activists with broader social and political structures. However, by encompassing both unconventional actions *and* structures, the aim is to recognise the culturalist challenges to the political process theory discussed by Sarah Maddison and Kyungja Jung, and Fiona Mackay in this collection. It is important to bridge structural and cultural theories, as the women's movement has always been active on many fronts – in both public and private spheres; in political and cultural spaces; and both inside and outside mainstream political institutions.

It is the use of 'outsider activity', both in terms of protest tactics and structures, that has changed most dramatically in New Zealand in four decades. I will argue that in contrast to the grassroots and public movement of the 1970s, the women's movement since the mid-1990s has been institutionalised and individualised, and that this change is not without problems.

The crest of the 'second wave'

Feminist publications and histories provide evidence of the many groups and individuals actively advocating for women's rights in New Zealand during the 1970s. There are discussions about the establishment of consciousness-raising groups, women's studies courses, protest groups, feminist publications and bookshops, conferences and conventions, and women's centres. The level of involvement of New Zealand women in this 'wave' of activism is indicated by the growing numbers who attended the three national women's conventions. The first women's liberation conference held in 1972 attracted several hundred participants; at the 1973 convention there were 1500 women; and in 1975, 2000 women braved a bitterly cold weekend to attend the Wellington Women's Convention. Given the size of the New Zealand population, this would be the equivalent of 30 000 women attending a conference in the United Kingdom.

The size and reach of the 1970s women's movement can also be demonstrated by looking at the number of grassroots groups that collectively made up the movement itself. By the end of 1972 in New Zealand there were at least 20 women's liberation groups in existence.[6] In one city, a new consciousness-raising group was established every month in the early 1970s.[7] There were also high levels of interest in lobby groups. For example, 210 women attended the first two meetings of the Women's Electoral Lobby (WEL).[8]

A broad range of tactics were used in the 1970s by women's rights and women's liberation organisations, including a substantial amount of street-level or contentious political action. The actions were often theatrical, militant, and public such as street marches where women dressed as Victorian women pushed twentieth-century prams and brandished banners proudly declaring: 'Liberate My Mother!' and '24 Hour Free Child Care!'[9] Direct action was taken over the government's lack of coverage of unpaid workers in a new accident compensation scheme: 'Four members of Palmerston North Women's Liberation paraded round the Square with large paper bags over their heads bearing the legend "Housewives are people too."'[10]

Alongside the direct action of the 1970s, women's groups also employed more conventional political tactics to push for social and political change, similar to the double militancy which occurred in Australia, Canada, and the United Kingdom discussed in earlier chapters in this collection. To focus only on contentious street-level protests ignores the multiple fronts on which feminist organisations have taken action. Women's groups presented petitions to parliament, wrote letters to MPs, and made submissions to parliamentary Royal Commissions and working groups. As Heather Devere and Jane Scott note:

> What was distinctive about the activity [in the 1970s] was its nature and range. The National Organisation for Women, for example, participated in mainstream political activity: lectures, petitions, house meetings, submissions, pamphlets, and letter writing. Groups such as Women for Equality carried out a variety of direct political action. Its members demonstrated against beauty contests and male-only drinking preserves, marched and performed guerrilla theatre against abortion law, and leafleted factories on equal pay.[11]

The New Zealand women's movement was segmented, decentralised, and diffuse in the 1970s. Activists frequently speak of the 'leaderlessness' of the 1970s feminist organisations. As Maud Cahill and Christine Dann note: 'dissatisfied with male domination in the protest movement [of the 1960s] as well as in wider society, but still influenced by the radicalism and militancy of the movement, women began meeting in small groups to form what became known as the women's liberation movement'.[12] Women set up refuges, rape crisis centres, and health organisations. Grassroots and flaxroots 'education' groups discussed the works of international and local feminists: 'We scoured the library shelves for Mary Wollstonecraft, John Stuart Mill, the books about the suffragettes. We eagerly devoured Betty Friedan's *The Feminine Mistique* and hunted the bookshops for each new publication...'.[13] And groups researched the position of women in society, turning out publications such as *Why Employ Women?* and *Jobs, Children and Chores: A Study of Mothers in Paid Employment in the Christchurch Area.*

Not all of the efforts of women during this decade were directed towards creating groups with unconventional structures. Prue Hyman notes: 'The categories of organisations into which feminists have put their energy include conventional political parties, the bureaucracy, pressure groups, grassroots organisations, and separatist activity'.[14] Women even used unconventional tactics to push for change in more conventional political organisations. For example, New Zealand Labour women picketed their own party conference in 1974 demanding women's issues be given greater priority.

While existing histories present a vibrant, diverse, and dynamic women's movement in New Zealand in the 1970s, from the mid-1990s the picture is markedly different.

Institutionalised and depoliticised

It is difficult to accurately gauge the current number of women's groups in New Zealand and their membership levels, however, a range of sources provide evidence of the continuing diversity of women's groups and feminist organisations in New Zealand. The Ministry of Women's Affairs' *2005 Women's Directory* names a total of 101 national organisations (such as unions, women's groups, health centres) that advocate for women. A 1997 study found '503 mainly Pakeha women-run organisations' from both the business and the non-profit sectors where the majority of decision-makers and staff were women.[15] Finally, there were 67 non-profit and community women's groups in New Zealand with active websites in 2006. There were websites for chapters of international 'service organisations' such as Soroptimists and Zonta; for home-grown organisations such as Supergrans which provides home-making advice to women; and for long-running groups such as the National Council of Women and the Maori Women's Welfare League. There are ten websites for professional associations, such as Women in Aviation and Women in Science. There are six websites for academic gender studies programmes and two for publications produced by women in academia. There are also websites for seven women's centres, six lesbian sites, and five sites for Maori women's groups.

Publications by women's groups give an indication of the size of these organisations after 1995. Many of the largest groups in New Zealand are traditional and long-standing women's groups. For example, the Federation of Women's Institutes claims 10 000 members,[16] and 300 women were expected at the 2006 conference of Rural Women (formerly the Federated Farmers Women's Branch).[17] There is also evidence of high usage of the services provided by feminist organisations. For example, the Auckland Women's Centre stated that in 2004–05 over 10 000 women used the Centre.[18] And 533 women 'attended all or part of'[19] the 2005 Janus Women's Convention (though this is a lower level than the 2000 women who were at the 1975 Women's Convention).

The existence of women's groups alone does not signal an active women's movement and it is important to look at whether these diverse groups use unconventional tactics and/or forms to challenge dominant norms. A protest event analysis using reports from three major metropolitan daily newspapers – the *New Zealand Herald*, the *Dominion Post*,[20] and the *Press* – provides one window into women's movement activity in New Zealand after 1995. There are limits to using newspapers as a data source in social movement research due to reporting biases. However, it is important to gain some sense of the 'public' face of the New Zealand women's movement during the last decade and it is through the mass media that most citizens gain messages about, and from, social movements. I am not making a claim of having located every protest action carried out by New Zealand women after 1995 but I am providing a broad picture of the reporting of activism. 'Protest events' are taken to include all forms of claims-making by women's groups, from pamphleteering, conferences, and workshops, to petitions, street-marches, and violent disruptive actions. This broad definition reflects the reality of women's activism by encompassing the political and cultural focus of social movements.

There were very low levels of disruptive protest action by individual feminists and by women's groups between 1995 and 2005 (see Table 1) when compared with the extensive list of 'protests' found in Christine Dann's history of the women's movement in the 1970s and early 1980s.[21] In total, only 55 reports of protest events were found in the three selected publications between 1995 and 2005. There were 14 reports of direct actions, often involving routine protest events such as annual Reclaim the Night marches. There were also four stories on disruptive actions between 1995 and 2005, such as the protest in which two pieces of beef were thrown on the catwalk in protest at the Miss Otago pageant in Dunedin.[22]

There were also reports of a range of more conventional political activities by New Zealand women's organisations after 1995. There were ten stories on speeches, petitions, and general comments by women's groups on government policies, such as in 2005 when Rural Women New Zealand presented a petition to a Labour party MP containing 18 000 signatures.[23] Nine newspaper articles covered educational or consciousness-raising events; while five stories featured commemorative events.

Table 5.1 Protest events by women as reported in selected New Zealand newspapers 1995–2005

	Event organised by/or attributed to:						
	Broad coalition	*Interest group*	*State watchdog*	*Academic/ education*	*Individual*	*Professional*	*Total (by year)*
1995	1	4			1	1	7
1996					1		1
1997		5					5
1998		1	1		1		3
1999		2			1		3
2000		1			3		4
2001	1	6		2			9
2002		2			2		4
2003		7					7
2004					3		3
2005	2	1			6		9

Source: analysis of news reports from the first week of each month from the *New Zealand Herald*, the *Dominion Post* (and its predecessors the *Dominion* and the *Evening Post*) and the *Christchurch Press*.

Many of the unconventional protest events that were covered in the news-papers scrutinised were small in size. The 1999 protest in Dunedin over a beauty pageant involved 12 tertiary students, and a 2003 anti-GE protest at Fonterra's headquarters involved 30 women and children from Mothers Against Genetic Engineering (Madge).[24] The largest events found in the protest event analysis were single-issue events. For example, 4000 people marched against the closure of maternity services at Kaitaia Hospital in 2002.[25]

Not only were reports of protest events infrequent and the size of events small, but a number of the newspaper reports told of the involvement of women within other broad issue movements. In 1995 there were media reports on a group of women hoping to fly to French Polynesia to protest about nuclear testing.[26] In 2003 there was media coverage of Madge's controversial anti-GE billboard campaign. These events were included in the analysis as feminist con-cerns have always been wide ranging and feminists have long played a role in other radical causes such as the anti-nuclear movement.

The protest event analysis also indicates a deradicalisation of the actions of women's groups after 1995. In the 1970s commemorative days, such as Inter-national Women's Day and Suffrage Day, were frequently used to protest about the position of women in society and to connect with earlier waves of women's movement activism. 'On Suffrage Day we dressed up as suffragettes and chained ourselves to the Cathedral railings under the banner "Yesterday's suf-fragettes: Today's marionettes." '[27] By contrast, in 1995 the *Evening Post* reported:

> The day associated with the slogan 'bread and roses' got off to an early start with a breakfast at Wellington Town Hall today. Just under 500 guests heard speeches marking International Women's Day by former Minister of Women's Affairs Margaret Shields and Sharyn Cederman, president of United Nations women's development agency Unifem NZ.[28]

An analysis of protest events reported in the publications of New Zealand women's groups after 1995 also shows that this period is markedly different from the women's movement ferment of the 1970s. There were reports in women's organisation publications of some groups mounting protest campaigns after 1995. For example, 'Women Vote No' was a campaign against voluntary superannuation launched in 1997.[29] And in 1999 a small group of feminists occupied The Rock 90.2 FM to protest against this radio station's sexist atti-tudes. However, discussions within women's groups own publications, like those in the metropolitan newspapers, paint a picture of disruptive protests as small and isolated events. Much of the focus of women's groups after 1995 was on the use of conventional political tactics and avenues to bring about social and political change. 'Traditional' women's groups such as the National Council of Women, Maori Women's Welfare League, and the YWCA; service provider groups such as Women's Refuge and Rape Crisis; and professional women's groups such as the Federation of University Women, were all actively involved in making submissions to parliamentary select committees, writing letters to members of parliament, and taking part in consultation processes with government departments between 1995 and 2005. For example, Rural Women made 51 submissions to government (central and local levels) between 2002 and 2005.[30] Every year the National Council of Women writes up to 100 submissions in response to proposed changes in legislation or government policy.[31]

Like newspapers, the publications from women's groups include reports on commemorative and celebratory events after 1995. For example, the Women's Studies Association newsletter[32] notes two celebrations in 1997: the 10th anniversary of Canterbury University's Feminist Studies, and a launch of a documentary on abortion services in New Zealand. Other publications noted events such as Suffrage Day breakfasts and annual candle-lighting ceremonies to celebrate the Federation of Business and Professional Women's 'International Night'.

The reliance on institutional means of seeking social and political change is problematic for those seeking to assert the continuing existence of a large-scale women's movement in New Zealand. However, focussing merely on contentious action can distort findings with regard to the vibrancy and life-cycles of movements. Is the lack of unconventional tactics by women's groups after 1995 made up for by the existence of groups using unconventional structures challenging the very systems in which they operate?

Women's groups using unconventional structures continue to exist in New Zealand, but the picture over the last decade is not of a flourishing grassroots activist movement. Publications from women's organisations note a litany of closures of feminist organisations in the last decade. In 1997, *Broadsheet*, New Zealand's longest running (and at that time only) feminist magazine, closed. One way movements reach and maintain contact with potential followers is through alternative publications[33] and the loss of *Broadsheet* was a major blow for feminist collectivism in New Zealand. In 2000, after 19 years of operation, Christchurch's feminist bookshop, the Kate Sheppard Bookshop, shut its doors. That same year the Society for Research on Women faded away. And in 2002 WEL formally wound up its national office. WEL, which in the 1970s boasted a national membership of 2000, held its final AGM in 2001 at a member's home.[34]

Alongside the closures of women's organisations and publications there are challenges to the women-only spaces and structures set up during earlier periods of activism. For example, since 1996 there have been debates within the Women's Studies Association newsletter about whether the Association's journal and conferences needed to remain as women only spaces. And at Victoria University of Wellington in 2005 the student association's Women's Right's Officer questioned the need for her position: 'I would prefer to see it put into something like an Equity Officer or a Rights Officer in general. I think that sort of role is so encompassing. With the Women's Rights Office, it's hard to fill ten hours a week'.[35]

The 1990s did see the establishment of a number of new women's groups – Lesbian Wellington, Maori Midwives, Not Just Gumboots and Scones (a website for rural women), and Supergrans. Between 2000 and 2005 there was the establishment of *Bent Magazine* the publication, the Cherry Bomb comic store, and a website for women working in the IT sector called Webgrrls. Late in 2005, a print run of 500 copies of a new feminist-zine called *Muse* hit the streets of the capital Wellington. However, overall since 1995 the picture from the publications and the websites of women's groups in New Zealand is not one of regeneration of broad-based grassroots organising but of a winding down of political activism by long-standing groups and service providers.

Change, adaptation, and political opportunities

There is little in the way of a recognisable mass women's movement in New Zealand after 1995, despite the continuing existence of feminist organisations and the ongoing commitment of individuals to feminism. So why has this change occurred?

Just as with the Canadian and Australian women's health movements discussed by Gwendolyn Gray in this collection, changing political opportunities have impacted upon the types of activism and modes of organising the New Zealand women's movement used over the past four decades. The broad political environment in which a social movement is embedded constitutes a powerful set of constraints/opportunities affecting the latter's development.[36] The adoption of neo-liberalism by successive New Zealand governments since the 1980s and, in particular, an adherence to public choice theories has hindered activism. Public choice advocates are suspicious of the motives behind collective action and this has impacted upon New Zealand governments reception of the claims-making of interest groups and social movements. Justifying Labour's 'blitzkrieg' approach to economic reforms in the 1980s (in which large-scale changes across a number of policy areas were simultaneously and rapidly implemented), then Finance Minister Roger Douglas explained that the strategy was explicitly designed to ensure that interest groups did not have 'the time to mobilise and drag you down'.[37]

Moves to formalise contracting between the state and non-government organisations have also affected the operation of many groups. As Devere and Scott note, the inadequate and unstable funding resulting from the contestable contracting-out of social service delivery to community organisations in the 1990s has led to a change in the nature of women's groups. They became administrators (planning projects to tender for funding contracts), social workers (meeting the immediate needs of individual women 'clients'), and mainstream political lobbyists (submitting women-friendly policy advice).[38] Della Porta has argued that policing of protest has shifted from overt repression to more subtle means of control.[39] I would argue that the accountability mechanisms placed on social movement organisations contracted by the state should be seen as part of that continuum of 'subtle' control.

The very outcomes of the women's movement activism of the 1970s and 1980s (both intended and unintended) are also part of the context that has reshaped women's activism in New Zealand. Women's movement activism in part led to participatory gains in the 1980s such as a rising number of women in public life (both in elected and bureaucratic positions), the establishment of the Ministry of Women's Affairs, the development of women's studies programmes within most New Zealand universities, and significant progress within trade unions and the Labour party. In particular, it is the way these outcomes have been framed in public debates that has affected attitudes towards collective action. Getting services provided or problems solved can give the impression that there is no longer a need for feminist activism.[40] The success of the women's movement activism of the 1970s and early 1980s has been framed as evidence that feminist activism is no longer needed. Former head of the Ministry of Women's Affairs Mary O'Regan notes: 'I have talked with young women in schools who think that women *have* equality now. I suppose they are influenced by the popular media, which gives that impression, superficially at least'.[41]

The success of individual women who have cracked (or chipped) the glass ceiling is also significant in undermining any 'collective' claims-making by feminists in New Zealand. 'When such consciousness calls for individual rather than collective or societal solutions to problems women face, it has defused an earlier gender consciousness'.[42] But as feminist Teresa O'Connor points out:

> To all those who would claim that because we have women as Prime Minister, Attorney-General, Chief Judge and Governor-General, not to mention chief executive of Telecom, women have true equality, I would say "rubbish".... Ask the appallingly-paid women cleaners who must leave their families at night to clean the nation's offices, or the caregivers of the elderly in the country, an overwhelmingly female workforce, how having Helen Clark, Margaret Wilson, Dame Sian Elias, Dame Sylvia Cartwright and Teresa Gattung in their respective positions has affected their pay packets or the status of the work they do.[43]

Individualism is also problematic in that it obscures the systemic oppression with which the 1970s women's movement was engaging. The assertion that women are oppressed by patriarchy relies on a belief that disadvantage and oppression is caused by structural phenomena and in an age of individualism it is difficult to gain support for this frame. The state has also ceased to be a target of feminist activism in New Zealand to a large degree, as it has been constructed as the 'saviour' of women, due to the disproportionate reliance of women on the state for employment, income support and services, as well as the number of women's groups reliant on state-funding for their survival. This echoes the concerns of Sarah Maddison and Kyungja Jung in this collection around the hegemony of liberal feminism.

The collective action frame is further undermined by debates around diversity and difference. The impact of diversity upon the New Zealand women's movement began in the late 1970s when women's liberation was increasingly rent by internal dissension, leading to the demise of many of the early women's movement organisations and the emphasis instead on more practically oriented single-issue groups such as refuges, rape crisis and women's health groups.[44] It is difficult under such conditions to mount a broad-based campaign for 'all women'. Collective identity formation is perceived as a major challenge by young feminists, as seen in the section by Fleur Fitzsimons in the 'New Voices' section of this collection.

There have been attempts to re-create a sense of the collective via web activity in New Zealand. YWCA in 1998 launched the Young Women of Aotearoa website to encourage young women to network, there is Womenz the 'webway to feminism in Aotearoa', and Webgrrls for IT women. However, studies of women's movement longevity highlight the importance of contacts made face-to-face, or shoulder-to-shoulder in protests, if a movement is to survive the doldrums.[45] Networks created on the web may not provide such a sound base for obligation and future commitment. What these new sites of activism indicate is that the nature of engagement in civic activism may be changing.

A mature movement or one in abeyance?

As was seen in the Introduction to this book there exist a range of theories about the process of social movement change and adaptation. One argument is that institutionalisation is a natural part of the life cycle of movements. Entry into the state can be a good bargain as movements are able to 'cash in' on resources mobilised in their takeoff and consolidation phase to access real political power.[46] Women's organisations in New Zealand did take advantage of political opportunities in the 1970s and early 1980s to consolidate their position within the state and in social service provision. However, the move inside the state and into more institutional structures alongside the state has been somewhat problematic.

The entry of feminists into institutional positions without a strong, active grassroots movement outside renders the women's movement vulnerable to backlash, state control, or merely a lack of resources. A study of Australian and Irish feminist organisations shows that successful intervention in policy required a coalition of grassroots feminists, national women's organisations, and 'feminist-friendly' coalitions.[47] The importance of coalitions is echoed by New Zealand femocrat Rae Julian: 'I feel secure as a feminist – a structural feminist who still believes that some changes can be affected from within the system, but only so long as there are the radicals outside to remind us of our accountability'.[48]

As noted in the Introduction, the absence of outsiders impacts upon the viability of feminist innovations inside the state. A backlash to feminist gains has been evident in New Zealand, though not to the extent suffered in the United States or Japan (see Joyce Gelb in this collection), in part because New Zealand has been under left-leaning coalition governments since 1999. However, even the existence of a left-leaning government has not completely insulated feminists working inside the state. In the last decade there have been repeated attacks on earlier institutional gains. For example, the Ministry of Women's Affairs attempts to give advice on gender impact of policies over a wide range of areas but their resources are few and their position is easily marginalised.[49] This problem of marginalisation is also evident at universities where the shift to formal women's studies programmes was applauded in the 1980s: 'The growth of Women's Studies in our universities and elsewhere gives us the best chance we have, I believe, of systematically exposing the power and prejudice from which it stems'.[50] In a commercial, mass tertiary education system, however, the viability of women's studies programmes is tenuous.[51]

Abeyance literature argues that in unfriendly political environments movements will strip down to their core in order to survive, and protect groups where people have high levels of personal commitment.[52] In their study of the United States women's movement between 1945 and the 1960s Leila Rupp and Verta Taylor argued that the unfriendly climate in these years explains why feminists directed very little effort into expanding the base of support for women's rights: 'Instead, the movement functioned primarily through channelling to pre-existing groups the individual commitment and the other resources necessary to survive when, for the most part, the odds were against its success'.[53]

Central to the idea of abeyance is the existence of a committed and connected core group of actors who can form a base for later activism. There is no evidence that New Zealand after 1995 had a core group of grassroots activists from which another wave of feminist activism might draw strength. There are individuals and some organisations that are committed to activism on behalf of New Zealand women, but the publications produced by women's organisations indicate that a small number of activists are spread thinly in a wide array of women's groups. There are frequent discussions attributing the closure (or threat of closure) of bookshops, newsletters and magazines, pressure groups, and women's centres to the loss of a key individual. For example, in 1995 it was noted that the Women's Learning Centre of Christchurch had 'reached a particularly crucial point in its development, as Marg will be moving to the North Island in January'[54] threatening the centre's future. And in 1996 there was the closure of the Affirmative Action newsletter as the woman behind it had decided to stand for parliament.[55] These difficulties faced by the New Zealand women's movement are in part about changing life cycles of the women activists at the heart of the movement. However, it does not bode well for the regeneration of the women's movement and continuity with the claims-making of 1970s feminists.

At the national level in New Zealand there has been a shift from political activism to cultural activism and service delivery as the core activities of feminists over the last four decades. However, the findings may in part reflect the way in which 'national' studies obscure sub-national activism, similar to the concerns raised by Fiona MacKay in this collection with regard to the United Kingdom. For example, continued strength is seen in Maori women's activism in New Zealand. The Maori Women's Welfare League, which was established in 1951, still has around 3000 active members and hundreds regularly attend national League conferences (the Maori population in New Zealand is around 500 000). Issues such as domestic violence, poverty, health and wellness, economic development, and Maori political participation are all tackled by the League. The lack of attention to the needs and claims-making of Maori women in discussions of the women's movement is problematic, but space constraints prevent fuller discussion here.

The findings of my study also highlight how protest event analysis (even when including activist publications) can obscure areas of strength in social movements. For example, it does not record the work carried out by service providers, such as Women's Refuge and Rape Crisis in New Zealand, in empowering *individual* women. As was noted in the Introduction, women's liberation activists have long been involved in their own separate service delivery structures, in cultural production and in the politics of everyday life.

While acknowledging that feminist activism in New Zealand may have hidden strengths, the mere fact that it is hidden from view is problematic. The work of feminist activism in the early twenty-first century is often carried out behind-the-scenes and as a result goes unnoticed by politicians, bureaucrats, and the wider public. Not only is the lack of a public face problematic, so too is the continued intrusion of successive New Zealand governments into cultural and non-government spheres. Invisibility on the one hand and the absorption of civil society into new forms of governance on the other, means that new recruits and supporters of the women's movement are left wondering if there is any viable collective to which they can attach themselves.

Conclusion

In New Zealand, older feminists are calling for younger women to take up the baton. 'Sadly, there is a generation of young women, largely white and middle class, reaping the benefits of the campaigns of their foremothers, who fail to understand why there is still a need for a women's movement'.[56] However the women's liberation movement of the 1970s changed forever the landscape of New Zealand society and politics. Perhaps it is time for new modes, new styles of activism, and new voices to come to the fore. Young women argue they are actively involved in civic activism. The Young Women's Caucus at the 2005 Janus Women's Convention told the 'older' activists:

> We want you all to know that we are here. We are struggling with you, behind you and on our own. Many of us are active already in many different ways. If there are not many young women present at this convention it is not because we are not passionate and active, but because of the many obstacles in terms of time and expense which stand in our way.[57]

There is some evidence of new sites of feminist activism opening up in New Zealand, however these are not identical to, nor continuous from, the 1970s women's liberation movement. As has already been noted there are new websites and feminist-zines appearing in New Zealand. There are 'rapid fire' campaigns organised via web-networks such as the 2006 campaign against the not-guilty verdict handed down to a police officer at the centre of an historical rape allegation. It seems that the regeneration of feminist activism in New Zealand may not simply be about the 'continuation' of the tactics and aims of the 1970s women's movement. Given all the progress made, and the shifting political terrain, a new movement may be needed. As Jacinta, a 'young woman' who attended the Wellington Women's Convention noted:

> I left thinking that while young women today are thankful for the efforts earlier feminists have made and benefits won … we will not be 'owned' by you. Your version of feminism may not be ours. Societies evolve, feminism must be allowed to evolve with it.[58]

Notes

1 Coney, 'Why the Women's Movement ran out of steam', p. 54.
2 Hyman, 'New Zealand since 1984', p. 33.
3 Munro, 'More reflections', p. 8.
4 The time frame was chosen to build on earlier reviews of women's movement activism in New Zealand. Dann, *Up From Under: Women and Liberation in New Zealand*; Cahill and Dann, *Changing Our Lives;* Hyman, 'New Zealand since 1984'.
5 Devere and Scott, 'The Women's Movement'; Cahill and Dann, *Changing Our Lives*; Duncan, *Society and Politics*; Du Plessis and Higgins, 'Feminism'.
6 Coney, *Standing in the Sunshine*, p. 142.
7 Mercier, 'Self-help liberation', p. 44.
8 Preddey, *The WEL Herstory*, p. 5.
9 Mercier, 'An odyssey', p. 50.
10 Dann, *Up From Under*, p. 11.
11 Devere and Scott, 'The Women's Movement', p. 390.
12 Cahill and Dann, 'Introduction', *Changing Our Lives*, p. 2.
13 Baynes, 'Waiting for the suffragettes', p. 37.
14 Hyman, 'New Zealand since 1984'.
15 Pringle *et al.*, *Broadsheet* Autumn 1997, p. 33.
16 Federation of Women's Institutes cwi.org.nz/ accessed 6 June 2006.
17 Rural Women, www.ruralwomen.org/ accessed 6 June 2006.
18 Auckland Women's Centre, www.womenz.org.nz/wc/wcentre.htm accessed 6 June 2006.
19 Janus Trust, Annual Report of the Janus Looking Back, Moving Forward Trust, p. 4.
20 Under the title *Dominion Post* I will include the predecessors to this newspaper, the *Dominion* and the *Evening Post*.
21 Dann, *Up From Under*. pp. 5–23.
22 (1999). 'Beef hurled in catwalk protest, *Press*, 4 October, p. 9.
23 (2005). 'Rural women battle on home front', *Dominion Post*, 3 December, p. 2.
24 Collins (2003). 'Dairy giant closes door on mothers' anti-GM group', *New Zealand Herald*, 2 October.
25 Gee (2002). 'Marchers protest at surgery cuts', *New Zealand Herald*, 5 June.
26 (1995). 'French ban women's protest', *Dominion Post*, 5 October, p. 2.
27 Dann, 'The liberation of women is women's work'. p. 78.
28 (1995). 'Breakfasts celebrate Women's Day', *Evening Post*, 8 March, p. 3.
29 Women's Studies Association NZ (1997). *Newsletter*, Spring, p. 13.

30 Rural Women www.ruralwomen.org/ accessed 19 June 2006.
31 National Council of Women www.ncwnz.co.nz accessed 19 June 2006.
32 Women's Studies Association NZ (1997). *Newsletter*, Summer, p. 7.
33 Ferree and Hess, *Controversy and coalition*, p. 78.
34 Preddey, *The WEL Herstory*, p. 21.
35 Legget, 'Out of the kitchen and into the fire'.
36 McAdam *et al.*, *Comparative Perspectives on Social Movements*, p. 12.
37 Douglas, *Unfinished Business*, p. 140.
38 Devere and Scott, 'The Women's Movement', p. 294.
39 della Porta, *Social Movements, Political Violence, and the State: A Comparative Analysis of Italy and Germany.*
40 Bagguley, 'Contemporary British feminism', p. 182.
41 O'Regan, 'Radicalised by the system', p. 167.
42 Katzenstein, 'Feminism within American institutions', p. 32.
43 O'Connor (2003). 'Women's movement still needed', *Nelson Mail*, 20 May.
44 Coney, *Standing in the Sunshine*, p. 143.
45 Rupp and Taylor, *Survival in the Doldrums*; Taylor, 'Social movement continuity'.
46 Offe, 'Reflections on the institutional self-transformation of movement politics', p. 243.
47 Shannon, *The Influence of Feminism on Public Policy*, p. 28.
48 Julian. 'Blinding revelation or dawning awareness?', p. 100.
49 Hyman, 'New Zealand since 1984'.
50 Stafford, 'Speech at the inauguration of the Centre for Women's Studies', Christchurch.
51 Hyman, 'Hui Raranga Wahine/New Zealand Women's Studies Association Conference', p. 8.
52 Taylor, 'Social movement continuity', p. 768.
53 Rupp and Taylor, *Surviving in the Doldrums*, p. 196.
54 Women's Studies Association, Newsletter, p. 5.
55 Glendining, 'Women's Studies Association Newsletter'.
56 O'Connor, 'Women's movement still needed'.
57 Young Women's Caucus, 2005, Janus Women's Convention.
58 Kapiti Women's Centre, 'Newsletter'.

6 The politics of backlash in the United States and Japan

Joyce Gelb

In their recent book *Rising Tide*,[1] Ronald Inglehart and Pippa Norris contend there is an inexorable tide leading towards gender equality in nations that have undergone modernisation and transformation into post-industrial societies. This chapter takes issue with this optimistic finding, highlighting issues related to gender equality, feminism and backlash against social change. While gains may be made for a variety of reasons – including domestic women's mobilisation, institutional responsiveness at the national level, and the forces of political globalisation and transnational feminism – such gains are not static nor necessarily permanent. Counter-mobilisation related to regime change, forces of partisanship, sometimes coupled with religion, as well the effective use of symbols and slogans, may reinforce traditional values related to women and act as a brake on progress towards gender equality.

This chapter explores the impact of the backlash against feminist progress in the United States (US) and Japan, two neo-liberal states with very different political and religious foundations. It also focuses on the interaction between social movements and countermovements, a relatively recent topic. In essence, as a social movement begins mobilising resources and gaining a degree of success, those who oppose its goals and/or feel threatened by them may coalesce into a vocal opposition.[2] Countermovements may seek to confront, undermine or neutralise their opponents, while seeking to raise the cost of mobilisation and access to the political realm.[3] While most of the analysis is confined to state interaction with feminist movements and the ideas of feminism, mass media coverage may encourage movement counter-mobilisation as journalists seek out opposing interests in response to movement claims.[4] The history of feminist advocacy and impact in Japan and the US has provided examples both of movement success, and of opposition that seeks to limit further change. These cases show that movements and policies often undergo cycles of intense activity as well as periods of greater quiescence in which activism is more muted.

The United States

It has been suggested that the US women's movement is one of transformation, expansion and diversification, with a rich resource base inside and outside of government.[5] Women's movements are comprised of interest groups and social movements using a wide range of strategies to pressure government, through lobbying, litigation, and political campaigning (including providing funding support for candidates). As with movements discussed in other chapters in this collection, movement activism has been somewhat cyclical.

While the Democratic Party has been a frequent supporter of some feminist goals, a period of 'backlash' against feminism has become evident since 1980, with the election of Ronald Reagan, and thereafter particularly from 2000 during the presidency of George W Bush. Opposition to women's movement claims is not new in the US. A virulent 'New Right' conservative movement initially mobilised in opposition to the Equal Rights Amendment and *Roe v Wade*, the 1973 Supreme Court decision that recognised women's right to abortion. However, the countermovement has taken on a new legitimacy in the last decade, due to its connection to an incumbent president and members of Congress and its incorporation into the Republican Party agenda. This group has been working to roll back women's progress in every aspect – including work, school, reproductive and health rights, and economic security. The Right is also strengthened by its ties to fundamentalist religious groups in the US, groups that wield important political influence. It has been suggested that the virulence of the anti-feminist movement in the US has no counterpart elsewhere in the democratic world.[6]

Examples of the backlash against feminism in the US are all too common. In one instance, the Department of Justice has dropped all cases challenging sex discrimination in employment;[7] enforcement of Title IX of the Educational Amendments Act of 1972 on equity in education and sports has been weakened; while a Department of Education Commission has been seeking ways to weaken further opportunities for female students. Proposals have been made to eliminate hundreds of thousands of children from childcare programs that were never inclusive to begin with, and tax cuts and budget cutbacks have led to cuts in services and programs while affording few benefits to moderate and low-income women.

Reproductive rights are being threatened and two newly appointed Supreme Court members with questionable credentials on women's issues will hold the balance of power on this issue. Moreover, the Bush administration has supported policies that prohibit servicewomen from obtaining abortions in overseas military hospitals unless the pregnancy resulted from rape or incest or endangers the woman's life – and in the case of rape, she must pay for her own procedures.[8] Programs related to women's health are being undermined and scientific information distorted, for example, the National Cancer Institute has posted information on its website that falsely links abortion and cancer.

Backlash is also evident in government appointments. Individuals hostile to women's interests have been placed on important advisory committees, including those related to domestic violence and reproductive health and the Food and Drug Administration (FDA). Some FDA members appointed by Attorney General Ashcroft represent the Independent Women's Forum, an organisation that has vehemently attacked and disparaged the Violence Against Women Act and urged the Supreme Court to declare the Act unconstitutional.[9] Dr David Hager, who has refused to prescribe birth control for pregnant women and suggested prayer to alleviate pain for women suffering PMS, is on the FDA' s Reproductive Health Drugs Advisory Committee.[10]

In terms of government machinery, within a few weeks of election, the Bush administration closed the White House Office for Women's Initiatives and Outreach, which had been established under President Clinton, and which monitored policy initiatives within the executive branch and served as a liaison point to the outside.[11] It also sought to close key offices of the Women's Bureau, which was established in 1920. The administration limited the role of the Defense Advisory Committee on Women in the Service and permitted its charter to expire. Only policies seen to encourage 'family values', as defined by conservatives, have been embraced by the administration.

One consequence of Bush administration policy in conjunction with right-wing forces has been to deny pregnant women the subsidised family-planning services available in most other advanced nations. This policy was initiated by the first Bush administration, overturned by the Clinton administration and reinstated with the election of George W Bush. Due to the pressure exerted by anti-choice groups, the number of abortion providers has declined by 37 per cent since 1982, and 87 per cent of US counties have no abortion provider – affecting close to 40 per cent of American women.[12] The administration, through the FDA, has also delayed permitting emergency contraception to be made available without a prescription, despite contrary recommendations from two FDA Advisory commissions. The Bush administration has reinstated the Regan era 'global gag' rule, which prevents US family-planning funding being given to overseas non-governmental organisations that use their own funds to counsel and refer for abortion services, provide abortions or engage in advocacy about abortion within their own countries.

At the judicial level, packing the courts with judges opposed to women's reproductive and other rights has been common – several US Court of Appeals judges with these characteristics have been appointed as 'recess' appointments, which do not require Senate confirmation. As courts in the US wield enormous power, given lifetime appointments and the ability to interpret the law, these nominations have grave implications for women's future progress. On 17 March 2007, in a blow to pro-choice and pro-feminist forces, the US Supreme Court upheld the so-called 'partial birth abortion ban', which prevents many abortions after the first 12 weeks of pregnancy.

Feminism has also been under attack in the US outside government. Susan Faludi, in her 1991 book *Backlash*, provided an early account of anti-feminist efforts to discredit the movement. Anti-feminists have included Camille Paglia and Elizabeth Fox-Genovese, as well as Nancy Friday with her popular book *The Power of Beauty* (1996). Other more liberal journals joined the attack including the *New Republic* and *Village Voice*. In 1995, the Million Man March by black men served notice on 'uppity black women'.[13] The white Christian group Promise Keepers similarly served notice on all women that they should be dominated by men, and stay home taking care of the children.

Right-wing attacks on feminism, which highlight the ongoing interaction between countermovements and feminists, have also been common on American college campuses. The Independent Women's Forum was established in 1991, and, along with other conservative organisations such as the Concerned Women of America, seeks to mobilise what are characterised as alternative 'feminist' organisations. The Forum's 'Student Activist Guide' provides guidelines for the establishment of campus-based chapters, much like those disseminated by pro-feminist groups. Emulating the approach of pro-choice and pro-feminist groups, they send speakers and establish chapters at college campuses. They are a branch of a new conservative 'Campus Coalition', which dispatches conservative speakers to colleges and universities across the nation.[14]

In August 2003, the Independent Women's Forum's campus program expanded to include holding alternative events such as 'She Thinks'. A right-wing women's group launched a national 'Take Back the Campus' campaign (representing a voice opposing anti-assault movements) to challenge feminist 'myths'. They have sponsored advertisements in the UCLA *Daily Bruin*, as well as the *Yale Daily* and *Dartmouth Review*. Among the ' myths of feminism' they seek to debunk are the incidence of violence against women such as rape, sexual assault and domestic violence, the accuracy of data suggesting that women earn less than men, or that Women's Studies is a source of empowerment for female students and so on.[15] The Clare Booth Luce Policy Institute is an effort to create a new group of smart savvy conservative women, with an emphasis on consciousness-raising among young women of college age, in order to persuade them that feminism is the source of their woes.[16]

Such interests claim the pay gap for women is phoney and refer to this as 'cockamamie', they disparage efforts to protect women against sexual harassment, attack Title IX as a 'war against boys', insist that contraception is a 'frivolity, not something women need' and consider *Roe v Wade* the worst abomination of constitutional law in American history.[17] They also view the Violence against Women Act as a waste of money and say it encourages mistrust of all men.[18] These views, once represented as those of fringe extremists, now affect all policies relating to women in the US.

The backlash has also impacted in different ways upon the activities of those who consider themselves part of the US feminist movement. Efforts to defend existing policy and hold the line have occupied feminist activists, who have found it difficult to develop new initiatives in this chilly climate for women. For example, on college campuses feminist students have had to organise themselves to respond to Katie Roiphe and other conservative spokeswomen, as well as to the Independent Women's Forum. But membership in mainstream feminist groups continues to be strong. A summer 2006 annual meeting of the National Organization for Women (NOW) attracted young women from over 550 NOW chapters across the nation. EMILY's List, which helps to support pro-choice candidates for national office, boasts over 100 000 members/contributors, up from just 25 original members in 1985; it is now the largest political action committee in the nation.[19] NOW and the National Abortion Rights Action League report memberships of 500 000 and one million respectively. These groups have sought to both build on existing campus-based women's groups and establish new ones with ties to the older feminist organisations.

Even in this conflictual atmosphere some positive gains have been made, including the passage of the Violence Against Women Act in 1994 and its subsequent reauthorisations. This type of gain is in part due to the political opportunities provided by federal systems, as well as to the continued advocacy of feminist groups, and is seen also in Australia and Canada (as observed by Gwendolyn Gray this collection). The federal system in the US has sometimes proved helpful to women's advocacy, particularly when the national government is hostile to feminist claims or reluctant to act. As of January 2007, the US Congress is once more ruled by a Democratic majority; with a female Speaker of the House for the first time in American history – Nancy Pelosi of California. Whether the new Democratic Congressional dominance will prove to be more hospitable to women's interests remains to be seen.

Japan

Backlash, and its impact upon the advancement of women-friendly legislation and policy, is also evident in Japan.

Japanese women's movements have a long history, dating back to the nineteenth century. They have tended to be localised and single-issue oriented, sometimes coalescing around issues of mutual concern at the national level. For example, movements focus on issues such as reproductive rights, domestic violence and equal employment. Unlike the US, religion does not play a major role in relation to women's issues, as religion itself occupies a far less central role for society. It is said that religion for most people in Japan is significant only at birth, marriage and death. Despite the absence of a connection between religiously-based and other right-wing groups in Japan, conservative efforts have similarly sought to turn back the limited gains made to date by women's groups. Women's role and opportunities in Japan have been circumscribed by the forces of tradition, which emphasise male hierarchy and a subordinate role for women in society. Women's role has traditionally been defined as that of 'Good Wife and Mother'; and despite the falling birth rate, this value system continues to limit access to the labour force and the 'public' sphere. This role definition manifests itself in an 'M' shaped curve which signifies women's entry into the labour force after school, with workforce participation then declining after marriage and childbirth, only to rise again somewhat when children are of school age.

The right-wing backlash against feminism is evident in government in Japan. The Liberal Democratic Party has dominated politics during the entire post-war period (except for a brief period in the 1990s) and opposition parties have not been able to break its hold on the political system. During the regime of Prime

Minister Junichiro Koizumi, from 2001 until September 2006, conservatism wore a more affable face, though the right-wing factions that dominate politics remained largely unchallenged. Koizumi recruited a number of female candidates popularly known as 'Koizumi's children' (also 'assassins'). This move was part of his effort to punish recalcitrant Diet members who opposed his plans for privatisation of the postal service, rather than strictly a move for gender equality.[20] Among the women candidates he promoted were Kuniko Inoguchi, Toshiko Abe and Motoko Hirotsu. Further examples of the affable face of conservatism in Japan came in 2001 when Koizumi appointed a record number of women to his first cabinet; five out of 17. However, Koizumi's modern exterior and media orientation should not obscure his conservative views; for example, he opposed any assumption of financial or other responsibility on the part of Japan for the so called 'comfort women' who were pressed into prostitution during the Second World War.

In the Abe administration, which was in power 2006–07, the appointees were very conservative anti-feminist women. They included Eriko Yamatani as one of the Prime Minister's five aides and Sanae Takaichi as minister of gender equality, a post diluted by the addition of numerous other responsibilities including innovation, technology and food safety. This move sent a clear signal of lack of interest in women's issues in the Abe administration. Apart from holding multiple portfolios, Takaichi was also noted for her opposition to the feminist cause of retention of dual surnames for married women. In March 2007, Prime Minister Abe denied that the Japanese government was responsible for forcibly recruiting the 'comfort women'.[21] In addition, Minister Hakuo Yanagisawa of the Department of Health Labour and Welfare was quoted as saying that women are best viewed as 'baby making machines' (though he later apologised). Whether Abe's regime represented an even more virulent and nationalistic approach to policy in Japan than that of his predecessors is still unclear, although it appears that this is the case given the examples cited above. Following Abe's abrupt resignation in September 2007, he was replaced by Yasuo Fukuda. Fukuda also had a history of controversial remarks on gender issues, having been reported in 2003 as saying to journalists that rape victims looked as though they were 'asking for it'. His Cabinet was similar to that of Abe, although gender equality was now grouped with population and youth.

Other instances of right-wing ascension in Japanese politics are also evident. In Tokyo the right-wing leadership of Governor Shintaro Ishihara led to the abolition of the Tokyo Women's Foundation in 2002, and budgets for women's centres supported by the metropolitan government have been cut. In Osaka, right-wing assembly members who alleged that gender equality efforts would destroy the family, society and Japanese culture, have prevailed. This led to a weak ordinance emphasising the differences between men and women being passed.[22] A group named Nihon Kaigi and its women's branch, Nihon Josei Kaigi, have attacked the concept of a 'gender equal' society promulgated by the 1999 Basic Law for Gender Equality, and called for recognition of male/female differences with an emphasis on the traditional role of women as homemakers.

In Chiba prefecture, efforts by the female governor Akiko Domoto to adopt affirmative action policies for companies bidding for government contracts have been stymied.

Hostility to women's issues has spilled over to other policy reform proposals including local ordinances on gender equality, education reform, sex education, and the retention of women's surnames after marriage. Observers have made a strong link between conservatism and nationalism as twin pillars of Japanese society that must not be challenged. Concern about role change for Japanese women has been accentuated by the low fertility rate (now 1.29 per woman) and the lessened rate of marriage, as well as its delayed nature.

As in the US, the backlash against feminism has also been fought out in the newspapers and other public forums. According to the Convenor of Japan Women's Watch, Hiroko Hara, the major goals strongly supported by radical fundamental religious groups are as follows:

1   To restore traditional family values and to build a society in which men work hard outside the home and women protect and take care of families at home. They argue that this would prevent juvenile delinquency and correct moral degeneration in the society; they do not accept diverse forms of families.
2   To gut sex education and recommend sexual abstinence for young people until marriage; and
3   To abolish women's/gender studies.[23]

In line with these objectives, female intellectuals such as Mari Osawa have been vilified in the press as 'radical feminists' who are challenging 'family values' and introducing Communist ideas in the guise of 'gender equality'.[24] More recently, noted feminist and Tokyo University professor, Chizuko Ueno, was barred from speaking in a series on human rights sponsored by the Education Department of the Tokyo Metropolitan Government in Kunitachi City. Tokyo Governor Ishihara contended that she had not been banned, just that the district had been 'warned' about her appearance.[25] In numerous public comments, Governor Ishihara reinforced the theme that gender differences between men and women should be enforced and the term 'gender free' was in need of a Japanese interpretation. He also claimed that aged women who have no reproductive capacity are useless to society.[26] Ueno's talk was cancelled, apparently due to concern about use of the term 'gender free', which is understood as a synonym for 'gender equal', a symbol unpopular with the Japanese Right. Ueno herself saw the suppression of the term as part of a 'conservative backlash' against 'the collapse of gender boundaries' by politicians, many representing the dominant Liberal Democratic Party. In addition to Ishihara, they included the then Prime Ministerial hopeful, Shinzo Abe.[27] Leading Japanese newspapers including the right-wing *Sankei Shimbun* and even the more mainstream *Asahi Shimbun* have engaged in unremitting front-page support for anti-gender interests.[28] Proponents of the backlash movement insist that societal disruption has been brought about by radical sexual education, and children should therefore be taught 'continence', rather than given empowerment. The Ministry of Education, Culture, Sports, Science, and Technology seems to be complying with this opinion.

There have been some gains by women's groups in recent years, despite the backlash. Activists were able to obtain a change in the Eugenic Protection Law, related to reproductive health and rights, when the much-disliked name, a legacy of the post-war period, was changed to the Mother's Body Protection Law (botai hogo ho) in 1996. Women's efforts were also responsible for the passage of the Law for the Prevention of Spousal Violence and the Protection of Women first passed in 2001, and then amended and reauthorised in 2006. These gains are notable in a political system that lacks transparency and accountability, as well as access to the policy process.

Women members of the Japanese Diet and women's groups have continued their advocacy in the face of the vigorous attacks on feminist concerns. For example, the Asia-Japan Women's Resource Centre responded to Minister Yanagisawa:

> Women are not child-production machines!
> We demand the Health Minister's resignation.[29]

Women's and other liberal groups have protested against Prime Minister Abe's denial of the existence of 'comfort women' during World War II in Japan. Abe told a Diet committee session on 6 March 2007 that there was no evidence that Japanese military officials took the women by force – such as by kidnapping – to brothels, again denying there was coercion by the military in any strict sense. He made this statement despite documented evidence showing that about 200 000 women were impressed into prostitution.

Separately, Chief Cabinet Secretary Yasuhisa Shiozaki told a news conference that overseas criticism of Prime Minister Abe's comments was based on an incorrect interpretation of his remarks: 'There may have been coercion in a broad sense in recruiting the women, but we do not believe that the women were physically taken by force by the military to the frontline brothels', Shiozaki said, noting that Abe was referring to a 'narrower definition' of coercion.[30] In response, the Action Network on Japanese Military Comfort Women called for a state apology and restitution to victims of Japanese actions, saying:

> Today we bring to you 14 406 signatures from Japan, Korea, Taiwan and Germany urging you to support the Kono Statement as a bare minimum. We also have put together a brochure explaining why your argument denying coercion does not stand. We earnestly hope that our Prime Minister will genuinely share the pain that we share with the surviving women, and that you will demonstrate to the international community that you are a true leader of an honest government, committed to fulfilling responsibility for the State's past wrongdoings.

As in the US, women's advocacy groups have sought to make common cause with members of the legislature and sympathetic bureaucrats wherever possible. Nonetheless, forcing women's groups to operate on the defensive means that gains appear fragile and subject to reversal.

Conclusion

These parallel examples of policy towards women in two neo-liberal states, the US and Japan, raise a number of questions about the future of feminism as a political movement and progress towards gender equality. In contrast to the find-ings of Inglehart and Norris, who seek to demonstrate a 'rising tide' of equality in all but the most traditional states, this paper has stressed the obstacles to the achievement of gender equality, suggesting that even modest gains for women can generate a virulent countermovement. In the US, this analysis has demonstrated the force of religion in retarding further gains in gender equality policy, in conjunction with the ascendancy of conservative interests that domi-nate the political system. With the ascension to power in Congress of a Demo-cratic Party majority, it is possible that more progress may be made in some areas related to policy for women.

In Japan, the political system is constrained by the Liberal Democratic Party hegemony and the prominence of conservatives within it, but it is worth noting that even some members of the Democratic Party of Japan share many of the anti-gender equality views noted here. We are reminded that politics is a dynamic process, and perhaps a cyclical one as well, in which yesterday's attain-ments may be turned to today's new challenges. For feminist mobilisations, the backlash in the US and Japan has meant a retrenchment to protect gains made, and little possibility of policy progress.

However, the picture in both countries does provide evidence of continued advocacy and activism by feminist and women's groups, even in the face of backlash and hostility. In the US, perhaps in reaction to the negative political atmosphere, feminist groups continue to claim a large number of adherents. NARAL Pro-Choice America, a Washington group that favours legal abortion, contacted 800 000 members and supporters on the night President Bush nomi-nated conservative John Roberts to the bench, an indication of its continuing large membership base. Other groups report the same. NARAL Pro Choice America claims a membership of about one million and is making special efforts at outreach to younger feminists, especially those on college campuses. A similar approach is being adopted by another feminist group, The Feminist Majority. These groups are also making extensive use of blogs and such interac-tive web-based efforts as Myspace to engage younger members.[31] In Japan, as noted previously, women's groups have protested against remarks made by government ministers, even the Prime Minister, disparaging women. So it appears that once made, gains are not easily eradicated and feminist movements in both Japan and the United States demonstrate resilience, even in the face of adversity. While there is no 'inexorable tide' towards equality, elements of societal change may be sustained, as least partially, through movement activism and continued advocacy.

Notes

1 Inglehart and Norris, *Rising Tide.*
2 Meyer and Staggenborg 'Movements, countermovements, and the structure of political opportunity'.
3 Zald and Useem, 'Movement and countermovement interaction'.
4 Meyer and Staggenborg, 'Movements, countermovements, and the structure of political opportunity'.
5 For an extended discussion see Gelb, *Gender Policies in Japan and the United States.*
6 Bashevkin, *Women on the Defensive*, p. 70.
7 National Women's Law Centre, *Slip Sliding Away.*
8 National Women's Law Centre, *Slip Sliding Away*, p. 9.
9 National Women's Law Centre, *Slip Sliding Away*, p. 8.
10 National Women's Law Centre, *Slip Sliding Away*, p. 49.
11 National Women's Law Centre, *Slip Sliding Away*, p. 10.
12 Gelb, *Gender Policies in Japan and the United States.*
13 Hooks, 'All quiet on the feminist front'.
14 International Women's Forum website, at www.iwforum.org.
15 Haller. 'Anti feminist ad campaign launched on campus', *Women's E News*, 31 May 2001.
16 Pollitt, 'Feminism and women'.
17 Quoted in National Women's Law Centre, *Slip Sliding Away*, p. 3.
18 National Women's Law Centre, *Slip Sliding Away*, p. 4.
19 *Women's E News*, 21 July 2006.
20 Under the Abe administration that succeeded Koizumi, virtually all of those ousted for their opposition to the privatisation plans have been reinstated to office. The Diet is Japan's national parliament.
21 (2007). *New York Times*, 7 March.
22 Gelb, *Gender Policies in Japan and the United States*, p. 125.
23 Hara, 'Challenges of women for women, against women in Japan'.
24 Gelb, *Gender Policies in Japan and the United States.*
25 (2006). *Asahi Shimbun*, 27 January.
26 CGS Online, 23 May 2006, 'Overview of the backlash in Japan', Center for Gender Studies, International Christian University.
27 Personal correspondence from Andrew Horvat, japanforum@lists.nbr.org. 26 January 2006.
28 Gelb, *Gender Policies in Japan and the United States*, p. 126.
29 Asia-Japan Women's Resource Center, 29 January 2007, www.ajwrc.org/english.
30 Onishi (2007). 'Abe rejects Japan's war files on sex', *New York Times*, 2 March.
31 An example of outreach to younger women can be seen at myspace.com (profile. myspace.com/index.cfm?fuseaction=user.viewprofile&friendid=92607334) accessed January 2008.

Part II

New spaces

7 Gender specialists and global governance

New forms of women's movement mobilisation?

Jacqui True

Globalisation has brought about greater awareness of gross abuses of social, economic, civil and political human rights and linkages between them as well as greater practical possibilities for solidarity across borders and struggles. In particular, the increasing integration of economies, polities and societies has created 'political opportunities' for new forms of women's movement mobilisation. Feminist struggles are increasingly taking place within and around global institutions and are no longer confined to local grassroots or national social movement activism.

Global governance organisations including the United Nations, the World Bank, the International Criminal Court; regional organisations such as the European Union and Asia Pacific Economic Cooperation (APEC); and international development agencies have developed new forms of expertise and professional practices associated with gender analysis. The governance of a progressively more globalised and feminised labour market and the external pressure of a globally mobilised women's movement have justified these organisations' focus on *inter alia* women's human rights, women's empowerment within anti-poverty programmes, and women's entrepreneurship in trade and development policy.

'Gender mainstreaming' within regional and global governance organisations has involved a range of initiatives to integrate gender perspectives into institutional and policymaking processes. Gender specialists have emerged as key agents in this mainstreaming process raising the question of the professionalisation of the women's movement and its autonomy from institutional power.[1] The roles of gender specialists are often ambiguous and the extent to which they have been able to mainstream an awareness of gender relations within policy and institutional processes is under-researched.[2]

This chapter has three main parts. First, it considers the studies of state-level feminist advocacy that suggest alliances between feminists inside bureaucratic organisations and outside in women's civil society organisations are crucial for mainstreaming gender in government policies and processes. Drawing on this significant insight, the chapter explores the recent rise of gender mainstreaming in global governance organisations. Second, the chapter analyses the role and location of gender specialists in gender mainstreaming initiatives in these organisations. Considering recent debates in feminist networks, it asks whether women's rights and gender equality outcomes at the global level would be better achieved if gender specialists served as separate bodies of expert knowledge or as diffusers of that knowledge to non-specialists in international organisations. Third, the chapter investigates the relationship between 'insider', gender specialists in global and regional governance organisations and 'outsider', global networks of women's rights activists. The chapter corroborates findings in other chapters of this book about the necessity of having dual entry points inside and outside institutional power for feminist activism to be successful. This is as true at the global level as it is at the domestic level and is intrinsic to the success of gender mainstreaming as a strategy for political transformation.

Agents of mainstreaming

Since the 1995 UN Beijing Conference on Women, international organisations and governments around the world have adopted 'gender mainstreaming' as the preferred strategy to advance equality between women and men. According to the Economic and Social Council of the United Nations, mainstreaming involves

> [M]aking the concerns and experiences of women as well as of men an integral part of the design, implementation, monitoring and evaluation of policies and programmes in all political, economic and societal spheres, so that women and men benefit equally, and inequality is not perpetuated.

This definition is used widely throughout United Nations agencies. The Council of Europe's definition of gender mainstreaming is also influential, especially in the European Union and its member states.[3] In adopting the idea of mainstreaming, global, regional and national-level organisations have sought to move beyond equal rights and equal opportunity approaches that treat masculine structures as the norm, and women and men's equality as an optional add-on. Feminists argue that the goal of gender equality can only be attained when institutional rules and norms change to reflect and represent women's interests.[4] By taking into account the differences and power inequalities between women and men, gender mainstreaming seeks to influence these institutional rules and norms but it does so through change in organisations.[5]

Addressing issues of equality and justice in global governance is crucially important, since decisions today that have major consequences for the life chances and well-being of citizens are being made in global and regional settings that are only indirectly connected to the democratic political institutions in which (masculine) citizens have traditionally had a stake and a voice. When it comes to mechanisms that hold them accountable to women and men whose lives they affect, international organisations lack democratic legitimacy compared with nation-state institutions. Robert Keohane calls this an 'external accountability gap'; that is, a gap between the jurisdiction of global and regional organisations and their impact.[6]

Using such normative arguments about democracy and accountability, civil society groups have challenged international organisations and called for them to be accountable to all those they affect. International organisations have responded in various ways to these challenges, including addressing gender bias and disparities by purporting to integrate gender perspectives into their institutional procedures and policymaking, and sometimes into their substantive policy and operational outputs. Mainstreaming seeks to advance women's interests and gender equality through enlightened global public policy but it also gives international organisations a way to respond to some of the concerns of key constituencies within global civil society, who are affected by the organisations' decisions but do not participate in them, either directly or indirectly.

Within international organisations, gender specialists and line policy analysts, rather than women's movements, are intended to be the key agents in the mainstreaming process, although movements from below gave rise to the theory behind gender mainstreaming. Indeed, the global spread of mainstreaming approaches has encouraged the rise of a feminist 'epistemic community'.[7] This epistemic community of feminist advocates, researchers and officials has used 'gender expertise' – both critical argumentation and evidence-based research – to substantively engage institutional power. But gender mainstreaming is not merely a new form of technical expertise associated with global governance and the production of appropriate subjects for a neo-liberal global order, where the efficiency of markets is privileged over all other social, political and economic goals. It is an explicitly feminist strategy for political transformation and the realisation of gender justice and equality.[8]

In nation-states, gender specialist positions and women's policy machineries have been the crucial agents of mainstreaming; giving women's movements access to institutions and building mutually beneficial alliances between movement activists and policymakers (as discussed in Part II of this collection). Political science research shows that the combination of a strong women's policy machinery and a highly mobilised women's movement has delivered the best public policy outcomes for women across countries.[9] There is no straightforward analogy between the efficacy of gender specialists in nation-states and global governance organisations. However, the experience of gender specialists within national bureaucracies, particularly in Australia and New Zealand, offers some insights for exploring the agency of gender specialists at the global level and their relationship to the women's/feminist movement.

Learning from the femocrat experience

The Australian case of feminists in the bureaucracy, coined 'femocrats', has been well studied and with the benefit of hindsight makes clear some of the potentials and the pitfalls of the 'insider' or elite strategy for bringing about feminist change.[10] In the 1970s and 1980s, Australian women took advantage of openings in the bureaucracy facilitated by progressive governments, weak norms of public service neutrality, and the development of centralised women's policy machinery to promote feminist policy agendas.[11] A powerful alliance emerged between femocrats within the bureaucracy and a strong women's movement outside. In particular, an effective advocacy body, Women's Electoral Lobby, developed the 'wheel' model of women's policy machinery and was successful in having it adopted at different levels of government. Many feminists moved from doing unpaid work for change in the community to positions in government as heads of women's units and women's officers.[12] Femocrats interviewed by Hester Eisenstein believed: 'to be a femocrat was to be one kind of activist but the strategy was predicated on the support and energy of a broad women's movement'.[13] As one interviewee remarked: 'your job in advocating for women is twice as difficult if there is not lobbying and organising coming from the outside'.[14]

In Australia many of the new femocrats in the 1970s and 1980s came from a background in women's liberation and the Women's Electoral Lobby.[15] For example, both a later head of the Australian Office of the Status of Women and first chief executive of the New Zealand Ministry of Women's Affairs had been activists in the women's refuge movement, hardly the standard curriculum vitae for civil servants![16] However, although they had put them there, femocrats were criticised by parts of the women's movement. These groups argued that femocrats were not true collectivist feminists, that they were elites, non-representative of most women or of the women's movement, and that by helping the state to extend control over women's lives and to co-opt feminist agendas they effectively legitimised patriarchal institutions.[17] Feminist insiders themselves struggled to maintain their allegiance to the feminist cause and their accountability to the government, their employer. Eisenstein sums up their dilemma: 'women's advisors were supposed to represent the views of women to government. But in fact, they were on the government payroll, and often wound up mainly representing the government to women'.[18]

The femocrat strategy materialised at the beginning of a period of fundamental structural change in Australia and New Zealand. This change involved a shift away from the post-war welfare state tradition towards a neo-liberal form of state where the market was increasingly preferred over the state in the delivery of core public services. In this political context Anna Yeatman argues that feminists in high level positions in the bureaucracy effectively represented class rather than gender interests.[19] However, Marian Sawer argues that this interpretation fails to explain why femocrats continued to pursue strategies such as community-based childcare programs rather than tax deductions when as high income earners this was clearly not in their material 'class-based' interests.[20]

The rise of neo-liberal discourse and the spread of the new public management model delegitimised advocacy for what were now called 'special interests' within government in both Australia and New Zealand (as discussed by Sandra Grey, and Sarah Maddison and Kyungja Jung in this collection). Whereas in Australia an early incarnation of gender mainstreaming was the women's budget program introduced in 1984 at Commonwealth (federal) level, which required all agencies including economic policy departments to disaggregate the gender impact of budgetary proposals, in New Zealand gender mainstreaming became an argument for closing down or downgrading the units associated with women's equality. The Equal Employment Commission was established and staffed with femocrats to address gender pay inequities for a mere two months before it was removed by another Act of Parliament under a new, more conservative government and a private sector trust was set up in its place.[21] The Australian Howard government followed New Zealand down this path in misinterpreting gender mainstreaming as meaning specialist units were no longer needed. Whereas in the 1980s, feminist knowledge and activist experience was valued with the provision of gender specialist positions in government, by the 1990s, where women's units remained in government, they were increasingly staffed with generic managers and economic analysts. These individuals were hired to be *principal agents* of government and *not advocates* for women.[22]

To cut a long story short, feminists entered Australian and New Zealand government bureaucracies but by the 1990s were confronting an increasingly hostile environment. But they did leave a legacy: the diffusion of feminist ideas on gender as a legitimate frame for policy analysis in government. Moreover, many of their ideas, such as gender budget analysis, time-use surveys for unpaid work, gender checklists and gender-impact statements subsequently spread to other countries and importantly, to international organisations such as the UN and the EU.

One of the most important lessons to take from the femocrat experience for those seeking to mainstream a gender perspective in global governance is the need to build and maintain alliances between feminist networks inside and outside organisations. Such alliances can help to build the knowledge, and to keep the pressure on organisations making it easier for 'insider' gender specialists to balance their policymaking and advocacy roles (as discussed in Part I of this collection). Femocrats in Australia relied upon the pressure of activists outside government both in instigating election promises and following up on them between elections. But since there is no electoral and little democratic accountability at the global level, this activist political pressure is even more crucial and needs to be ever vigilant to progress the work of gender advocates within international organisations.

The femocrat experience suggests that institutional gender mainstreaming is an integral and historical dimension of women's movement mobilisation. At the global level, mainstreaming need not conform to an expert-bureaucratic model, where gender specialists are the main actors disconnected from women's activism in civil society.[23] Some analysts have argued that the movement of feminists into Antipodean governments led to the fragmentation of the national women's movements while others contend that the outcomes of state restructuring for women would have been worse had there not been feminist advocates in government.[24]

With economic liberalisation and increasing global integration, the forms of women's activism are changing. If the 1990s is a story of declining women's movements in western states, it is also a story of the impressive growth and solidarity of a truly global women's movement. More so than ever before, feminist politics today involves intensive and vigorous advocacy beyond borders. The phenomenal increase in transnational feminist activism is due to the political opportunities created by the globalisation of markets, governance, and normative structures such as international law, and the sharing of political struggles through internet communication and other new technologies.[25] Thus, feminist activism today routinely involves political engagement within and around regional and global governance organisations, which have the policymaking power to set and enforce international rules and standards, and establish influential international norms. Global politics is characterised by high levels of civil society activism around particular issues and advocacy campaigns. Thus, whereas gender mainstreaming in national bureaucracies may have had a demobilising effect on women's movements in recent years, at the global level women's activism has increased exponentially as western and non-western women's movements have pooled their energies and linked a myriad of locally-specific campaigns for women's human rights and gender justice (such as seen in the case of the urban safety movement described by Caroline Andrew in this collection).

Women's global activism reached a high point at the 1995 UN Beijing Fourth World Conference on Women. At Beijing governments agreed on a wide-ranging Platform for Action (PFA) that was largely the result of women's lobbying efforts. Gender mainstreaming was a cross-cutting theme in the PFA as well as one of the 12 critical areas of concern focused on institutional mechanisms for the advancement of women. Acknowledging the potential for marginalisation in all initiatives that seek to redress gender inequality and injustice, including mainstreaming and those that provide separate units and programmes for women, the PFA states: 'women/gender units [in government/governance] are important for effective mainstreaming, but strategies must be further developed to prevent inadvertent marginalisation as opposed to mainstreaming of the gender dimension throughout all [government/governance] operations'.

Containers or diffusers of gender knowledge?

Among feminists there has been some debate over the role of gender specialists and gender mainstreaming as a strategy for global policy change. Opinion is divided over whether the accountability for addressing gender injustice should be primarily with gender specialists and agencies that have the achievement of women's rights and gender equality as their primary mission, or whether this accountability should be shared with non-gender specialists and all of an organisation, as in gender mainstreaming. The UN currently has a dual strategy with an extensive system of gender focal points and four small agencies dedicated to gender equality issues: the United Nations Development Fund for Women (UNIFEM), the Division for the Advancement of Women, the International Research and Training Institute for the Advancement of Women and the Office of the Secretary-General's Special Advisor on Gender Issues. In the EU, gender mainstreaming has been interpreted as not requiring specialists, as a methodology for policymaking that beyond its initial institutionalisation could be designed and implemented by anyone.[26]

Many, including feminists and institutional actors, have called for the diffusion of responsibility for gender equality. With respect to international development organisations, Caroline Hannan-Andersson argues that the role of gender specialists must be strictly catalytic and not inhibit a shift of responsibility for gender mainstreaming to management and operations units.[27] Contrary to this view, some feminists argue that making gender mainstreaming everyone's job effectively means that it becomes no one's job. UNIFEM gender specialists Anne-Marie Goetz and Joanne Sandler put it bluntly: 'gender mainstreaming is everywhere – there are 1300 gender focal points in the UN system – and yet nowhere'.[28] Everyone does it or is expected to, so no one needs to be employed to specifically focus on gender issues. Since 11 September 2001. the focus on security politics and UN reform has diminished the political urgency and space for promoting women's rights that existed in the 1990s.[29] In this current global context the strength of gender mainstreaming in extending a gender perspective across all policy areas and jurisdictions is also precisely its weakness. Goetz and Sandler argue that it serves to dissipate the expertise on women and divert resources away from specialist knowledge to training non-gender specialist staff and producing bureaucratic tools like checklists, action plans, scorecards, implications statements and so on that can be used by anyone.[30]

Feminists both for and against gender mainstreaming strategies stress the knowledge gap in international organisations. There are too few gender specialists in global governance organisations, especially in the security and trade policy areas. However, the gender mainstreaming discourse has not provided a strong rationale for organisations to invest in specialist knowledge and expertise. Within the UN there are, as noted, a growing number of gender focal points but only a small number of high-level appointments of gender experts. Gender focal points serve as desk information sources and facilitators of gender analysis but they are not dedicated gender specialists or fully accountable for the outcomes of gender mainstreaming. The international security and trade policy areas illustrate some of the trade-offs associated with prioritising gender mainstreaming over specialist gender positions or agencies in global governance.

Significant in this area is Security Council Resolution 1325 on Gender, Peace and Security, which was passed in October 2000. Potentially revolutionary, the Resolution acknowledges the role of women as well as men in peace and security, and contains a mandate for ensuring women's rights to participate in peace processes and post-conflict reconstruction and their protection in armed conflict. Cohn notes that the expanding group of advocates in and around the UN has relied on gender mainstreaming as the mechanism for implementing these changes.[31] Resolution 1325 calls for the integration of gender across UN security policy and operations, including the need for better representation and participation of women, gender analysis and sex disaggregated data, and research on peacekeeping and peacebuilding operations.

Following the passage of this resolution, it took four years of recommenda-tions and consultancy reports before the UN appointed the first Gender Advisor at the Department of Peacekeeping Operations.[32] This advisor is charged with operationalising Resolution 1325 in UN peacekeeping policy. Yet UN consul-tants Rehn and Johnson-Sirleaf (now President of Liberia) warn that 'limiting this function to one person is setting them up to fail'.[33] Subsequent to cases of UN peacekeepers' sexual exploitation and abuse of local and trafficked women in Bosnia, a focal point on sexual exploitation and abuse was also added in the Department of Peacekeeping Operations. At the operational level, 11 out of 18 peacekeeping missions around the world now have gender advisors or units. According to the UN Secretary-General the role of these advisors in gender units is 'to promote, facilitate, support, and monitor the incorporation of a gender perspective in peacekeeping operations'.[34] Among their tasks are making contact with local women's organisations, promoting registration of female voters and training female candidates for campaigns and elections as well as coordinating gender mainstreaming across departments and developing gender-sensitive pro-grammes and training for UN personnel and police.[35] This is a tall order for a single unit or position.

The UN Department of Peacekeeping Operations 2005 progress report on gender mainstreaming observed that personnel and partners are 'often unin-formed about the nature, type and impact of gender mainstreaming'.[36] Gender mainstreaming remains a task assigned to and carried out by the gender units. The report states: 'the notions that gender advisors are catalysts in gender main-streaming efforts and that gender mainstreaming is the responsibility of all staff have also failed to be universally accepted'.[37] Gender specialists in gender units continue to take the lead in promoting gender equality and little or no gender expertise was found in other departments.

In the trade policy area, the gender mainstreaming strategy has also had its limitations in terms of the development of specialist knowledge. In 2002, APEC, a regional trade policymaking body made up of 21 member states, established its framework for the integration of women, and importantly, a gender focal point network to implement the new framework. The network aimed to link non-specialist officials directly with substantive gender expertise in the organisation through designated 'gender focal points' in each of the four committees and 11 working groups across the organisation. It took more than three years for the institutional framework to be designed and agreed on by Trade Ministers, let alone implemented.

The APEC gender focal point network is innovative in two ways. First, as the name suggests, it takes a network form to ensure that gender is mainstreamed throughout the regional organisation as a cross-cutting rather than a sectoral issue. Second, the mainstreaming design rests heavily on gender expertise developed not in member states but 'transnationally across the economic sectors such as agriculture and tourism, represented by APEC working groups (which may include private sector representatives)'. In addition, gender-based analysis is a requirement of all projects funded by APEC's Budget and Management

Committee. Projects must address specific gender questions and criteria in both their proposal and evaluation stages. But working groups are also encouraged to develop specific projects that utilise sex-disaggregated data, analyse the gender dimensions of regional trade and economics, and increase the involvement of women in projects and policymaking. In theory, the APEC mainstreaming framework appears sound. However, in practice, it assumes that officials can easily assess gender and trade expertise and that the gender checklist requirement on requests for funding is enough of an incentive to get officials to use that expertise. There are no earmarked resources for the development and consolidation of knowledge about gender dimensions and impacts of trade policy. This is left entirely up to voluntary bureaucratic activism and the interest of member states, and in the end relies on regional feminist advocacy and research around the Women's Leader's Network officially outside of APEC but mirroring its agendas.[38]

What is telling about the story of feminist engagement with the UN Security Council and with APEC is that, despite their different regimes and locations, the impetus for the policy and institutional change came from women's movements. Resolution 1325 is the only UN resolution to have a transnational lobby group devoted to monitoring and evaluating its implementation as well as doing much of the work to make 1325 known at the grassroots level across conflict zones. In the case of APEC, the Women's Leader's Network, although officially outside of the formal organisation of APEC, is currently the only women's network to have infiltrated a trade organisation and become part of its regular agenda while seeking to change it. However, once the two organisations developed institutional mandates for mainstreaming gender, both of which stress the rights of women to participate in decision-making, these mandates have provided an ongoing political opportunity structure for challenging the democratic accountability of the organisations to women citizens in particular, and for the development of new alliances and networking among feminist activists, scholars and policymakers inside and outside institutional power.

Opening spaces for women's movements

One of the most effective ways feminists have learnt to prevent the marginalisation of women's concerns and gender issues is to build alliances between insiders (gender specialists) and outsiders (women's movements). It is hard to see, for instance, how gender mainstreaming could work as a policy strategy inside organisations without the support and scrutiny of women's movements outside. Yet theories of gender mainstreaming do not stress the substantive representation of women's interests in policy discussion or require experts to consult with, or be accountable to, women's movements. For instance, the influential Council of Europe definition of gender mainstreaming was conceived by a group of specialists with no input from any grassroots feminist activist. From its very inception in institutions, mainstreaming was seen as a part of the normal policymaking process with little room for dialogue with civil society or activists.[39] Are there linkages between gender specialists in international organisations and grassroots women's activism? For instance, have gender specialists sought to foster the participation and support of women's organisations in civil society as a way of institutionalising global organisations' external accountability to feminism/women's movements?

The movements for gender integration in the International Criminal Court (ICC) and for the inclusion of women in building peace around the UN Security Council Resolution 1325 are two recent examples of successful cooperation between gender specialists inside international organisations and feminist activists outside. In both cases, sustained advocacy by women's organisations working with committed insiders led to the adoption of gender-sensitive international laws and is helping to ensure their practical realisation.

The ICC's Rome Statute was influenced to a significant degree by the lobbying efforts of the Women's Caucus for Gender Justice (WCGJ), an expansive transnational network of women's organisations and individuals. The drafting was informed by feminist critiques of justice and power and, as a result, gender was mainstreamed throughout the Statute. The Statute covers administration of the ICC, including the gender balanced recruitment of judges and other personnel, and gender-sensitive court procedures, especially for the protection of victims and witnesses. The substantive legal provisions make gender-specific crimes of sexual violence into war crimes, crimes against humanity, and acts of genocide. In addition, the Rome Statute provides mandates for the Court appointment of gender experts and legal expertise on violence against women and children (Article 36 [8] b and Article 44 [2]).[40]

Louise Chappell argues that gender advocates inside and outside reinforced each other's efforts to ensure that women's access to justice was placed (and remained) on the agenda of the ICC and the ad hoc tribunals. The WCGJ in particular 'played a pivotal role in bringing to the attention of official delegates the importance of considering gender issues in their discussion' and many of the 'insiders', especially senior prosecutors and judges have taken up these demands in their subsequent decision making.[41] The Women's Initiatives for Gender Justice continues to monitor the implementation and mainstreaming of gender in the Statute by informing women about job openings in the court, lobbying to ensure that equal numbers of women are elected to the court, and providing gender legal advice and training to the court's staff.[42] For their part, gender experts holding new specialist positions within the ICC encourage the input of women's organisations in their ongoing work to make the Statute an effective human rights instrument.

In the UN, collaboration between UNIFEM gender experts and women's networks led to informal meetings with the Security Council that facilitated the adoption of Resolution 1325 on Gender, Peace, and Security.[43] The nongovernmental transnational women's advocacy networks that lobbied for Resolution 1325 included the International Women's Tribune, Women's Caucus for Gender Justice, International Alert, the Women's International League for Peace and Freedom, the NGO Working Group on Women, Peace and Security and

ACCORD. 'What makes 1325 unique', Carol Cohn argues, 'is that it is both the product of and the armature for a massive mobilisation of women's political energies'.[44]

Although gender mainstreaming is being implemented by gender specialists through the UN Inter-agency Taskforce on Women, Peace and Security, and a member-state group, 'Friends of 1325', there is also a critical role for advocacy networks in the gender and security mainstreaming process. Feminist advocacy networks have conducted 'research at the grassroots level to build up knowledge in the area of gender and peacebuilding and to provide multilateral and bilateral donors with proven strategies to improve their capacities in this field'.[45] All major donors now have dedicated gender expertise or policies on peacekeeping and peacebuilding, although they have interpreted and operationalised the gender mainstreaming mandate in different ways. Advocates have also used 1325 to demand women's inclusion in peace negotiations and have begun to monitor the Resolution's implementation by holding regional consultations, creating new information-sharing web portals, and developing measurable indicators of progress. As Cohn observes, 'feminist insiders and outsiders at the UN have put tremendous, creative thought and energy into making [Resolution 1325] a living document – an ongoing commitment for the Security Council rather than a one time rhetorical gesture'.[46] Their collaboration has helped to widely disseminate and raise awareness about the resolution's mandate in local as well as international settings with the aim of making it meaningful on the ground.

Cohn cites the case of the Democratic Republic of Congo, where local women's organisations and the Gender Advisor in the UN Peacekeeping Mission worked together to implement 1325.[47] Having already lobbied their government extensively for two years to implement 1325, and written to the Security Council, they lobbied the director of the UN Mission for a gender office and perspective in the Mission when it arrived in 2000. A gender advisor was appointed in 2002 and since then the women's organisations have been 'working closely with her on projects such as translating 1325 into the four official languages and strategies for inserting a gender perspective into all levels of government'.

Another example from the UN Mission in Kosovo (UNMIK) shows how collaboration between the international gender specialist and women's organisations can make a difference. Lesley Abdela, the British-appointed gender specialist for the Organisation for Security and Cooperation in Europe (OSCE), part of UNMIK, urged the international organisation to consult and involve Kosovo women's groups in the post-conflict reconstruction process. When the OSCE did not respond, she wrote a letter to Kofi Annan asking him to intervene. The UN Secretary-General's intervention ensured that the women's organisations were included. However, Abdela, the gender specialist, was fired for breaching organisational protocol.[48] This example makes clear that there are risks as well as trade-offs involved in the alliances between feminist insiders and outsiders, even when there is a payoff for women's rights or gender equality.

Not all insiders would be willing and able to pay the price that Lesley Abdela did to change a policy or a process for feminist goals.

Towards critical interventions

For some feminists, activism is by definition oppositional and 'grassroots'.[49] In this view, gender specialists who are for the most part elite institutional actors could not possibly be seen as part of women's movement mobilisation. However, if we understand feminism as a discursive movement, constantly being reflected on and reformulated by individuals and groups, then gender specialists clearly contribute to this movement as a political struggle over the meanings of gender and their embeddedness in material structures of inequality.[50] Everyday feminists – those who share and practice the values of the movement against masculinist domination – are typically non-activists.[51] You do not have to be a feminist activist, engaging in street protest, to do gender mainstreaming, but mainstreaming gender inside powerful organisations can be a form of everyday feminist activism. Moreover, if we can show that gender mainstreaming is not merely used as a problem-solving device or a means to ends other than gender equality, but used strategically by gender specialists for even small achievements towards breaking down masculine hegemonies in international organisations and their institutional and policy norms, then it follows that we should see these actors as part of the feminist movement. It is inevitable that the role of the gender specialist involves complicity with institutional power in some respects, being constrained as well as enabled as a feminist agent by the institutional norms reproduced in organisations over time.[52] Institutional and organisational change, especially in multilateral organisations with diverse staff backgrounds and wide-ranging policy agendas, is complex and difficult.

To a greater extent than in national bureaucracies even, the capacity of gender specialists in global governance organisations to change policy processes and outcomes towards greater gender justice rests on the ongoing advocacy, knowledge, and pressure of broader women's movements. As shown by the alliances between gender experts and feminist advocates in the framing and implementation of new rules and norms around the ICC and the UN Security Council Resolution 1325, successful feminist change requires leveraging institutional and non-institutional entry points for activism. However, some issue areas such as international criminal law and organisations such as the ICC have been more amenable to activism from the inside and the outside, and as a consequence, gender mainstreaming has made greater inroads in these areas. International trade and security are policy areas that have traditionally involved secret or closed-door multilateral discussions and negotiations among state parties from which civil society has been denied access to observation let alone participation. They are also areas where the unequal gender impacts are deeply structural and therefore difficult to see without extensive analysis, and where gender inequalities have been seen as best addressed by local and national governments rather than by international organisations or global civil society. Thus security and trade organisations have been especially challenging institutional settings for women's movements to enter and to put gender issues on the agenda. But that is why the cases of UN Security Council Resolution 1325 and APEC's Framework for the Integration of Women are so significant. They represent markers of the new transnational spaces of women's activism, and of the global democratic potential of that activism.

Notes

1 Antrobus, *The Global Women's Movement*, p. 151. See also Beveridge and Nott, 'Mainstreaming: A case for optimism and cynicism'.
2 See Pollack and Hafner-Burton, 'Mainstreaming gender in global governance'; Bergeron, 'The post-Washington consensus and economic representations of women in development at the World Bank'; Prugl and Lustgarten, 'The institutional road towards equality'; Rahmani, *Gender Mainstreaming in the United Nations Human Rights Treaty Bodies*; True, 'Mainstreaming gender in global public policy'; True, 'Gender mainstreaming and regional trade governance in the Asia-Pacific Economic Forum (APEC)'.
3 See Verloo, 'Displacement and empowerment'.
4 Goetz, *Getting Institutions Right for Women*.
5 Prugl, 'From equal rights to gender mainstreaming', Prugl and Lustgarten distinguish organisations from institutions; the former are localised bureaucracies but also households, firms, the latter are rules and norms, often embedded in organisations over time.
6 Keohane, 'Global governance and democratic accountability'.
7 Walby, 'Feminism in a global era'.
8 Prugl, 'From equal rights'; Verloo, 'Displacement and empowerment'.
9 Weldon, *Protest, Policy and the Problem of Violence Against Women*.
10 Eisenstein, *Inside Agitators;* Yeatman, *Bureaucrats, Technocrats, Femocrats*; Sawer, *Femocrats and Ecorats*; Chappell, *Gendering Government*.
11 Chappell, *Gendering Government*.
12 Eisenstein, *Inside Agitators*, pp. xiii, 32.
13 Eisenstein, *Inside Agitators*, p. 212.
14 Eisenstein, *Inside Agitators*, p. 203.
15 Eisenstein, *Inside Agitators*, pp. 74, 91.
16 See Sawer, *Sisters in Suits*; O'Regan with Varnham, 'Daring or deluded', pp. 176–180.
17 Eisenstein, *Inside Agitators*, p. xv.
18 Eisenstein, *Inside Agitators*, p. 89.
19 Yeatman, *Bureaucrats, Technocrats, Femocrats*; Eisenstein, *Inside Agitators*, p. 195.
20 Sawer, *Sisters in Suits*, pp. 78–103.
21 See Mintrom and True, *Framework for the Future*.
22 Eisenstein, *Inside Agitators*; Teghtsoonian, 'Neoliberalism and gender analysis mainstreaming in Aotearoa/New Zealand'.
23 Daly, 'Gender mainstreaming in theory and practice', p. 447; Beveridge and Nott, 'Mainstreaming: A case for optimism and cynicism'.
24 Sawer, 'Feminism and the state', p. 101; Domett and True, 'Perspectives: The fight continues for gender equality'.
25 For data on the exponential increase in international NGOs on women's rights in recent years see Smith, 'Characteristics of the modern transnational social movement sector', pp. 42–58.
26 Stratigaki, 'Gender mainstreaming vs positive action'.

27 Hannan-Andersson, 'Moving positions forward: Strategies for gender and development cooperation'.
28 Goetz and Sandler, 'Should we swap gender?'
29 Sen, *Neolibs, Neocons and Gender Justice: Lessons from Global Negotiations*.
30 Goetz and Sandler, 'Should we swap gender?'
31 Cohn, 'Mainstreaming Gender in UN Security Policy'.
32 The Women's International League for Peace and Freedom advocacy website monitors the implementation of SC Resolution 1325 and documents the series of recommendations and UN responses culminating in the Department of Peacekeeping Operations Gender Advisor position. See www.peacewomen.org.
33 Rehn and Johnson-Sirleaf, *Women, War, Peace*, p. 68.
34 UN Secretary-General, *Women, Peace and Security*.
35 Purkarthhofer, 'Gender and gender mainstreaming in international peacebuilding'.
36 The United Nations Department of Peacekeeping Operations, *2005 Progress Report*, p. 9.
37 United Nations Department of Peacekeeping Operations, *Progress Report*, p. 3.
38 See True, 'Gender mainstreaming and regional trade governance in Asia-Pacific Economic Cooperation (APEC)'.
39 Verloo, 'Displacement and empowerment'.
40 Spees, 'Women's advocacy in the creation of the International Criminal Court'.
41 Chappell notes that rulings of Justice Mumbo at ICTY and Justice Pillay at ICTR were both influenced by the arguments of feminist advocates ('Gender Mainstreaming in International Institutions').
42 Afrin and Schwartz, 'A human rights instrument that works for women', p. 156.
43 Hill *et al.*, 'Nongovernmental organisations' role...'.
44 Cohn, 'Feminist peacemaking', p. 8.
45 Barnes, 'Reform or more of the same?').
46 Cohn, 'Feminist peacemaking', p. 8.
47 Cohn, 'Feminist peacemaking', p. 9.
48 Abdela, 'Kosovo: Missed opportunities, lessons for the future', p. 93.
49 Antrobus, *The Global Women's Movement*, p. 150.
50 See Prugl, 'From equal rights'.
51 Mansbridge, 'What is the Feminist Movement', pp. 27–34.
52 See Kronsell, 'Studying silences on gender in institutions of hegemonic masculinity'.

8 Campaigns for candidate gender quotas

A new global women's movement?

Mona Lena Krook

Women form more than half the population in most countries around the world, but until very recently, constituted only a small minority of all political representatives. This pattern has begun to change as women's groups around the world have mobilised for measures to increase the proportion of women elected to political office. While only about 20 countries had some sort of quota policy prior to 1990, quotas appeared in more than 50 states in the 1990s and more than 40 more since the year 2000.[1] The global diffusion of any policy is a notable development, but the rapid diffusion of candidate gender quotas *per se* is particularly remarkable. This is because positive action for women in electoral processes challenges, and even contradicts, a number of other recent trends in international and feminist politics, namely rising neo-liberalism, supposed decline in women's movement activity, growing scepticism about the unity of 'women' as a category, and ongoing challenges to links between descriptive and substantive representation. The spread of gender quotas thus raises two related sets of questions. First, why have quotas been so readily adopted in diverse countries around the world? Second, does the apparently widespread support for quotas constitute a demand articulated by a new global women's movement, or instead, reflect a more cynical attempt among elites to mask other struggles under the guise of concern for the political status of women?

This chapter addresses these questions in three parts. The first section discusses basic features of gender quotas and makes the case for viewing them as a global, rather than a national, phenomenon. The second section outlines possible explanations for quota diffusion, focusing on the major actors and motivations behind quota reforms. The third section builds on these arguments to 'map' various quota campaigns to explore the degree to which they can be deemed to form part of a broader global women's movement, given that feminist and non-feminist actors are frequently involved on both sides of these debates. The final section concludes with some thoughts about the consequences of these findings for viewing campaigns for gender quotas as part of a new global women's movement aimed at empowering women around the globe. It calls for more careful attention to the multiple possibilities – both intended and unintended – of quota reform, and thus to the varied contributions and challenges of gender quotas to feminist theory and practice.

Gender quotas as a global phenomenon

Gender quotas currently exist in more than 100 countries, and their numbers continue to grow, with new policies being proposed and debated nearly every month. As they have spread around the world, they have converged around three basic types: reserved seats, party quotas, and legislative quotas. Reserved seats are usually enacted through constitutional reform and set aside a guaranteed – and often limited – number of seats for women among elected representatives. They are distributed in various ways but are most often allocated by designating certain districts as 'women's districts' for the period of one election cycle, or by granting political parties the right to appoint a certain number of women in accordance with the percentage of votes received in the most recent elections. Party quotas, in comparison, are adopted voluntarily by political parties, who pledge to increase the percentage of women among their party's candidates or elected representatives. These measures establish a desired proportion of female candidates, although the actual wording of the reform is sometimes gender neutral, setting a minimum or maximum representation of either sex. Legislative quotas, finally, involve constitutional and/or legal reform and require all parties to nominate a certain percentage of women, often, but not always, with oversight from central government authorities.

Despite the differences among these three categories, a number of important patterns emerge in terms of the form and timing of quota adoption in countries around the world. First, the type of quota pursued is strongly correlated with world region: reserved seats appear mainly in Africa, Asia, and the Middle East; party quotas are most common in Western Europe; and legislative quotas are found primarily in Latin America.[2] Second, the adoption of quota policies is clearly clustered around particular years: after several years of stagnation, the number of countries with quotas increased slightly over the course of the 1980s and then jumped dramatically during the 1990s and 2000s. Third, these developments intersect: the first wave of quota policies was largely reserved seats in Asia, the second wave was mainly party quotas in Western Europe, and the third wave has primarily involved party and legislative quotas in Africa and Latin America.[3] These patterns suggest that gender quotas are a global phenomenon that is powered at least to some degree through policy diffusion across national borders. This view contradicts most existing research on gender quotas, which tends to approach these policies in the context of national, rather than international, developments. A global lens indicates that it might be fruitful to investigate possible connections between individual quota campaigns, and the role played by domestic and transnational women's movements.

Explaining quota diffusion

The existing literature offers mainly domestic explanations for quota adoption related to the mobilisation of women's groups, the calculations of political elites, and the connections between quotas and reigning political norms. One group of scholars argues that although male elites are often responsible for the decision to adopt quotas, simply because they constitute the majority of party leaders and legislators, these measures are usually put on the political agenda only after women have organised in favour of quotas. These women may include grassroots women's movements, cross-partisan networks of female politicians, women's sections inside political parties, individual female leaders, and members of women's policy agencies. Similar to many other chapters in this volume, these researchers often emphasise the importance of the combined efforts of women 'inside' and 'outside' elite circles for the proposal – and ultimate adoption – of gender quota policies.

A second set of scholars focuses on political elites and the strategic advantages they may perceive for supporting gender quotas. Most point to the role of party competition, noting that elites often embrace quotas after one of their electoral rivals establishes them. However, others uncover other strategic incentives, like seeking to sustain a faltering regime, consolidate control over political rivals, or demonstrate commitment (often superficial) to promoting women's rights. A third group of scholars views quota adoption as an extension of existing or emerging notions of equality and representation. This normative approach may take a number of different forms, depending on how quotas relate to reigning political principles like equality and fair access, difference and group representation, and democratic transition and innovation.[4]

Despite this tendency to focus on gender quotas in relation to national-level debates, more recent work – observing that quotas have now appeared in many countries around the world – has begun to develop a fourth broad set of explanations focused on international norms and the role of transnational information-sharing. It points to the significance of international meetings and conferences that generate recommendations for member states to improve women's access to political decision-making, as well as the importance of transnational organisations and networks that exchange information on strategies for promoting women's political representation across national borders. These dynamics, however, play out in at least four ways through distinct configurations of actors and motivations for quota reform. The first two dynamics involve a strong role for international and state actors, while the second two entail much more initiative from national and transnational social movement actors.[5]

International imposition occurs when international actors are directly involved in quota adoption, either by making the decision to apply quotas or by strongly compelling national leaders to do so themselves. The international community usually exerts this pressure in cooperation with local women's movements and transnational non-governmental organisations (NGOs), but sometimes acts in a more unilateral fashion and imposes gender quotas despite women's opposition to these measures. In these cases, international organisations frame the new policy as a central feature of a modern state. States comply for a variety of different reasons, but often because they seek to cultivate international legitimacy, either to foster perceptions of domestic legitimacy or to avoid being viewed as pariahs in the international community.[6] As such, their behaviour may reflect a degree of socialisation to international norms, or may simply indicate strategic action on the part of international and state actors to achieve other political ends. Among quota campaigns, this dynamic is present mainly in post-conflict societies, where international bodies have assumed a central role in post-conflict reconstruction.

International blockage affects quota campaigns when international actors seek to prevent the adoption of gender quotas, despite mobilisation by local women's groups and transnational NGOs in favour of quota policies. These attempts to subvert or undermine quota adoption, however, may be overcome when domestic pressures exceed the degree of international intervention into national political processes. This dynamic finds parallels in research on competing sets of national and international norms, which seeks to explain why norms are implemented in some instances but not in others, and why some norms are enforced and others are not.[7] In these cases, international organisations are captured, either unwittingly or as part of their strategic framing processes, by implicit beliefs that prevent change in traditional gender norms.[8] This dynamic is relatively rare in quota campaigns, as international actors in general tend to support commitments to increase women's political representation, but has been notable in the cases of East Timor and Iraq.

International tipping occurs when international actors influence quota campaigns already in progress by providing new sources of normative leverage in national debates. While international documents and meetings serve as catalysts by introducing or popularising new ideas and strategies for increasing women's representation, most of the 'work' in these campaigns is done by domestic actors who organise both nationally and regionally, often in the run-up to international women's conferences.[9] In these cases, international events aid domestic policy entrepreneurs by intensifying focus on their particular issue area, leading them to point increasingly to international rules to gain support for gender quotas. Two of the most prominent international agreements in this regard are the 1979 UN Convention on the Elimination of All Forms of Discrimination against Women (CEDAW) and the 1995 Beijing Platform for Action (PFA), which call on member states to foster women's full and equal participation in public life. The visibility of these events and agreements, combined with the rapid adoption of quotas in their wake, leads many to mistake their role as catalysts for a role as the cause or origin of specific quota policies. This is especially the case in Latin America, where scholars focus on the role of the Beijing PFA in spurring the rapid diffusion of gender quotas, when in fact domestic campaigns were already underway in most of these countries before Beijing.

Transnational emulation, finally, inspires quota campaigns when local women's movements and transnational NGOs share information across national borders. In most instances, activists seek to overcome unfavourable domestic conditions by borrowing ideas from other groups through direct relational ties, like personal contacts, and non-relational channels, such as journalistic accounts and academic writings.[10] Some engage in horizontal emulation by simply copying the strategies of others to devise the best course of action, but most have contact with transnational networks that serve as conduits of information on various policy models and tactics for change, and act as allies in convincing governments to adopt new policy innovations.[11] While some of these instances are truly global, many occur at the regional level among countries that share historical ties and often involve efforts to 'translate' lessons to suit specific domestic contexts, even when this entails distorting lessons from other countries or devising new 'home-grown' solutions to similar policy challenges.[12] This dynamic generally takes one of three forms: personal contacts among individuals regarding specific quota strategies, transmission between countries with similar languages or parties with similar ideologies, and lessons learned through the creation of myths and innovative local solutions. This diversity stems from the fact that transnational sharing introduces a more active role for domestic campaigners, who draw insights from multiple sources but then select, borrow, and modify these strategies in order to make them 'fit' their particular context.

Mapping quota campaigns

All four of these latter dynamics involve international and transnational actors and, combined with the three domestic explanations, point to a diverse array of players in quota campaigns around the world. Viewed from a broader global perspective, these various narratives reveal three main groups of actors and at least seven possible motivations for quota reform. The three categories of actors who participate in quota campaigns are located in civil society, the state, and international and transnational spheres. Civil society actors include grassroots women's movements, women's movement organisations, some individual women and women's sections inside political parties,[13] and individual women active inside and outside parties. Most of these actors mobilise for gender quotas, but some occasionally organise against quotas. They are frequently the actors who initiate quota campaigns, which they direct towards state actors, sometimes with ideas or help from international and transnational actors.

State actors, in contrast, encompass national women's policy agencies, national leaders, governing coalitions, representatives in parliament, party leaders, and judges in national and local courts. They are often the most powerful voices for and against quotas because of their broad visibility and their capacity to institute or reject quotas within political parties and national assemblies. They occasionally propose quotas, but are most often the targets of campaigns waged by civil society and international and transnational actors.

International and transnational actors comprise international organisations of global and regional scope; groups formed under the auspices of international organisations; transnational NGOs; and transnational networks of activists, politicians, and scholars. In a handful of earlier cases,[14] colonial governments also played a central role in instituting quota reforms. These actors almost invariably support gender quotas but at times prove to be an effective obstacle to quota adoption. For the most part, they provide inspiration and resources for civil society actors in their quest to convince state actors of the virtues of gender quotas.

The seven motivations that may lead these actors to pursue quota reform include principled stands, electoral considerations, empty gestures, promotion of other political ends, extension of representational guarantees, international pressure, and transnational learning. Almost all of these motivations contain both normative and pragmatic elements, and in many cases, several distinct motives operate simultaneously. Principled stands are present when women's groups pursue quotas out of the belief that women should be better represented, elites undertake repeated quota reform out of concerns to improve women's political access, political parties and state adopt quotas to promote equality or redefine citizenship in more inclusive directions, and international and transnational organisations recommend quotas as a way to foster gender-balanced decision-making. Electoral considerations come into play when elites decide to introduce quotas after one of their key rivals adopts them. Empty gestures are related to electoral considerations and generally occur where political elites view quotas as a relatively easy way to demonstrate commitment to women's rights without necessarily altering existing patterns of representation. In these cases, leaders enthusiastically embrace gender quotas out of the belief or knowledge that these policies will not personally affect them, will never be implemented, or will be deemed unconstitutional before they can ever be applied.

The promotion of other political ends comes into play when elites view quotas as means for consolidating power over party representatives and political rivals and demonstrating autonomy from other branches of government. The extension of representational guarantees operates when the adoption of gender quotas builds on guarantees already given to other groups based on language, religion, race, ethnicity, youth, or occupation. International pressure influences quota adoption when leaders include a range of different social groups in an attempt to establish the international legitimacy of a new regime, conform to emerging international norms following the direct intervention of international and transnational organisations, or maintain colonial-era policies following independence or secession. Transnational learning, finally, occurs when women's groups share information with each other across national borders on successful strategies for increasing women's representation, or transnational organisations and networks transmit information to domestic groups to suggest new tactics for reform. These processes rarely reveal direct application of lessons learned, but frequently involve efforts to 'translate' quotas to suit specific domestic contexts.[15]

Looking at these accounts together, it becomes clear in many cases that feminist and non-feminist actors are involved in pressing for quota adoption, influencing to at least some extent the degree to which these policies can be considered 'feminist' reforms. Perhaps most importantly, the adoption of gender quotas does not always stem from principled concerns to empower women in politics. Rather, most quota policies are the result of a combination of normative and pragmatic motivations; the relationship between gender quotas and feminist projects of empowerment remains an empirical question, not a theoretical given. Evaluating individual quota campaigns thus requires careful attention to the alliances – both intended and unintended – that come together to promote quota reform, in order to establish whether these policies originate in women's movement activity, as well as what they might mean for broader feminist aspirations.

Although the potential alliance combinations are endless, it is possible to discern a number of common coalitions that come together during quota campaigns, more often than not involving a combination of feminist and non-feminist actors. Attention to these varied alliances is crucial for assessing the degree to which quota campaigns – viewed broadly – can be linked to the emergence of a new global women's movement. A first alliance operates strictly at a domestic level, bringing together women in civil society and women in the state, who both take principled stands on the need for increased female representation. Examples include campaigns that mobilise women's movement organisations and/or women inside the political parties, who work with members of women's policy agencies to support quota reform.

A second set of alliances join women in civil society and men in the state. While civil society groups generally assume principled stands, male elites within the state typically espouse quotas for pragmatic reasons: they respond to electoral considerations, make empty gestures, promote other political ends, or extend representational guarantees. In some cases, women inside the parties gain concessions when they convince party leaders that promoting quotas will attract more female voters. In others, women's movement organisations press for quotas, and elites take up this demand in order to appear open to demands from civil society or to consolidate control over their political rivals. In these instances, quotas do originate with women's movements, but serve other – sometimes pernicious and even anti-democratic – goals.

A third type of coalition occurs between women in civil society and various kinds of transnational actors, including transnational NGOs and networks. Both groups are generally inspired by principled concerns, but transnational actors are also motivated by the possibility of transnational sharing. Indeed, most transnational networks exist to serve as conduits of information on various policy models and tactics for change, as well as to act as allies in persuading governments to adopt new policy innovations. In quota campaigns, this dynamic is present in countries where women's movement organisations learn new tactics for reform through their involvement in various kinds of regional networks. It also exists in cases where women inside parties discover in the course of meetings of international party federations that quotas have been used effectively in similar parties abroad.

A fourth kind of alliance links women in civil society with global and regional international organisations. While both sets of actors are publicly committed to gender quotas for principled reasons, they also exert international pressure in order to gain compliance with emerging international norms. This partnership is particularly effective when states are sensitive to international scrutiny, where elites come to view quotas as a means to cultivate international legitimacy, foster perceptions of domestic legitimacy, or avoid being viewed as pariahs in the international community.

A fifth type of coalition appears between women in civil society across two or more countries. These groups – generally women's movement organisations or women's sections inside political parties – espouse similar normative beliefs regarding the need to increase the number of women in elected office. Their interest in exchanging information on concrete strategies for adopting and implementing quota policies, however, means that they are also motivated by a need for transnational sharing. These groups often organise sessions during meetings of regional and global organisations, but they also frequently initiate their own contacts by planning conferences, arranging personal visits, and circulating memos. In some cases, their contacts are facilitated through the financial and logistical assistance of national and transnational research centres on women and politics.

Notably, all five alliances involve women's groups in civil society, who often team with various kinds of state and/or international and transnational actors in order to press for the adoption of gender quotas. In one sense, these patterns suggest that quota debates are a distinctly national-level phenomenon, focused on shaping the outcomes of elections in particular countries. In another sense, however, these reforms appear around roughly the same moment in time, indicating that the adoption of these policies is influenced to some extent by events and actors operating internationally and transnationally. Four of the five coalitions offer insight into this apparent contradiction. Given the nature of quota measures, which seek national- and party-level reforms, women's groups that advocate these policies must target local and national political elites. However, at the beginning and often in the course of their mobilisation, these individuals and organisations almost always make connections with similar women's groups in other countries, work to some degree with members of transnational NGOs, and/or draw in some way on the moral leverage of international organisations, in order to devise effective strategies for achieving quota adoption. Whether weak or strong, these ties point to a network of quota campaigns that – despite their manifestation in various national contexts – do form part of a broader women's movement operating on a global scale. These patterns provide further illustration of the multiple groups of actors involved in women's movements worldwide, as alluded to by many of the other authors in this volume.

Conclusion: quotas and global feminist activism

Candidate gender quotas have now spread to more than 100 countries around the world, most within the last 15 years. This chapter argues that quota policies are often the result of the combined efforts of feminist and non-feminist actors, who may embrace quotas for distinct and even contradictory reasons. Despite the involvement of non-feminist actors, the chapter maintains that quota campaigns can – and should – be viewed as part of a new global women's movement. Quota debates address national-level processes, and individual campaigns often promote slightly different kinds of quota reforms, tailored to the features of the political culture and the electoral systems of various states.[16] However, similarities in the form and timing of their adoption suggest that these reforms are influenced at least to some degree by events and actors in the international and transnational spheres, who serve as concrete agents of cross-national diffusion. Although specific connections between quota campaigns take a number of different forms, together they contribute to broader global awareness on the need for gender-balanced decision-making.

Nonetheless, an important question remains concerning the feminist nature and consequences of quota reform. The distinct normative and pragmatic motivations behind quota adoption suggest that quotas may take on different meanings across political contexts, with varied implications for feminist theory and practice. Scholars have signalled at least four negative possibilities in this regard. The first is that quotas may contribute – within a global context of growing neo-liberalism – to an increasing separation between political empowerment, on the one hand, and social and economic empowerment, on the other.[17] Quotas may thus appear to be a major concession to women's movement demands, but in fact serve two decidedly non-feminist ends: to demobilise feminists through the guise of empty promises, and to mask enduring – and, some might argue, more pressing – inequalities among women themselves, particularly along class and racial lines. The second is that quotas may result in the election of more women, but only those who will reinforce rather than challenge the status quo. The third is that quotas may reify 'women' as a political category, creating the false impression of a unified group that does not in fact exist.[18] This is likely to restrict the scope of women as political actors, as well as the recognition of the diverse needs of women as a group, by anticipating that women can only represent 'women's issues'.[19] The fourth is that quotas may reduce women's effectiveness as political actors, both individually and collectively, because they may be viewed as representatives who did not earn political office 'on their own'.[20]

On the whole, the evidence for all four claims is mixed. First, although neo-liberalism is often associated with the end of special measures to help under-represented groups, concerns to improve economic efficiency have in fact bolstered the case for quotas. Indeed, international actors like the UN and the World Bank often explain their support for these measures on the grounds that the increased representation of women contributes to greater gains in social and economic development. Similarly, the passage of quota policies has varied effects on women's movements: while in some countries quota reforms result in a decline in women's movement activity, in others they spur continued mobilisation to ensure that quotas are implemented in line with the spirit of the reform. Second, although some work suggests that women elected through quotas are more loyal to party leaders than women who win open seats, the presence of quotas does not always preclude the ability of women to represent women's concerns. Indeed, in some cases these policies confer a special mandate on women who are elected this way, precisely because their election is intended specifically to improve the representation of women as a group. Third, although a lot of evidence suggests that female candidates are often viewed as representatives of 'women', quota policies vary importantly in the degree to which they essentialise women: some measures are sex-specific, indicating that women are the group that requires special treatment, while others are gender-neutral, providing for a minimum representation of both women and men. Fourth, some women do encounter obstacles to their political credibility when they enter political assemblies as 'quota women'. However, many more gain increased confidence over the course of their tenure and bring a range of women-centred issues to political attention.

All of these patterns suggest that gender quotas have a somewhat complicated relationship with feminist projects of empowerment. The available evidence reveals that quotas often facilitate women's election to political office, but also potentially undermine other feminist beliefs and goals. However, while they can reach the political agenda for feminist and non-feminist reasons, and can serve both feminist and non-feminist ends, they often renew feminist engagement with the formal political sphere, with crucial consequences for women as a group. The presence of multiple – and often contradictory – motives and effects requires careful attention in individual cases to the ramifications of quota adoption for feminist theory and practice. Assessing the precise meaning of quota reforms thus remains an empirical question: while some policies are deeply informed by feminist projects, others depart dramatically from feminist concerns. For this reason, analysing the dynamics at work in individual campaigns is crucial for gauging whether gender quotas promote the ultimate goal of female political empowerment, the overarching goal of all global women's movements.

Notes

1 Krook, 'Reforming representation'.
2 Krook, 'Gender quotas as a global phenomenon'.
3 For more details, see Krook, 'Reforming representation', pp. 312–313.
4 For a more extended discussion, see Krook, 'Candidate gender quotas'.
5 For a more extended discussion with case details, see Krook, 'Reforming representation', pp. 311–322.
6 Krook, 'Reforming representation'; Towns, *Norms and Equality in International Society*.
7 Checkel, 'Why comply?'; Legro, 'Which norms matter?'.
8 Carpenter, 'Women and children first'.
9 Alvarez, 'Translating the global'; Tripp, 'Transnational feminism and political representation in Africa'.
10 McAdam and Rucht, 'The cross-national diffusion of movement ideas'.
11 Keck and Sikkink, *Activists Beyond Borders*; True and Mintrom, 'Transnational networks and policy diffusion'.
12 Joachim, 'Framing issues and seizing opportunities'; Strang and Meyer, 'Institutional conditions for diffusion'.
13 There is a debate in research on gender and politics as to whether or not women's groups inside political parties can be called a 'women's movement'. I place them among other groups in 'civil society', in light of their similar distance from centres of power and their parallel struggles to influence the actions of political elites.

14 This is the case in India, as well as the two states that eventually seceded from India, Pakistan and Bangladesh.
15 Krook, 'Reforming representation'.
16 Dahlerup (ed.), *Women, Quotas, and Politics*; Krook, *Politicizing Representation*; Russell, *Building New Labour: The Politics of Party Organization.*
17 Phillips, *Which Equalities Matter?*
18 Mansbridge, 'Should Blacks represent Blacks and women represent women? A contingent yes'.
19 Childs and Krook, 'Gender and politics'.
20 Goetz and Hassim (eds), *No Shortcuts to Power*; Rincker, *Women's Access to the Decentralized State.*

9   Women in cities

New spaces for the women's movement?

Caroline Andrew

The objective of this chapter is to describe activities in Canada and around the world that relate to women's urban safety. I try to analyse their relationship to the women's movement: can they be considered part of the women's movement and, if so, are they new spaces for feminist action? In order to answer these questions, I shall use two characteristics of social movements discussed in the Introduction to this book; first, the opposition to dominant norms and, second, the use of unconventional actions and/or structures to bring about social change. These raise very interesting questions in the case of the activities around women's urban safety, as these activities seek close relationships with municipal governments but this, in itself, can be seen as an act of opposition to dominant norms. In addition, they usually employ unconventional structures and often use unconventional actions.

But first, what are we looking at and what have been the catalysts for this activity? The examples in this chapter all relate to local/municipal activities relating to women's urban safety. At the same time they are activities that focus on global-local linkages. I am going to look at two levels of examples: the four largest Canadian cities (Montreal, Toronto, Vancouver and Ottawa); and the way in which activities related to women's urban safety have moved around the world. These two sets of examples come out of work I have been doing associated with a network organisation called Women in Cities International (web site: www.femmesetvilles.org), as well as secondary literature.

A safety audit is both very simple and very complex; it is a group of users of urban space, led by women, who walk around their shared space and observe what makes them feel unsafe in this space. They then prioritise recommendations for changes, both physical and social. At a more complex level, it is a challenge about knowledge and whose knowledge counts. Women are empowered to make decisions about their environment and to organise politically to ensure that their lived expertise is listened to and acted upon. It is also a useful image because it has moved around the world – from Durban in South Africa, through Petrovadosk in Russia and Barcelona in Spain and on to Mumbai and Delhi in India. The safety audit has also moved across Canada. Invented in Toronto, it was adopted with enthusiasm in Montreal, where there have been more than 100 safety audits in different neighbourhoods, housing projects, public buildings and public transportation systems. We will look more closely at the safety audit later on in this chapter, but first it is important to situate the emerging activism of women's groups at the urban level.

Urban activism

Women's urban safety as a new space for the women's movement is linked to globalisation and the related, and somewhat contradictory, pressures for the decentralisation of political action. Globalisation has helped bring about the creation of large and diverse urban centres. One of the significant characteristics of these centres is the extent of fear that exists within them, particularly in cities marked by diversity, such as all the largest Canadian cities. As Leonie Sandercock writes 'there is a political economy of city fears (whether these fears are real or imagined), and an unavoidable question is whose fears get legitimised and translated into policy responses, and whose fears get silenced or marginalised'. Sandercock argues that such discourses of fear pose a threat 'to the sustainability of cities of difference, to a democratic civic culture and the vibrancy of the urban public realm – that is, to the very possibility of cosmopolis'.[1]

Women's urban safety activities stemmed from exactly what Sandercock describes. Women saw their fears being marginalised while other groups' fears of strangers led to all kinds of policy responses, including questioning of immigration, more severe sentencing, more police and more money spent on police. Such responses did not relate to creating vibrant urban public space but rather to the privatisation of this space.[2]

Women also felt marginalised by the fact that often their fears were judged irrational as official data showed that women were not the group most subject to urban violence. This ignored the point that fear influences behaviour and that women were more constrained in their movements in the cities because their feelings of insecurity influenced their use of urban space. This sense of the limits being placed on urban citizenship was a strong mobilising factor, and one that mobilised women on a cross-class basis. Women went from being frustrated by the marginalisation of their views on urban safety to a more rigorous analysis of municipal government and the reasons for their marginalisation. The 'main business' of municipal government has been the enhancing of private development through the provision of infrastructure and the promotion of economic development. Women began to make the connection between their marginalisation from local government, the power of male business interests and the ensuing production of a city whose built form added to feelings of insecurity. Women's groups made links between an agenda for the city as a place to live and urban safety. Creating partnerships between community-based women's groups and municipal government can be seen as oppositional to dominant norms and an attempt to become part of those dominant norms.

Globalisation, particularly through the development of technology, has also fuelled women's urban safety activities through the greatly increased possibilities for electronic links across the world. Urban safety has always been an area in which examples from one place have had a great influence on other places and these possibilities have simply multiplied with the web.[3] Globalisation offers the context for understanding Women in Cities International, a Canadian organisation with international links and international aspirations. It began in the early 2000s when a number of individuals who had been working for the larger Canadian cities or in organisations funded by the cities began talking and realising that the government cutbacks of the 1980s and 1990s had led to the elimination of cross-Canada contacts that had existed prior to the 1990s. A desire to recreate these links and extend them internationally led to a decision to organise an international conference in Montreal in 2002. The international links were extensions of the kinds of contacts that individuals had developed, notably with the UN Habitat Safer Cities programme, the International Union of Local Authorities and with the Huairou Commission, the UN-recognised NGO created at the time of Beijing that represents women's grassroots organisations on a wide range of UN related women's issues. These contacts have been built up through the work of Canadian activists trying to advance women's issues at UN conferences (like Anne Michaud, at that time the staff person for the City of Montreal's Femmes et Ville programme).

The conference led to the formal creation of Femmes et Villes International, so as to have a legally constituted group that would qualify for grants. The name was chosen to be close to, but different from, the name of the Montreal municipal programme. The word 'international' was added, signalling the aspirations of those creating the group. Femmes et Villes International was created as a bilingual organisation and the English version, Women in Cities International (WICI), has over time become the more common name.

At the same time, as many authors have pointed out,[4] globalisation has also been associated with measures of decentralisation. The reasons for this are multiple; national governments wanting to cut their budgets and shift responsibility to lower levels or concentrate on measures of global competitiveness, but also grassroots pressure for meaningful participation in decision-making and policy-making, plus the growing importance of local identity politics based on spatialised groups and fuelled by fears that globalisation will eliminate local specificity. By shifting more power to local governments, areas of activity important to women opened up at the local level. Women's groups, who in Canada in the post-war period had been most active and most engaged at the federal and Quebec levels of government, found themselves with strategic decisions to make. Was this decentralisation simply neo-liberalism and, if so, should it be resisted or complied with? Were there real opportunities in decentralisation, either to reach new groups of women or to invest in new policy areas? A major debate on decentralisation emerged, with activists taking up the full range of positions from active struggle against decentralisation to interest in the potential gains to be made through strengthening the local presence of the women's movement.[5] This debate was particularly strong in Quebec, where the movement was closely associated with the affirmation of the Quebec state and, in addition, where the women's movement was highly institutionalised at the level of the Quebec state.

In the Canadian context, decentralisation to the larger cities is also fuelled by the growing ethno-racial diversity of the large Canadian cities. Recent immigration is almost exclusively a metropolitan phenomenon, with almost half of recent immigrants located in the Greater Toronto region. This means that those interested in successful measures of integration are becoming more aware of the potential of local action and decentralisation. To give only one example, the movement for voting rights for non-citizens is closely connected to those pushing for greater powers for the City of Toronto and for the potential capacity of the new City of Toronto Act to allow municipal definitions of citizenship. The gendered understanding of the impact of ethno-racial diversity or, perhaps more accurately, the intersectional understanding, has been heightened by the research work of the five Metropolis research centres across Canada. Metropolis is an international network of researchers interested in better understanding the integration and settlement of immigrants and much of the research has been sensitive to the intersections of ethno-racial diversity and gender.

Decentralisation movements outside Canada have also contributed to Canadian feminist thinking. The Declaration of the International Union of Local Authorities (IULA) on women and local government was a document that had a major impact in Canadian cities and was also much used to argue that this interest in the relationship of women to local government was a world-wide phenomenon. The International Union of Local Authorities is the international federation of national bodies of local authorities and, in the case of Canada, the Federation of Canadian Municipalities (FCM), as a member of IULA, adopted the Declaration. The Declaration became a useful tool for groups in Canadian cities that wanted to advance women's issues within their municipal governments. In Ottawa it was used to set up a Task Force on Women's Access to Municipal Services and in Montreal as a way of advancing the programmes of Femmes et Ville.

The spread of safety audits

As stated earlier, this chapter focuses on one particularly interesting tool that has moved around the world in relation to women's urban safety; the safety audit. It was first used in Toronto in 1989 by METRAC (The Metro Action Committee on Public Violence against Women and Children), an organisation created by the Metropolitan Toronto Council of that time following a report from the 'Task Force on Public Violence against Women and Children' which, in turn, had been created following a series of rapes/murders in Toronto.

As noted earlier, the safety audit involves people who use urban space going around as a group and observing this space from the point of view of identifying features that make them feel unsafe. Sometimes the group is totally made up of women, but at other times it is a mixed group of women and men, and still other times a group including municipal employees or municipal elected officials as well as community women. They then discuss what they have seen and create a list of recommendations that reflect the priorities of the group. Following this, the recommendations go to the local municipality where there either is, or is not, a process of implementation. We will come back to this point as it is a crucial question for safety audits.

Various lessons can be derived from the widespread use of safety audits. As Carolyn Whitzman has argued,

> [T]hese resources work at the community and individual levels to improve spaces and to improve women's ability to influence local politics and planning issues. They work not only to make public spaces safer, but also to increase access to community spaces that might empower individual women (such as health centres, educational institutions, and employment).[6]

Her analysis helps to explain the popularity of safety audits and their importance for linking community-based women's activity to municipal government. They are based on a view of the importance of partnering between insiders and outsiders (other chapters in both Parts I and II in this collection note the strength that comes through double militancy). Safety audits can frame activity around women's views about their environment in ways that put this activity clearly within the areas of responsibility of municipal governments. Depending on location, safety audits can touch on parks, public transportation, zoning, lighting, policing, public buildings and public spaces, signage and other dimensions of public attractiveness, all of which are clearly seen to be areas of municipal government responsibility.

Safety audits can meet a series of objectives. They are a tool of overall community development as well as one specifically relating to women ('Safer for women, safer for all'). Municipal governments can see them as core business and they are a coalition activity in the sense of bringing together different actors with very different motivations (protecting women, creating the conditions for equal urban citizenship for women, reinforcing the expertise of safety planners and community police, enhancing 'the production of critical, oppositional knowledges' by social movements).[7] Finally, they illustrate global-local linkages in the way they have moved around the world. As mentioned earlier, they have been used in Durban, Petrovadosk, Barcelona, Mumbai, Delhi and Gotenberg as well as a large number of Canadian communities, both large and small.

On the other hand, there are issues that can challenge the effectiveness of safety audits. The link between the recommendations of the audit and the implementation capacity and will of the local municipality is certainly the area where safety audits run into difficulties. Safety audits depend on implementation as otherwise they will be processes of frustration and not of empowerment. But there have been considerable variations in the ways municipalities have responded to safety audits; some, such as the old City of Ottawa, set up an administrative process by which the recommendations were examined and priorities set for implementation.

Diversity, in terms of ethno-cultural groups, age and disability, is also a challenge to safety audits. Safety audits work best when the most disadvantaged groups participate but this does not often happen. Sometimes there is a lack of will on the part of the organising committee and sometimes, it would be fair to say, it is due more to lack of contacts. This remains a problem because we know that the process is much better if it does include women coming from doubly, and triply, marginalised communities.

Changing opportunities and safety audits

It is important to situate safety audits and their relation to decentralised activity for women's urban safety within the debates they have been associated with. Four of these are particularly pertinent: reactions to neo-liberalism; the relationship of service delivery to advocacy; the institutionalisation of social movements; and, debates around urban citizenship and the politics of everyday life.

The growth of feminist activity at the local level is linked to political changes brought about by neo-liberalism (decentralisation, shrinking the state and using groups from civil society to deliver state services), and certainly here the context has been more in terms of the 'abeyance' hypothesis than in terms of the 'flourishing' hypothesis posed in the introduction of this book. Successive federal governments in Canada, and perhaps particularly the one in place in 2007, have moved away from the earlier support and fostering of the national women's movement. The political environment fuelled by the electoral success of neo-liberal governments in British Columbia, in Quebec and at the federal level, and the use of resources of government to reframe public debates, has greatly reduced the visibility of gender equality as a public policy goal in Canada. The federal government slashed the budget of Status of Women Canada in the autumn of 2006 in a period of huge federal surpluses. In addition to reducing funding, the government explicitly eliminated advocacy (and research) from any activity funded by Status of Women Canada.

These changes have given rise to an important debate within the women's movement around the relationship between service delivery and advocacy. As neo-liberal governments want to reduce the size of the state, they have both decentralised and privatised service-delivery functions. The privatisation has been at times to the for-profit private sector and at other times to civil society groups. A great number of local women's groups depend financially on agreements to deliver services that could be, or in some cases were, public services. This often makes the groups reluctant to criticise the sources that are financing them and keeps them quiet about government policies they might otherwise have wanted to denounce. This has created a huge debate around whether service delivery activities are incompatible with advocacy, either for theoretical or very practical reasons relating to time and resources. Has, therefore, the emphasis on service delivery lessened the advocacy activities of the women's movement?

There is also a related, but separate, debate about the impact of the institutionalisation of social movements. Within this debate, institutionalisation is discussed in a number of ways – from participation in networks and partnerships that involve the state to incorporation into state structures and programs.[8] For the most part these groups seek institutionalisation, both in order to make demands on the resources of the state, and as a strategy to transform the 'main business' of municipal governments by including women's groups as, if not central, at least legitimate actors. Legitimacy is often seen to be crucial in terms of the relationship of these groups to women in their community, in building a sense of entitlement so that their issues as women are seen as legitimate issues within the local political sphere.[9]

Women's urban safety activities also relate to the debate about urban citizenship[10] and to what we might call the politics of everyday life. The debates about urban citizenship emerge from the understanding of the ways in which different scales of political activity are created and recreated over time and space. This is not an either-or proposition; there can be a multiplicity of sites of struggle from the body to the global but at certain moments and in specific contexts, different levels can become more salient. The arguments about urban citizenship relate to these questions of rescaling, and authors such as James Holston[11] link urban citizenship to the kinds of political struggles around urban public services and issues that arise in terms of the right to the city. These issues are very much the politics of everyday life – for example, decent public transportation, housing that is not only decent and affordable but well situated, top quality day care and so on.

What these debates do is set up a series of alternative interpretations for understanding the evolution of the women's movement. Three interpretations will be developed here and returned to following the description of the activities. The first interpretation stems largely from the debate around institutionalisation. This would be to see our activities as a sectoral sub-set of the institutionalisation that has overcome the Canadian women's movement. As there are groups that work on pay equity or the place of women in the armed forces, there are groups that work on engendering municipal governments. These groups also relate to the sector of the women's movement that works on violence. A sub-set of these groups are those who work on the interface of issues of violence against women at a local and spatially defined community or municipal level. So our first interpretation would be that these new spaces correspond to an institutionalisation of the women's movement, both by sector and by level of government.

The debates around service delivery and advocacy suggest a second interpretation – that these activities can be better understood as a state-led project aimed at co-opting women's activism. Funds are given by the federal or provincial governments to deliver services or programmes at a local or municipal level that involve those groups in activities that take up all their energy and leave no time for advocacy.

And, finally, the arguments about decentralisation and those about urban citizenship suggest a third understanding – that these activities represent an emerging global women's grassroots/local governance movement that affirms the right of all women to urban citizenship, to full access to good urban public services and to the freedom of identity and movement within communities and cities.

These interpretations have been simplified and possibly caricaturised in this attempt to distinguish them. However, they do lend themselves to different understandings of the development and the current state of the women's movement. The first would suggest that the women's movement was continuing to exist in parallel with movements of institutionalisation and professionalisation,[12] and that this is a less visible phase of the women's movement as the work is very much segmented by policy sector and by scale of activity. The movement is alive and there continue to be advances in the ways in which women's equality is inserted into public or public-private policies, but within an overall political environment less interested, or more hostile, to the women's movement. The second interpretation would suggest that the Canadian women's movement is somewhat in abeyance. Women's organisations have been channelled into delivering services for governments that are less and less interested in directly dealing with women's equality. Keeping organisations busy with the delivery of services could be seen as an effective state strategy for the management of this issue. The third interpretation fits the idea that the global women's movement is investing in new spaces – cities and local governance – in ways that build on global links, similarities, solidarity and the recognition of difference. To cut immediately to the conclusion, it is clear that elements of all three hypotheses co-exist and, the concluding section will suggest ways in which these activities can strengthen elements that support the third, 'flourishing in new spaces' hypothesis.

Safety audits and the women's movement

Coming back to the activities relating to safety audits and, more generally, to activities around women's urban safety in the larger Canadian cities, there have been audits done of parks, transportation systems, shopping centres, public buildings and housing complexes, in neighbourhoods that are suburban, inner-city and periurban, and with groups of women who are neighbourhood-based or from different backgrounds – the elderly, immigrant women, young women. There have been reports, many publications and some implementation. These activities have been described elsewhere,[13] and therefore we will focus here on the lessons to be learned for our understanding of these activities within the women's movement.

First, there are important links between women's urban safety activities and activities related more generally to mainstreaming gender issues in municipal government (the power of mainstreaming is discussed in the chapter by Jacqui True). In some cases, safety was an area for initiating activities linked to women in order to raise consciousness about gender at the municipal level and, to go back to our original point, to reshape the 'main business' of municipal government. This was certainly true in Ottawa with the work of WISE (Women's Initiatives for a Safer Environment) – the current name for the organisation funded by the City of Ottawa to work on safety audits and public education initiatives around public safety. It is also the case in Toronto with the Safe City Committee and in Montreal with Femmes et Ville and a community-based committee. These safety-oriented activities relate, and are linked, to activities aimed at mainstreaming gender. The Ottawa-based project, A City for all Women Initiative – Initiative: une ville pour toutes les femmes – includes safety as one area within its work with the city while respecting the role of WISE as the lead agency in Ottawa in this policy area. Its own work centres on the development of an equality guide for city managers and on training for civic engagement undertaken with community-based groups. Women's urban safety has permitted entry into discussions about the nature of current municipal government and a vision for its transformation, linked broadly to its community and fully committed to implementing an equity lens across the full range of municipal policy.

A second and often depressing lesson is that the development of activity relating to gender and municipal policy-making is certainly not linear. Both Toronto and Montreal are less active since municipal amalgamation (and in the case of Montreal, de-amalgamation as well) and, in Vancouver, a council-approved plan for gender equality was discontinued by the new council in the spring of 2006. New activity does emerge; Montreal has recently created a women's advisory council to the City (Le conseil des montréalaises), the Toronto Women's Call to Action may be renewing activism in Toronto, the Vancouver plan may have some on-going influence and Ottawa is piloting the gender equality guide within the largest department of the city. The variability of the activity relates to the continued fragility of a gendered perspective in municipal activities and the dependence on specific individuals, both those within the municipal government (elected and appointed) and those within community-based women's groups.

The third lesson is about how to combine 'insider' and 'outsider' strategies and how to understand the roles both of 'insiders' and 'outsiders'. One useful starting point for building a strategy for local action is the image used by Carolyn Whitzman of the necessity of four legs for a good table; elected officials acting as champions for gender equality, strategic femocrats, organised community-based women's groups and good research. This view implies a strategy of combining the insiders and the outsiders and being conscious of the balance between the two approaches. Insiders have been both elected politicians and appointed officials, and results have been most positive when both are involved. Elected officials such as Leah Cousineau in Montreal, Barbara Hall in Toronto and Diane Holmes in Ottawa were strong champions of women's equality as well as important municipal politicians and therefore able to bring political weight to bear on issues. Although women elected officials have often played this role, there have also been males, such as Jack Layton in Toronto, who have moved the gender equality agenda forward. It is also important to have municipal appointed officials interested in advancing this agenda. Carolyn Whitzman working for the Safe City Committee in Toronto and Anne Michaud of Femmes et Ville in Montreal are two clear examples of femocrats working with elected officials and with community-based groups. The outsiders of the insider–outsider combination are the community-based groups that can put pressure on the municipal council from outside, while working at the same time with the appointed officials and the elected representatives. This requires both a close relationship and an understanding that some distance and a certain autonomy is important for the community-based groups.

The fourth lesson relates to the importance of coalition politics,[14] as a way of understanding the potential strength of community-based politics. Conway describes coalitions in ways that are useful to the understanding of these community sites:

> Coalitions are spaces of experimentation and this is particularly important in a period of flux and uncertainty in both practice and theory. Because coalitions are constituted by a fundamental recognition of diversity and respect for pluralism, the knowledges that arise in and through coalition politics are particularly prescient for the building of a world with the space for many worlds, to use the Zapatista formulation. The knowledges produced in coalitions demonstrate the possibility of action premised on partial and provisional knowing – on politics that is simultaneously committed and open to what it does not yet know.[15]

The coalition character of the work raises questions of their relationship to the women's movement. Can social movement actors work in coalitions that include very different kinds of groups and still be considered to represent social movements? This is one of the challenges of understanding coalition politics and the ways in which they do, or do not, oppose dominant norms. Coalitions also have the potential of drawing new groups of participants into political activity. Some of the projects described have certainly done this and, if Conway is right that coalition politics creates openness to what we do not yet know, the women's movement may gain support as people work together and learn about each other's visions

A final lesson relates to the local–global interface. From the point of view of local action, the link to the global has been extremely positive. In the Canadian context, as stated earlier, the local is very much characterised by ethno-racial diversity and the global links that diasporas have to their countries of origin. Multiple sites are contributing to the local level. The global dimensions of women's urban safety also give the issue a higher and more important profile; if it is difficult to advance the agenda in the local municipal council it is inspiring, and encouraging, to know that women across the world are engaged in the same struggle. One example of this was in the summer of 2006 when WICI received funding to bring participants to the World Urban Forum in Vancouver for networking sessions on gender equality and women's urban safety activities. Several women involved in local community-based Canadian projects were included and the impact on the participants was considerable; they felt clearly part of a world-wide movement linking urbanisation and women's equality.

How to understand the activity?

We come back to our three possible interpretations of the current activity relating to women and cities: that it represents the women's movement's institutionalisation; that it represents a strategy of government control by channelling women's activism into service delivery; and, finally, that it represents an emerging grassroots global movement to create cities in which the full diversity of women enjoy equal access to high quality urban public services and an inclusive urban citizenship. The descriptions of these activities, and of the lessons drawn from these activities, have illustrated that elements of all three interpretations co-exist. There is an enormous variety of front-line interventions that relate to violence against women and the expansion of services brings with it the need for coordination of these services. As decentralisation increases, this coordination has an increasingly local dimension, although, of course, provincial and Canada-wide coordination structures also continue to exist.

If the expansion of services relates to community pressure, it also relates to government moves to deliver services through community agencies. The argument that the increase in services being delivered by community agencies diminishes advocacy also appears to be confirmed by our examples, as with relatively limited resources groups put energy into service delivery. This is perhaps even more striking in the current Canadian political climate. In the autumn of 2006, the federal government cut the budget of Status of Women Canada, which led to the closing of the Policy Research Fund. In addition, the guidelines for funding were altered to eliminate any mention of advocacy. By dismantling the capacity of Status of Women Canada to encourage women's groups both to do research and to do advocacy, their service orientation becomes even more pronounced.

At the same time, our third interpretation can also be maintained, that these activities illustrate world-wide linkages across communities whereby women are learning from each other about how to try to transform the 'main business' of municipal government. Through these concrete but often unconventional practices, women are working to improve public services to disadvantaged groups of women and therefore realise the potential of urban public spaces to create an inclusive citizenship.

If all three interpretations co-exist, and this would be consistent with our understanding of coalition politics, how can we strengthen the third interpretation while understanding that there will be a coexistence of all three, and perhaps more, interpretations?

A first step would be to go back to the definition of social movements and to think strategically about the role of the 'outsider' in opposing dominant norms, using unconventional methods and reinforcing the unconventional structures of the 'outsider' organisations. Too often, 'outsiders' feel the pressure to behave like 'insiders' and forget that their strength is in being on the 'outside'. It is a complicated and delicate balance to use unconventional methods and yet remain in close contact with the 'inside'. As the Introduction states, we are not necessarily talking about the demonstrations of the 1960s but rather making clear that there is a vision of a different world and that the group shares the vision and is working towards it. This is not easy, but it is not impossible. We need perhaps more brainstorming on how to be genuinely unconventional in the twenty-first century.

However, this call for more explicit strategic thinking is extremely difficult to answer in the context of inadequate resources. This is the dilemma of the groups involved in engendering local governance and working to create safe and inclusive communities – teetering between being new spaces for the women's movement and being new spaces for government co-option.

Notes

I would like to acknowledge the support of Status of Women Canada in funding Women in Cities International to develop a guide on creating partnerships between community-based women's groups and municipal governments.

1 Sandercock, *Cosmopolis II*.
2 Fraser, *Unruly Practices*.
3 Whitzman and Lahaise, 'London inspires Montreal which inspires Toronto which inspires London…', pp. 22–23; Whitzman, 'Women and community safety', pp. 24–27.
4 Massey, *Space, Place, and Gender*; Hamel *et al.*, *Urban Movements in a Globalising World*; Conway, *Identity, Place, Knowledge*.
5 Masson, 'Engaging with the politics of downward rescaling'.
6 Whitzman, 'Women and community safety', p. 25. For more analysis of safety audits, see Andrew, 'Les femmes et le local'; Andrew, 'Getting women's issues on the municipal agenda'; Andrew, 'Resisting boundaries?'; Andrew, 'Women in the urban landscape'; Vezina, *Initiatives Municipales Prenant en Considération les Intérêts Particuliers des Femmes*; Women in Cities International, *Building Community-based Partnerships for Local Action on Women's Safety;* Women's Action Centre Against Violence (Ottawa-Carleton), *Safety Audit Tools and Housing*.
7 Conway, 'Reinventing emancipation', p. 1.
8 Hamel, 'The fragmentation of social movements and social justice'.
9 Klodawsky and Andrew, 'A city for all women initiative'.
10 Andrew, 'Gendering nation states and/or gendering city-states'.
11 Holston, 'Urban citizenship and globalization'.
12 Bondi and Laurie, 'Working the spaces of neoliberalism'; Larner and Craig, 'After neoliberalism?'; Hamel *et al.*, *Urban Movements in a Globalising World*.
13 Whitzman, 'The "voice of women" in Canadian Local Government'; Michaud, *Women's Safety;* Andrew, 'Women in the urban landscape', p. 189; Andrew (2006), 'Où sont les femmes? Where are the women?', Conference Presentation, Montreal, Une ville à la mesure des femmes.
14 Conway, 'Reinventing emancipation'.
15 Conway, 'Reinventing emancipation'.

10 Cyberfeminism in action

Claiming women's space in cyberspace

CJ Rowe

While contemporary women's movements may be less visible in the streets, they have found a new frontier in cyberspace. Consciousness raising has graduated from small groups of women in their kitchens, sitting rooms and community centres to the Internet, and the local has become the global. My chapter looks at the new possibilities the Internet has opened up for women's movements and presents a case study of the research done by a Canadian organisation called Womenspace. It argues that cyberfeminism is flourishing rather than representing a movement in abeyance, reinforcing the view that women's movements cannot be defined by a particular repertoire of collective action.

This chapter examines both theoretical debates over cyberfeminism and the ways in which feminists are utilising the new tools made available to them through information and communication technologies (ICTs). They are using these tools to grow, expand and come up with new ways to act and react to governmental policy and social norms. It will also explore the barriers faced by women and feminists when they choose or try to acquire the necessary equipment (for example, computers and software), skills and time to even get online. In addition, other groups are finding a new space on the Internet, including fathers' rights groups, and perpetrators of sexual violence such as pornographers.

What is cyberfeminism?

Cyberfeminism and the debates around what cyberfeminism is have been around since the mid-1990s. This is a feminism that goes beyond looking at the impact of new ICTs on women to recognise the ways in which our conceptualisations of gender and technology have shifted and the ways that these new conceptualisations shape our lives.

Cyberfeminism can be found in both theory and practice on the Internet. Current literature on cyberfeminism presents it variously as a social theory, as a process, and as a way that women have come together online to create their own spaces on the Internet. Faith Wilding, one of the theorists of cyberfeminism, views it as something that is open, fluid and not yet defined by those who are engaged in its development as a new feminist theory. She states that '[c]yberfeminists have the chance to create new formations of feminist theory and practice which address the complex new social conditions created by global technologies'.[1] Wilding argues for a definition of cyberfeminism that connects theory with practice in order to best understand and situate women's lived encounters with ICTs.

Some of the difficulties faced by those searching to define cyberfeminism may have been rooted in the fact that feminism itself does not adhere to any standard definition. There is no one feminism but many different branches of feminist theory. At its basis, however, is the recognition of the organisation of the social world by gender, where women as a group are systematically oppressed under patriarchy. Feminism is a form of thought that starts from women's standpoints and looks to explore and uncover patriarchal social dynamics. Feminism is also committed to social change and this social change is rooted in the actions of women who are working to circumvent patriarchal structures in favour of a more egalitarian world.

Like feminism, cyberfeminism is open to definition, however, it centres on gender and technology as its overreaching elements. Cyberfeminism looks at technologies and explores the intersection between gender, culture, the body and technology.[2] It is also engaged in both theory and practice. While this theory is critical of the ways in which information technologies have been integrated into and affect our daily lives it is unwilling to remain within the realm of criticism and works towards exploring the potential that ICTs hold for change and challenge in our patriarchal society.

Cyberfeminists recognise that technology is a complex territory, one that exists in a social framework that is already established in practice and is deeply embedded in economic, political and cultural environments. They also acknowledge that these environments are sexist and racist and are deeply entrenched in social class. The Internet does not constitute a utopia of non-gender. It comes out of systems designed to serve war and is part of masculinist institutions. In order to fully harness the Internet, we must first acknowledge and fully take into account the implications of its founding formations and the present political and economic conditions that drive the Internet. Wilding notes that

> [I]t can be seen as a radical act to insert the word feminism into cyber space, to interrupt the flow of masculine codes by boldly declaring the intention to bastardise, hybridise, provoke, and infect the male order of things by politicising the environment of the Net.[3]

Cyberfeminists can use feminist theoretical insights and strategic tools on the Internet to battle the very real sexism and racism encoded in software and hardware on the Internet thereby politicising this environment.

There is the real fear that cyberspace will simply recreate the same tired old stereotypes of gender, given that it too is structured by patriarchal and capitalistic social relations. However, women must be willing to make the trip into cyberspace in order to challenge the recreation of gendered bodies by men and women alike. Cyberfeminists have been harnessing the Internet for their social actions, to distribute news, share resources and to promote action issues. Cyberfeminists can and have borrowed from past feminist thinking, experience and knowledge to carry forward their work on the Internet. The goal to create a feminist politics on the Internet is ever evolving and includes the empowerment of women and girls and the creation of new possibilities to promote action in our global world.

So cyberfeminism, while deeply entrenched in theory, is fundamentally based in our daily lives. Feminists and feminist organisations are using ICTs to claim space in cyberspace and are harnessing the tools available to them to move their issues and concerns forward. Womenspace, a Canadian non-profit organisation that promotes women's participation in information and communication technology, is one example of a group harnessing the Internet to move feminist ideals forward. Womenspace's activities include the development of online resources and learning, research, education and initiatives which support the use of the Internet for women's equality. Feminists and equality-seeking organisations are harnessing these new mediums to build coalitions, search out resources, browse government websites, share information and network.[4] In this way the Internet is challenging feminists to create and use new spaces, cyberspaces, to build communities, to share perspectives and ideas and to forward feminist actions all from their computers.

The Internet has become a useful tool for existing feminist organisations, for new cyber-feminist communities, and it has also become a home to individual feminists who create their own blogs and post their personal perspectives. On the Internet you can find the webpages of women's organisations, personal blogs, communities and magazine-type websites, all created to promote feminist messages. Feminists are not the only ones, however, finding a home in cyberspace – so are many other individuals and groups with different ideologies and world views. For example, while feminists are harnessing the Internet to forward their goals so are anti-feminist and father's rights groups.

Our spaces on the Internet

Much like the consciousness-raising groups in the 1960s and 1970s the Internet offers space to share injustices with others, to voice concerns, and to devise solutions. The real power in the Internet lies in its ability to interconnect people and ideas. The scope of its capacity allows for a dynamic source of networking and activism, a medium through which feminist consciousness can be built upon and feminist goals can be furthered. Now we can share and shake up things from our desks no matter where our offices and computer connections originate.

The Internet has become an important tool and space for feminists to share information with others, including non-feminists. The Internet and the process of searching for a key word demystifies feminism as it places the focus on the issue and solution rather than the negative association that many people still feel around the term 'feminism'. It allows people who may be looking for information on 'custody' or 'equal pay' to access feminist resources without having realised that feminism is what they were looking for. Women and men 'get the chance to grasp their connection to feminism without first having to confront and overcome their biases against it'.[5] It has also created a space where feminists can keep each other up to date on action alerts, legislation, news, and projects. Feminists can organise actions and lobby the government with the help of Internet tools such as letter writing campaigns, online petitions, and emailing legislative representatives. An example of this in relation to women's health movement is discussed in this book by Gwendolyn Gray.

Over the years, women have been developing feminist ways of using the Internet. A variety of tools and techniques have emerged to help us tell our stories, celebrate achievements, get together, connect though networks, share research, support one and other, examine issues, build communities, learn from one and other, and coordinate efforts. Some of the ways that feminists employ the Internet include:

Coalition building

Building coalitions both on and off line is a valuable technique. The Internet provides women and representatives of women's groups with tools and space to come together to share resources, efforts, tools and skills to raise awareness around the issues at hand. Canadian examples of such coalitions include Coalition for Women's Equality (www.womenvote.ca), the Ad Hoc Coalition for Women's Equality and Human Rights (www.womensequality.ca) and Canadian Feminists Alliance for International Action (www.fafia-afai.org).

News

Another way in which women and women's organisations have harnessed the Internet is by creating websites that help share feminist news, information and resources. Some examples of these sites include Womennet (www.womennet.ca), NetFemme (netfemme.cdeacf.ca) and Women's eNews (www.womensenews.org). In New Zealand, the sharing of resources is often supported through webspaces run by women's centres such as the space set up by the Auckland Women's Centre (womenz.org.nz).

Promoting actions

One way in which women promote actions is through list-serves. List-serves enable women to come in contact with others with similar experiences on issues, help women find resources on specific issues, share useful resources with others and share information on how to start groups, work on issues, or join in campaigns. Examples of such list-serves include PAR-L (www.unb.ca/-PAR-L), Femme et PoliTIC (netfemme.cdeacf.ca), DAWN Ontario (dawn.thot.net) and the Coalition for Women's Equality's Election 2006 (www.womenvote.ca). In Australia, Pamelas-List (www.nwjc.org.au/pamelaslist.htm) links representatives of some 60 national women's organisations for high-level information exchange and co-ordination.

Online resources

With the help of the Internet, women and women's equality-seeking groups have found it easier to share their resources. This is particularly true for those working in the area of violence against women. The British Columbia Rural Women's Network recently launched their Online Safety Toolkit (www.onlinesafetytoolkit.com) and Shelternet (www.shelternet.ca) helps women in Canada find shelters and provides resources in 10 different languages. In Australasia, women's health organisations frequently use webspaces to provide information services (www.womenshealth.org.nz and www.awhn.org.au/content/view/ 49/59).

It is not only NGOs that are providing information resources for women online but also governments and multilateral bodies. Invaluable information on how political parties across various nations are doing with regard to their international treaty obligations towards women are to be found through the UN WomenWatch portal (www.un.org/womenwatch). This portal enables women's groups to monitor the comments of relevant UN treaty committees, such as CEDAW, on their country's implementation of Convention obligations towards women. It similarly enables monitoring of implementation of the Beijing Platform for Action and other international obligations such as the Millennium Development Goals. Other organisations that provide invaluable resources for women's groups include the Inter-Parliamentary Union, whose site (www.ipu.org) monitors the parliamentary representation of women and provides a regularly updated ranking of national parliaments. The International Institute of Democracy and Electoral Assistance similarly monitors the adoption of electoral quotas around the world and their effects (www.quotaproject.org).

Community building

The Internet goes a long way to help feminists build online communities. These websites are designed to target women with particular interests. Some sites, such as www.gurl.com, are designed for young women and include online games, advice columns and members' only forums, while other sites, such as Womenspace's interactive website www.womynsvoices.ca, are designed to target feminists interested in issues affecting women and ICTs, from issues such as e-democracy to violence against women. A third example of online community building is the babble section of the rabble.ca website (rabble.ca/babble/). Rabble.ca is a registered not-for-profit organisation that 'was built on the efforts of progressive journalists, writers, artists and activists across the country'. The babble section of the website is the site's more interactive space 'where rabble-rousers mix, mingle and mix it up, whether it's to comment on an article, post your own version of events, to follow breaking news or join in rule-breaking discussion'. An attractive and highly interactive example of a webzine written primarily by and for a younger generation of feminists, is 'The F Word: Contemporary UK Feminism' (www.thefword.org.uk). It includes a blog with 'the latest news of interest to UK feminists'.

Feminist blogging

It has been argued that blogging is democratising the world of information and empowering the individual. You will find sites comprised of individual women writing about their daily lives with a feminist lens, to networks of bloggers linked together on a single blog site. Blog sites tend to link the personal with the political and allow readers a chance to be interactive with the author(s) of the blog.

BlogHer (blogher.org) is 'where the women bloggers are' and the mission of this site is to 'create opportunities for women bloggers to pursue exposure, education, and community'. Together, this blog site is working towards building a guide to women bloggers. The community has a long term vision to be:

- A do-ocracy where BlogHer doesn't serve women bloggers, but rather creates opportunities for all women bloggers to help ourselves and work together to voice and achieve our individual goals – professional, technical, social and/or personal;
- A robust BlogHer Network equipped with the tools we need to deliver on the education, exposure and community of women bloggers, branching out beyond a single blog to create a true community resource and meeting place;
- A community that regularly meets in person, at regional, local and specialised meet-ups, as well as at our annual conference, to continue our conversations. We are committed to extending our conversations and network even to these who cannot attend these meeting in person.

Another blog space of interest is feminist blogs (feministblogs.org/) which bills itself as 'an independent alternative to malestream media'. Here you will find commentary on politics, media criticisms and more by various authors.

An innovative approach to a blog spot is Holla Back NYC (www.hollaback-nyc.blogspot.com/), a site designed to empower New Yorkers to holla back at street harassers. The site urges folks to holla back 'whether you're commuting, lunching, partying, dancing, walking, chilling, drinking, or sunning. You have the right to feel safe, confident, and sexy, without being the object of some turd's fantasy. So stop walkin' on and holla back: send us pics of street harassers'. Along with pictures of street harassers, blog entries include a description of the harasser, where the incident occurred and how it made that person feel. It is an empowering site in that it gives contributors an outlet to express their emotions at being harassed on the street. Since the inception of this site many other holla back sites have popped up around the world.

Finally, an example of an individual feminist making an impact online is blackfeminism.org (blackfeminism.org). The site is described as 'one woman's opinion on race, gender and politics'.

All sites noted in this section are cyberfeminist sites in that they are created by women in order to put women's voices and feminist perspectives on the web. They are taking up space and spreading their messages and in so doing they are empowering women to share their stories and feel safer on the streets.

The digital divide and access to cyberspace

While it could be argued that feminism is flourishing on the Internet it could also be argued that access to the Internet and its resources is limited due to the 'digital divide'. The 'digital divide' is a term used to describe the gap that exists between those who have and those who do not have access to technology. This largely reflects socio-economic factors – who has the time, the money, the appropriate literacy, the telephone or broadband connections to use the Internet. The digital divide reveals the differences in how people can or cannot use access to the Internet to improve their lives, to express their views and to connect with other people.

In Canada the right to access and use ICTs is increasingly being considered a basic need that most people can achieve via personal ownership, public access, or through the workplace. However, people's access to ICTs varies in Canada. These differences are noticeable when one's geographic location is taken under consideration in trying to access or use ICTs. Large gaps in access begin to appear between urban and rural communities. This gap between access to and use of ICTs grows even larger when factors such as gender, income level, education, ability, and age are examined. While many Federal initiatives are trying, and have tried, to address some of these factors through programs funded by Industry Canada (such as Community Access Programs and VolNet), they have been unsuccessful in connecting all Canadians. Further, while the British Columbia government has in the past funded some women's service agencies through the Ministry of Women's Equality to give women basic skill development on computers and the Internet, this was a one-time, short-term funded initiative. Such short-term funding, and in some instances the location of the programs at places like transition houses, made it difficult for women to integrate these new skills at a time most convenient to their learning needs.

Government and regulatory interventions remain essential to ensuring universal access to network connectivity and advanced applications and services. Despite a number of attempts to integrate gender more fully into Canadian ICT programs and policies, there is still a gender gap and digital divide in the use of technology in both paid and unpaid work, leisure, study and employment. Women have less online access than men, for all the usual gender-related reasons – time, money, control, learning opportunities, other commitments and prioritising others' needs. 'Men have more opportunity to access online because they are more likely than women to hold jobs working with computers, with online access. Women are likely to be confined to word processing, data base entry, etc.'[6] Because of geographic, technological, gender and socio-economic barriers faced by women a genuine universal access to and effective use of ICTs and the array of applications that come along with such technology (including e-government, e-learning and telemedicine) they are being left behind.

A Womenspace document titled 'E-Quality for Women' notes that access is an important issue for Aboriginal women, especially those living in remote and isolated communities:

> In some communities, the fast Internet connection is costly and that limits the use of the Internet's full potential. On the other hand, in some communities, the fast connection is established only on computers situated in public places, and those are not easily accessible to all women. Outdated equipment in addition limits the access to Internet for some Aboriginal women and women's organisations.[7]

The gender gap in ICTs has the potential to exacerbate inequalities already present in our society. To ensure that some women are not left out, barriers such as illiteracy, language, limited resources, isolated location and time constraints must be addressed.

Canadian women often lack the necessary resources to make use of the Internet, including: finances (cost of hardware and software, Internet connection), available time, equipment near one's home or women's centre, broadband access, training and skill development opportunities, technical support (often more difficult for women in rural areas) or tools for increasing accessibility for women with disabilities. Women are also often a low priority when sharing a home computer with a spouse and children.[8] The widespread adoption of ICTs combined with the federal government's move towards e-government pose complex challenges for Canada and its commitment to equality and democracy.[9] Womenspace has been diligently working with the government over the past four years to include women in e-government.

The digital divide and women's organisations

Womenspace's research has found that while women's organisations have received bare bones funding to acquire computers very little funding has been afforded to women's groups in the area of ICT training and literacy. Women's organisations in Canada do not receive adequate funding to allow them the time or staff power to utilise the Internet properly. Womenspace has found that:

- Staff at many women's organisations and shelters are taking on their Internet work as volunteer work as they do not have the time or energy to do this type of work during their paid hours.
- Individual women and women working at women's organisations, shelters and services are not using the Internet or aren't using the Internet to its full

capacity primarily because they have a lack of technical knowledge or confidence in using ICTs.

- There is a lack of long-term stable funding to women's groups, which
  leaves such organisations to manage the additional, unfunded expenses of
  equipment maintenance, up-grades and training for users and staff to do on
  their own time.
- Lack of funding leaves women's organisations with an unacceptable level
  of uncertainty and renders staff decisions and programme development difficult if not impossible.
- Women's groups need commitment of adequate and stable funding in order
  to establish, maintain and improve their initiatives and programmes.
- For many, the issue is still that the technology gets in the way. Women's
  groups cite lack of time to learn how to use it. There is still the need to see
  beyond the hardware and software to how to apply the technology to the
  mission of organisations. An inability to engage online is often the result of
  lack of time and/or resources.
- Language and the preponderance of English on the Internet can have the
  effect of discouraging participation and can be a threat to cultural diversity.
  Nicole Pigeon has noted that one of the barriers to francophone women's
  participation in ICTs is a lack of francophone content reflecting the lives of
  women in minority communities.[10]

The role of women's organisations in the promotion of women's online participation is key in helping to prevent increasing inequality in civic participation,
education, employment and community building in the future. It is a critical
factor in supporting women to find relevant resources online, use online forums
for community building, government services provision and in future developments for e-democracy.

We must keep in mind that the barriers that women's organisations face are
not unlike those confronting women in society. Generally poorly funded and less
eligible for government ICT access and learning programs because they service
women, women's equality organisations are struggling to find sufficient time
and money to participate online. The most disadvantaged groups are particularly
concerned about being left behind in the digital age. Developing policies for
women's use of the Internet needs financial support, and women's groups must
come together and act at the different decision-making levels: local, regional,
provincial and national.

The online backlash and other challenges to cyberfeminism

While the Internet has become a space for networking, problem solving, and
community and coalition building among feminists and equality-seeking organisations, it has also facilitated attacks on feminism by those wishing to undermine women's equality, including 'father's rights' groups. The Internet has
become a forum though which these groups have found an easy and cost-

effective way to disseminate information, recruit new members and target individual feminists and women's organisations. The Internet is a powerful communication tool that is being used by all those wishing to spread their message to a larger audience therefore it is not surprising that feminists and equality seeking groups are not the only ones benefiting from the availability of ICTs.

The Internet has become the forum of choice for 'father's rights' groups precisely because it allows them to avoid interacting with those who disagree with their views.[11] 'Father's rights' groups complain about civil rights activists who critique their manifestos while their online homes provide them with 'safe spaces' to spread their messages and to target equality-seeking organisations and individual feminists. The Internet also helps 'father's rights' groups to identify and bring in new members who are enticed to join with the help of communications and outreach through private chat rooms, emails and web-boards.[12] Their proliferation is also due to the ease with which anyone can set up a website and run it from a single person's home/office, meaning there is no real need for an organisation as such.

The examination of the presence of 'father's rights' groups on the Internet has led to the revelation that there is an extensive Internet network of such groups around the world, including some major groups with chapters spanning many Western countries.[13] Surfing through these sites and reading their resources revealed a disturbing reality involving the expression of an often hateful, violent and unrestrained discourse against feminists and women.

'Father's rights' groups are not the only ones finding a home on the Internet – so are pornographers, traffickers and sexual predators. Like all other new communication technologies over the past few centuries, from printing to film, phone, and video, the Internet has become a forum for pornographic images, stalkers, voyeurs and abusers of women.[14] Creating and distributing pornographic images on the Internet has become a multi-billion dollar industry, one that is being fueled by a global economy.

The Internet gives sexual predators the ability to exploit women anonymously and from the privacy of their own homes. The types of sexual exploitation on the Internet include, but are not limited to, trafficking, sex tourism, promotion and exchange of information on where to buy prostitutes, live videoconferencing, pornography and cyberstalking. Because new technologies have been largely unregulated and because the Internet has created a global village that extends past jurisdictional boundaries, it is difficult for law enforcement officials to monitor and control. In addition, the incentives to conduct these types of activities are high as it is a profitable endeavour and the Internet holds the power to make anyone 'anonymous'.

On-line hate and obscenity pose barriers to women's equality and risk poisoning both cyberspace and 'real space'. Although it is important for legislators in Canada and around the world to explore the need for regulation in cyberspace, the reality of the difficulties involved in policing this global network remains daunting. It is imperative that governments implement programs that increase public awareness about the material available on the Internet, so that global citizens are given the capacity critically to evaluate the material present online. There is also a need to educate the public about existing alternatives for filtering out material they may deem offensive. Although present laws play an important role in society, their adaptation for regulating such material in cyberspace would prove difficult and possibly useless, therefore making education and self-regulation imperative in handling this new and evolving communications medium.

Is cyberfeminism evidence of the women's movement flourishing in a new space?

The advent of the Internet and the movement of feminism into cyberspace has brought new possibilities to feminist action. It has given us new ways to connect, share knowledge, lobby the government, and promote our organisations. It has also given us a global voice in that we can create and write our own blogs, we can join feminist communities of bloggers and join discussions raised on feminist list-serves and webboards. In some respects it does seem like feminism is flourishing in this new space. However, as we have seen there are various barriers raised by the gender digital divide and it is safe to say that not all feminists can access the Internet and the feminist spaces it allows.

The potential that is held in this new space is largely untapped but there are innovative feminists working online to pave the way for all women to find a safe and encouraging space on the Internet. There are those who are devising new ways of contacting government officials in order to facilitate lobbying efforts; there are those who are creating software that is user friendly and designed to teach as the user begins to use various web applications; there are those who are paving the way in the creation of feminist-driven sites that allow women to speak out and share their stories of harassment; there are those creating list-serves to help distribute calls to action, job postings and rants about daily struggles. Feminists are connecting online and in this sense feminism is flourishing in new spaces. Cyberfeminism is an ever growing and evolving feminism. It is a theory of resistance, empowerment, practice and pleasure, one that offers a new perspective in understanding the complex interactions of gender, technology and culture.

Notes

1 Wilding, 'Where is feminism in cyberfeminism?'; see also Brayton, 'Cyberfeminism as new theory'.
2 See Braidotti, 'Cyberfeminism with a difference'; Galloway, 'A report on cyberfeminism'.
3 Wilding, 'Where is feminism in cyberfeminism?'.
4 Pollock, 'Web strategies for equality'.
5 Richards and Schnall, 'Cyberfeminism: Networking on the Net'.
6 Pollock and Sutton, 'Women and the Internet', p. 7.
7 Golic, 'Aboriginal women and the Internet report'.
8 Pollock and Sutton, 'Women and the Internet'.

9 Paragraph 3 of Canadian Research Alliance for Community Innovation and Networking (CRACIN)'s Written Submission to Telecommunications Policy Review Panel, 15 August 2005.
10 Pigeon, 'Francophone women's groups in minority situations'.
11 Rowe, 'Father's rights groups and the backlash against feminists in the online world'.
12 Bouchard *et al.*, 'School success by gender'.
13 Bouchard *et al.*, 'School success by gender'.
14 For more information on cyberstalking see Rowe, 'Stalking meets the Internet'. For an article and resources on digital voyeurism see Rowe, 'Digital voyeurism'; and for an article on ICTs and pornography see Hughes, 'The use of new communication and information technologies for sexual exploitation of women and children'.

Part III
New feminist activists

11 New voices

The final section of this book is given over to young women who are self-identified feminist activists. They have experienced life in a time that could be described as 'post-women's liberation'. They were born in or after the time when street activism by women's organisations was at its height. As we noted at the beginning of the book, changes over the last four decades may require renegotiation of the identity of women's movements. Feminist activism may now take forms that would be unrecognisable to their 'foremothers'. So how do young feminists in Australia, Canada, Japan, Korea, New Zealand, Scotland and the United States – conceive of their 'movement' and its relationship to the past? Academic and activist Sarah Maddison introduces the chapter, followed by Erica Lewis, Jackie Steele, Melanee Thomas, Seyama Noriko, Eun Sang Lee, Fleur Fitzsimons, Claire Duncanson, and Ingrid Hu Dahl.

In strong hands: young women and the future of women's movements

Sarah Maddison

What does the future hold for women's movements? Whatever the history and trajectory of the movements described in this volume – whatever their successes or failures – there is always an eye to the future. Around the world, many older women's movement activists express concern about the presence or absence of the next generation of feminist activists; the young women who will carry the movement forward, defending past gains and facing future challenges.

This section gives voice to some of the women from the next generation of feminists, in the shape of eight young women activists from Australia, Canada, Japan, Korea, New Zealand, Scotland, and the United States. These women discuss their activism in a changing world and how they relate to the feminist movements of earlier decades. For readers who remember the brief but explosive 'generational debates' between feminists of different ages in women's movements in the United States, the United Kingdom and Australia in the mid-to-late 1990s, these voices are reassuring. If these young women are in any way representative of their generation then women's movements the world over have much to look forward to.

Remembering the 'generational debates'

The debates that flared during the 1990s highlighted important differences between younger feminists and their 'older sisters' in the movement. A flurry of publishing during this time produced books and articles from both sides of the 'generational divide'; texts that spoke with passion, and often anger, about the ways in which young women were or were not taking on the responsibilities handed down to them from older feminists. There was criticism from older women about what they perceived to be a lack of action by younger women. Young women responded angrily pointing out the many ways in which they were indeed active as feminists: ways that were different, and perhaps challenging, to an older generation.

To a young woman who was active in the Australian women's movement during the 1990s these debates about generationalism in the movement were engrossing. The debates were, after all, about me and my peers. I was swayed by the different points of view put forward by younger and older women: No, there didn't seem to be many young women in the more 'traditional' women's movement organisations such as the Australian Women's Electoral Lobby (WEL), so perhaps such organisations *were* no longer relevant. But if being a young feminist meant only being sassy and 'doing-it-yourself', as some writers suggested,[1] where did that leave the future and the possibility of young women shaping social and political institutions? For many older feminist activists the lack of visible activism from young women and falling membership in their organisations contributed to a feeling of failure. Such disappointment was sometimes expressed as hostility towards younger women.

In light of these debates – now over a decade old and with little or no remaining currency in the broader political culture – it is important that the voices of contemporary younger activists are included here. It is crucial that the field of social movement studies should include space for the voices of activists in both the research process and as a critical audience. Such involvement will inevitably focus our attention on our 'local knowledge' rather than our 'general knowledge'[2] as it develops in dialogue with the activists themselves, from their own perspectives and giving them a voice in the process. Creating this space brings into focus a far wider range of social movement activity, including those activities that take place quietly, 'behind the scenes', and yet without which no publicly visible movement could be possible. Such a focus on submerged networks constitutes social movement actors as 'diffuse and decentralised'[3] and takes account of periods away from the public spotlight.

This approach to social movement research is also entirely congruent with forms of feminist standpoint theory. Although not without its critics, the feminist standpoint is important, not least because it arises from 'a committed feminist exploration of women's experiences of oppression'.[4] I have suggested elsewhere that the intersections between feminist standpoint theory and the more constructivist approaches to social movement theorising can allow us to conceptualise what might be called the *activist standpoint*.[5] The standpoints of feminist and other activists can be understood through analysing the ways in which they construct their own experiences and understandings.

Social movement research that develops from an activist standpoint privileges the perspectives of the activists themselves as knowing, politicised subjects who, in the case of young feminist activists, articulate contemporary women's movements through their own feminist discourse and action. Such research provides the space and opportunity to 'give the voice back to the protestors we study'.[6] In this sense it is particularly gratifying to hear the voices of young women included in this collection.

International perspectives

The young women whose voices you will hear in the following section reflect the diversity of young women's lives and experiences, and the ways in which such diversity translates into feminist activism. Many of their stories raise questions about the legacies of earlier periods of women's movement activism and the implications for the future trajectories of these movements should these legacies be eroded in new political contexts. For example, several of the young women in the following pages underscore the importance that academic women's studies programs have had on their developing feminist consciousness and activism. What will be the implications of the current trend away from 'women's studies' towards the more male-inclusive 'gender studies', or even in some instances, 'Gender and Cultural Studies'? This is a new trajectory that is certainly evident in universities in Australia, New Zealand and the United Kingdom. Might this trend also spread to countries such as Korea and other nations where the relationship between women's studies and the women's movement is ingrained in movement history? How will this affect the future trajectory of the women's movement there?

The young women also return to questions that were central to the generational debates discussed above, and indeed to earlier periods of women's movement activism. Identity and diversity are fore-grounded in their stories in a number of ways. The challenge of reconciling multiple identities, deriving from gender, sexuality and race, both enriches and complicates these women's engagement in feminist activism, much as for older women in the 1970s, 1980s and 1990s. For many, these issues have been further explored in intergenerational feminist relationships that are clearly important to these young women. Mothers, grandmothers, teachers and other feminist mentors have inspired, guided and challenged these younger activists, who have sought out these connections and evidently prize them.

In sum, these contributions highlight the strength and diversity among younger women's movement activists in culturally and geographically diverse locations. Some locate their activism in the cultural sphere. Other areas of activism are diverse: in academia, the non-government sector, and in coalition with other social movements. Regardless of this diversity, all these young women understand and articulate the continuing necessity of women's movements around the world in the continuing struggles for women's rights, recognition and equality. These voices are strong and persuasive, and demand to be heard.

Erica Lewis – Australia

Erica like many others came to feminism after coming up against the patriarchy with a solid thump at University. She says that she has been fortunate to be mentored by wise women from Women's Electoral Lobby (WEL) and the YWCA and to have come through the student movement with talented and committed feminists who continue to provide inspiration and support for her work.

Erica has been active in global, national and local forums: she was an intern with the World YWCA at the United Nations Commission on the Status of Women; served as the foundation co-ordinator for the WomenSpeak Network; and was spokeswoman for the successful abortion law reform campaign in the Australian Capital Territory (ACT). She currently serves as WEL Australia National Secretary and Vice-President of YWCA Australia.

The tales of the women's movement's victories of the 1970s and 1980s are an amazing legacy and one I worry I cannot live up to. While I know that I and my peers will have our victories, I worry about preserving the gains of the past.

One of my mentors tells stories of how she came to the women's movement, bored with making sandwiches and doing other 'women's work' for the causes of the 1960s and 1970s. For many women today there is not the same need to work in women-only spaces. My peers are members of parliament, union organisers and activists in faith-based, human rights and environmental organisations. We study. We hold jobs in the business, public and community sectors. We raise our children and look after our parents. It does not mean that we have defeated the patriarchy; my friends have many war stories to tell. Nor does it mean that we have abandoned feminism, it remains central to our lives.

These victories have changed the way women live and work, and women's organisations must update their structures and strategies to reflect this. We need to build organisational capacity to better support the campaign and policy work that most of us participate in women's organisations to do. We need to strengthen our financial base so that we can buy in skills where we need them, and decrease our reliance on volunteers and their elusive free time. Women's organisations were campaign innovators in the 1970s; we need to regain that position by updating our campaign strategies and making better use of new technologies. These challenges are not unique to the women's movement, but have been amplified by our victories.

Some of the campaigns with the biggest impact in recent years have been run as collaborations. The Australian Capital Territory (ACT) abortion law reform campaign, which resulted in the removal of abortion from the ACT criminal code, was not owned by any single women's organisation, but instead was run by a broad range of women's and community health organisations building on our expertise and different strengths.

The WomenSpeak Network has been an experiment forced on the women's movement by changes in government funding, but one that I believe has allowed us to strengthen our networking and collaboration. In the late 1990s the Australian Government moved from providing a large number of small operational grants to women's organisations to providing four larger national secretariat grants and smaller project-based grants. Some organisations like WEL and the Association of Non-English Speaking Background Women of Australia have received no government funding since that time. One of the striking successes of the WomenSpeak Network has been its use as a forum to build campaign partnerships, whether for UNIFEM and the White Ribbon Campaign, or the re-establishment of a national immigrant and refugee women's organisation. The combined meetings of the four national women's secretariats have created large and regular meetings of women's organisations.

Feminism will remain a radical movement and threat to many in power, particularly those whose position is maintained by the oppression of women and by gender stereotypes. Feminism also remains an attractive philosophy that continues to recruit, whether or not all its adherents identify as feminists. Increasingly men are recognising the damage that the patriarchy does to them, as well as to women.

Last but not least: please remember young women are not the leaders of tomorrow. We are leaders of the women's movement today. However, do not think that means we want to do it without earlier generations of women's movement activists. We want to recognise that different challenges face different generations and that the strength of the women's movement lies not in a homogenised image of woman, but in our diversity, disparate experiences and our collective strength.

Jackie Steele – Canada

Jackie F Steele credits her grade 10 maths teacher for inspiring her to become a political woman. For the past four years, Jackie's passion for feminist electoral reform has been invested in the Collectif Féminisme et Démocratie (Québec), a group promoting women's equal representation in democratic institutions. At the pan-Canadian level, she has supported the National Association of Women and the Law on issues such as child custody, women's political participation, and religious arbitration. Locally, Jackie performs with the Oto-Wa Taiko drum group (Ottawa). She believes that political women everywhere are the driving force behind democratisation and human rights advocacy, making the twenty-first century a very exciting, if dangerous, time to be a feminist activist!

As a PhD candidate in political theory and an activist in the pan-Canadian and Québécois feminist communities, my convictions find expression in inter-disciplinary/intercultural pursuits and in a lifelong commitment to political contest. Feminist debates have given me the opportunity to work in solidarity with diverse women in promoting greater equality. For me, the goal of feminist theory and feminist movements is to further democratise social, economic, cultural and political power. This begins with producing social relations where difference and/or vulnerability do not lead to domination and denigration.

What I have learnt from contemporary feminist legal/political philosophy, reinforced by engagement in the Québécois feminist movement, is that equality is an ideal to be realised through the protection, in law and in practice, of diverse ways of being in the world. Feminism affirms and promotes the rights and responsibilities of women to shape their own individual and collective destinies. In 2008, feminist movements are producing political women and men, both at the grassroots and elite-level, who are willing to challenge anti-democratic attitudes and practices in order to bring us closer to the ideal of political equality for all women.

If 'the personal is the political!' was the credo of twentieth century second-wave feminism, the twenty-first century echo is 'the political is deeply personal!' In 2008, feminist voices must be heard everywhere, especially in the halls of formal political power. Accountable or not, democratic or not, states continue to be the agents empowered to ratify free trade agreements and UN Conventions, to approve Security Council resolutions, to mobilise public funds for war rather than childcare, and to act *in our names* in ways that compromise rather than further the human rights of women. Contesting discrimination and promoting the full inclusion of women in decision-making must remain at the forefront of feminist activity, together with grassroots participation in democratic debates and the strategic expression of democratic dissent. Such coalition-building activities link the 'individual-local-national-transnational-individual' chain of life. Feminist affirmation of diversity and demands for social inclusion are an invitation to Canada to follow Québec's lead and renew its role as an international catalyst for democracy and social justice.

'LIBERTÉ, DIVERSITÉ, SOLIDARITÉ' are at the heart of democracy. Our ability to affirm a 'free and democratic society' for *all* women and men in Canada depends upon the presence of political will, at the grassroots and elite levels, to promote the agency and well-being of all sexuate beings, whose distinct aboriginal, national, ethno-cultural, linguistic, physical, religious, spiritual, political and philosophical selves are cause for celebration, not marginalisation. The effective right to self-government begins with the recognition, by each and every woman, of our innate ability to decide for our own lives, supported by a conscious decision to exercise political power in solidarity with all women. Our project? To network transnationally and in doing so, expand the possibilities for realising the human potential of each and every girl on earth.

Melanee Thomas – Canada

Melanee sees her mother as her inspiration to get involved in the women's movement. As a child, Melanee first watched her mother walk on an illegal

*picket line, and then watched as her mom dealt with tremendous cuts to the
health care system from the front line. Melanee's early interest in politics was
sparked by watching Kim Campbell win the 1992 Progressive Conservative
leadership convention, becoming the first female Prime Minister in Canadian
history.*

*As a former Students' Union President, 2003 YWCA Young Woman of Dis-
tinction, the first ever Executive Director of the Council of Alberta University
Students, and executive member of a local Equal Voice chapter, Melanee is an
active feminist and activist. She was an NDP candidate in the 2004 and 2006
federal elections and is completing a PhD in Political Science at the McGill
University.*

At first glance, feminism in Canada has achieved quite a lot. The formal legal
barriers women faced have been toppled, and women's equality has been
entrenched in the *Charter of Rights and Freedoms*. The women who came
before us made the clear gains that my generation of women currently enjoys.
My generation of Canadian women has grown up with feminism, whether we
are aware of it or not. It has never occurred to some of us, myself included, that
we could not be the Prime Minister, a CEO of a Fortune 500 corporation, or the
leader in any field we chose. However, when we express this to other young
feminists, their response often is, 'Really? Are you sure being PM is a totally
reasonable aspiration, given how women are treated in politics by the media and
other politicians? Are you sure you're not just being too optimistic?'.

While feminism remains central to some young women's lives, others do not
learn the true history of the women's movement in Canada. Instead, we are
taught that those who came before us were simply essentialists rather than the
true transformers. As a result history continues to repeat itself. For example,
many young women are not aware that women in Canada still earn about two-
thirds of their male counterparts and that women's progress in fields such as
business and politics is still hampered by glass ceilings. Those of us who are
aware of these realities respond with roughly equal rates of optimism and
pessimism.

While I tend to side with the optimists, I must admit that current events are
quite disheartening. Status of Women Canada has been directed by the federal
government to stop its advocacy work on behalf of Canadian women. In some
provinces women's legally guaranteed access to abortion procedures is so
restricted that the issue has sparked a *Charter* challenge in court. While these
two examples seem deplorable, most gender-based oppression in Canada has
taken on an insidious nature, and young women are all too often naïve until we
are hit between the eyes with our first blatant experiences of gender discrimination. These first unfortunate experiences often cause us to question our perceptions of equality and examine how gender constructs our reality.

As a candidate for public office, I was often confronted with traditional sex
stereotypes by other candidates, constituents, and the media. Some would argue
this was due to my age, but the fact that my mother's experience as a candidate
for the same party in a neighbouring constituency during the same campaign

period echoed my own, suggests these stereotypes are easily applied to all generations of women. It is the older generations of women who have been fighting since the beginning who continue vital claims-making activity. I fear that if young Canadian women's consciousness is not raised, we may lose the gains earlier generations of women fought so hard to achieve.

It may be doubtful that women will lose the right to vote or legal freedom from discrimination based on sex or gender. However, these formal provisions do not end bigotry or misogyny, nor do they eliminate the idea that it is acceptable to colloquially or casually discriminate against women because of their sex. A disturbing example of this occurred early in 2007 when the editorial board of a student-run newspaper at one of Canada's largest universities argued that sexual assault and rape are appropriate subjects for satire. Many feminists, both women and men, spoke out against this and took action, but the fact remains that a portion of the population still thinks this discrimination is acceptable when it clearly is not.

Canadians say they value fairness and equality. To pursue that end, the women's movement in Canada will continue. Personally, I will continue to act as an agent of change through academia and activism, and will likely return to electoral politics at a later point in my life. My generation of women is beginning to see what our mothers and grandmothers already saw, and this will spark some of us to action. While it may have never occurred to a young Canadian woman that she could not be Prime Minister, that thought still occurs to some Canadians. This needs to change, and some of us will not rest until that does, in fact, change.

Seyama Noriko – Japan

Seyama Noriko has a Masters degree from Ochanomizu University (one of the two women's universities in Japan). Her Masters thesis was on the Women with Disabilities Movement. Noriko is a video activist, who directed together with Chieko Yamagami the documentary video '30 Years of Sisterhood – Women in the 1970s Women's Liberation Movement in Japan'. She was born in 1974, so was not a participant in the Women's Liberation movement but believes in the importance of leaving records of the movement for the future. The following are her thoughts from making '30 Years of Sisterhood'.

Over the last 30 years, the women's movement in Japan has gone through a transition in terminology (meanings) and standard bearers, as it changed from Women's Liberation to Feminism to Gender Studies. As has often been pointed out, the terminology has become highly abstract. As a result, thoughts and discussions have become monopolised by academics, excluding the broader constituency of women. I was concerned that this was not what the movement was meant to be. I wanted to explore this problem and find an effective method of solving it. In order to avoid the complications produced by the use of abstract terminology, I wanted to record the women's movement through visual images. This was the starting point of my exploration.

I thought the Women's Liberation movement in the 1970s made it possible for women to voice the difficulty of living in Japanese society as 'a woman'; this had continued to be an obstacle in their lives even after sex equality had been explicitly declared in the Constitution. It aimed to liberate women rather than to achieve well-defined targets. What was important was that those who participated in this movement were willing to accept themselves as they were. They did not negate themselves in order to conform to social expectations and they tried to connect to other women in the same situation.

Through visual images, I wanted to convey the fact that there were groups of women who positively took the challenge and worked on it; in the same way we are working on our problems today. I wanted to do it in an open way where I could expect the viewers to see the common ideas they might share with the women in the documentary. As it turned out, showing the documentary opened a way to reach a broader audience than conventional meetings based on texts on women's issues. Viewers shared time and place by watching the video together and talking together afterwards. They were readily engaged in the questions left open-ended in the video and started to talk about them. It was rewarding because this allowed us to think further about the meaning of Women's Liberation.

Reactions to our work differed by generation and experiences with the 1970s movement. Many young viewers said that it was the first time they had seen Women's Liberation activities and participants first hand. And most of the middle-aged viewers seemed to have learned about Women's Liberation activities through the mass media, which had ridiculed them. So they also said it was the first time they had seen and heard the real voices of participants in the movement.

Participants in the 1970s movement who are still active in some way told us after the show that they felt uncomfortable because they were being treated as part of past history, while the goal of the movement was still to be attained. But those who had distanced themselves from the movement felt they now had a better understanding of the women's movement. The screening also led some viewers to wonder what had happened to other social movements, which did not appear in the video.

The benefit the younger generation acquired from the video was that they learned first hand that there were real people who had attempted to find a solution to the problems faced by women and to take action through Women's Liberation, not through a theoretical development of Women's Studies. They also said they saw the problem as that Women's Liberation had been treated as a laughing stock at the time and still continued to be treated the same way in present society. Some people felt envious about the activism they saw in the video; they felt unhappy they had not shared the happy moment. One of the serious discussions was about why the 1970s Women's Liberation movement had not been passed on to the next generation.

As a whole producing this video and showing/discussing it seemed to have the positive effect of connecting women in the past, present, and future.

Compared with the 1970s, women have made a number of advances. But women and the women's movement today are also being challenged by a so-called backlash. In these circumstances, the history of the women's movement could end up being buried, if we do not record it ourselves. While there is still time, it is important for us to think seriously about what we want to tell, to whom, in what voice, and how we can best accomplish those tasks.

I myself want to continue to record herstories by various methods, taking up the lived realities of women in the past and connecting them to women today who are living various realities. I am sure the women of women's liberation can reach out to the next generation if they can talk from their reality. We are still oppressed by the tight gender roles of this society. So I still want to hear how women in the past could survive and act, and how they feel now, and to learn from them.

Resources

sisterhoodjapan.blogspot.com
www.jca.apc.org/video-juku/index-eng.html
www.renren-fav.org

Eun Sang Lee – Korea

Eun Sang Lee is currently deputy director of the Korea Sexual Violence Relief Center (KSVRC). She has worked for KSVRC as a volunteer and staff member for many years and also worked for the Sexual Harassment Counselling Centre of Ewha Womans University and Seoul Women's Foundation. She is interested in sexuality issues in this gender-unequal society. She believes that a feminist movement will create an alternative society where women enjoy their lives with safety, health, and peace.

My experience of growing up as a woman in Korea played a major role in my developing an interest in women's issues. Although my parents tried to provide me with plenty of educational and cultural opportunities, I realised that our society is simply not open enough to give equal opportunity to women.

I did a graduate degree in women's studies at Ewha Womans University – my first step towards becoming a feminist activist. The Ewha women's studies program was the first to be established in Korea and became a foundation stone of the feminist movement, producing many feminist activists.

After receiving my masters degree in women's studies in 1997, when I was 27, I started working at the Korea Sexual Violence Relief Center (KSVRC). KSVRC was established in 1991 by women who aimed to create a society free from sexual violence. As the first specialised sexual violence counselling centre, KSVRC has played a major role in leading the movement against sexual violence in Korea. In addition to developing and providing a feminist counselling service for survivors of sexual violence, it designed a range of programmes including a feminist self-defence workshop, the 'Take Back the Night' campaign, 'Survivors of Sexual Violence Speak Out', and other education programmes.

KSVRC has had a number of major achievements, including sexual violence law reform, sexual harassment law reform and the implementation of policies to counter sexual violence. The main purpose of our advocacy activities was to have our government take responsibility for sexual violence issues. That is why we asked them to enact laws, support survivors of sexual violence, implement policies to prevent sexual violence and properly budget for jobs in the area. I believe the Korean feminist movement was right to urge the government to fund their responsibilities in relation to sexual violence. Sexuality issues in Korean society are very significant in achieving gender equality. To empower women we need to understand how sexuality controls women's lives and infringes women's rights in many ways.

Now that there are many anti-sexual violence centres that receive government funding we worry about the institutionalisation of the feminist movement, with some even saying it is in crisis. There cannot be one right way that everybody has to follow. Calling for budget allocation was a necessary step to get our government to take responsibility; we still need to demand a larger budget and to monitor how the budget is used. At the same time we must be very careful not to become subordinate to government, and to keep our radical identity as feminist activists. Some may ask: 'Is it possible not to be co-opted when you receive government funding?' There is no easy answer. We are trying to receive less funding from the government, because we think that the government should now be able to handle the budget themselves. We will continue to advise them how to use the budget properly and how to build cooperative partnerships between government and NGOs.

I believe that a feminist movement is a path that our society needs to follow to achieve equality between all kinds of difference. Equality will bring us safety and peace, and a different relationship between genders, races, ages, nations, cultures and individuals.

We may encounter a lot of obstacles on the way to building the good society because the path is not wide and it may be bumpy. However, that does not mean the way is only hard and wearying, in fact I find it exciting and attractive. Because I always try to be sceptical about 'the universals' and find new values and norms, I feel changes in my community earlier than others. I meet 'minorities' who have fresh ideas from radical points of views, and I hardly ever feel alienated from my work, as my life and work share the same goals.

Fleur Fitzsimons – New Zealand

Fleur Fitzsimons considers her grandmother the greatest influence in her life and the person who inspired her to become involved in the feminist movement. Currently, Fleur is a Union Organiser for the Public Service Association. She has held various positions in the student movement including President of the Victoria University Students' Association and the New Zealand University Students' Association. She is a claimant in a Human Rights Commission case against the New Zealand student loan scheme claiming that it is unlawful discrimination against women. Fleur shares her insights on the importance of feminism.[7]

I have been part of numerous discussions among young women about the role of feminism in our lives, and our role in feminism. While some of the discussion has focussed around liberal feminism versus radical feminism or lesbian feminism, moving beyond the labels and on to the issues we as young women face has provided the most fruitful debate about the role of feminism among young women.

While 'consciousness raising' groups rarely exist in a formalised sense, there are discussions and debates about the role of women in New Zealand society and globally. On a local level, young women are involved in movements and debates about a wide range of issues including the lack of affordable childcare, the gender pay gap and the fact that it will take us, as women, twice as long to repay our student loans compared with men. In a global sense, many young women are concerned about the devastating impacts of American aggression throughout the world, human rights injustices and the impact of globalisation.

Women involved in these movements and discussions are some of the most passionate, committed women I have ever met, however, they do tend to be a minority. As young women, our major challenge in building a united, feminist movement is making opportunities to talk to other young women about their concerns and working together to develop a strong movement among women on issues that affect our lives.

Clearly, we will not build a feminist movement for the sake of it. We will build it because we know that discrimination against women is alive and well in New Zealand. We will build a feminist movement to do what feminism has always been about – that is, collectively fighting for women.

Claire Duncanson – Scotland

Claire is working on her doctoral thesis on military masculinities at the University of Edinburgh. Before returning to university to do a PhD, she worked as a campaigner for Amnesty International and Jubilee 2000 in Scotland, and for Global Perspective in Kenya. Although Claire can not pinpoint who or what initially inspired her feminism, she has been influenced by many wonderful women throughout her education and career.

To an outsider, the activism I am involved in might not seem particularly feminist. But all the campaigns I am involved in, from environmental, to human rights, to peace, are informed by feminism. Feminism. There's always the dilemma of whether to abandon the word and its excess baggage or to embrace it. For me it's about weighing up the benefits of being freed from the shackles of all those misunderstandings, stereotypes and fears expressed by the friends and acquaintances that refuse the label, and the duty to combat the myths, resurrect the term and fill it with renewed vigour.

Sometimes the dilemma seems less urgent than getting on with it. In 2007, the UK government pushed through a decision to replace the UK's nuclear weapons system, at a cost they claim to be £25 billion, but which others estimate is more likely to be £76 billion. When I protested against this injustice, feminism informed my understanding, my motivation and my tactics. When I joined the Faslane 365 blockade[8] at the gates of Faslane, the UK's nuclear weapons naval base in the West of Scotland, however, it was alongside men as well as women. Although I believe that it is partly men and masculinity that are responsible for nuclear weapons and war, I think it is important to join with men in campaigning for change. The experience was as inspiring as I hoped it would be.

One of the most interesting campaigns I have been involved in has been to involve Scottish men in campaigning to stop violence against women. Again, this work is informed by a feminist understanding of violence against women: that it is committed by men against women because they are women, and that it is rooted in unequal power relations and serves to reinforce those relations. In trying to encourage a Scottish version of the White Ribbon campaign, however, it has been fascinating to work with men who are dedicated to challenging constructions of masculinity which are linked to power, violence and control, and to encouraging alternatives.

The reason I am more than happy to combine feminism with working with men is not just because of an awareness that we cannot tackle problems such as nuclear weapons and violence against women if we do not include as many people as possible, men as well as women. It's not just because things will only change when men change, so we need to engage men and persuade them to change. More than a numbers game or an exercise in personality conversion, it's a belief that inequalities and injustices will only be eradicated if we tackle the way in which our entire society – including our systems of language and thought – is structured by gender. It is the association of disarmament with femininity, with being soft and weak, that makes it so difficult for the Government to think of alternatives to developing new nuclear weapons. It is the association of manliness with being strong and in control which contributes to violence against women. Challenging gendered dichotomies such as hard/soft, tough/tender, strong/weak is what feminism means to me, and it has to be the work of both women and men.

Ingrid Hu Dahl – United States

Ingrid Hu Dahl is a mixed-race woman of colour dedicated to empowering young girls through music in same sex environments and supportive spaces. She has a Masters degree in Women's & Gender Studies from Rutgers University (NJ) and is a founding member of the Willie Mae Rock Camp for Girls (Brooklyn, NY). She has been in bands since the age of eighteen and has learned a lot about the US from touring across the nation as a queer, androgynous musician. She has given workshops to teens and lectured at various universities on feminist art history, gender & homophobia, and women's leadership. Dahl makes art (film, performance, paintings, photography, craft) that questions role-play, identity, and representation. She believes in the power of laughter, new ways of seeing, and recognising young people as a source for social change.

During graduate school, I learned feminist theory by day and lived as an artist and rock musician by night. I experienced a tangible connection between these two worlds. I felt the history of those before me, encouraging me to discover new fields and act in multiple arenas. I would think of generations of feminist activists as I wrote lyrics and painted, exploring alternative forms of feminist inquiry.

As a feminist musician, I have developed a form of activism designed to raise the volume of young girls' voices by teaching them how to be loud, expressive agents, especially by forming rock bands. As a founding member of the Willie Mae Rock Camp for Girls, I use music and feminist knowledge to encourage new ways of seeing that can enhance girls' self-esteem. My mission to empower young people (as a method for social change) echoes what I needed in my youth – a rock camp, female role-models and mentors, a space where I could learn about the sexism and racism I experienced on a daily basis, gain confidence in my voice, and become an active agent who could combat these oppressive forces.

I founded the Willie Mae Rock Camp for Girls in 2005 at the age of 25, after spending a summer working at the Rock n' Roll Camp for Girls in Portland, Oregon. The Portland camp attracted many girls of mixed racial backgrounds. In conversations with a fellow mixed-race queer young woman of colour, I began thinking about the unique potential that an all-female space provided to explore the very real, daily practice of racism, sexism and homophobia in society. We decided to design a feminist workshop at the camp that would build upon the girls' experiences of oppression and binary thinking that we personally had never been encouraged to discuss as children or teens.

Leading with inquiry, we sought to help the campers unlearn their oppression and uncover valuable knowledge they already had within. Through the workshops, the girls began to formulate their own answers, assisting each other in finding strength to see difficult truths. Through intensive interaction, we helped heighten their capacities to imagine new possibilities for gender equality and identity formation through praxis, knowledge production, dialogue, and *action.*

Our rock camp does not ask girls to compromise their identities. Instead we draw on their musical talents and interests to offer them tools to explore social pressures and question the injustice in the world in which they live. We help them see how gender intersects with other forms of oppression – racism, homophobia, classism, and look-ism. By examining these intersections, we create ripple effects as the 80 campers and counsellors draw on collective experiences that cut across borders of race, sex, sexuality, and class. By 2007, we had presented our 'Image vs. Identity' workshop to more than 600 young women from coast to coast.

As a site for feminist pedagogy linking groups of campers and counsellors who are close in age, the rock camp fosters intergenerational mentoring and learning on many levels – creative, analytical, and theoretical. We see past feminist activists as heroes who braved verbal and physical attacks to break silence, setting an example for us to follow. The emerging activists at rock camp are intelligent, inquiring young women who are braving social change by making music with one another, *acting* rather than *appearing*.

Recognising the power of young people, my activism starts with a rhythm and beat, builds momentum and volume of youth voice, and provides young people the space to design social norms and new cultures built on love and respect. When we share our own experiences as feminists with young girls, we interrupt boundaries that delineate 'us' from 'them' in order to explore common social positions and power differentials that affect half the world's population. By working with young women, we attempt to forge practices of freedom and empowerment that enable girls to find their own paths while building allies for the difficult project of social change.

Notes

1 See for example Bail, *D.I.Y. Feminism*.
2 Jasper, *The Art of Moral Protest*, p. 377.
3 Taylor, 'Mobilizing for change in a social movement society', p. 222.
4 Stanley and Wise, 'Method, methodology and epistemology in feminist research processes', p. 27.
5 Maddison, 'Feminist perspectives on social movement research'.
6 Jasper, *The Art of Moral Protest*, p. 379.
7 This has been reprinted from the Janus Women's Convention Newsletter, February 2005, New Zealand, with permission of the Janus Women's Trust.
8 A 365-day blockade organised by a coalition of peace movement and anti-nuclear groups www.faslane365.org.

Bibliography

Abdela, Lesley (2004). 'Kosovo: Missed opportunities, lessons for the future', in Haleh Afshar and David Eade (eds), *Development, Women, and War: Feminist perspectives*, Oxford: Oxfam.

Afrin, Zakia and Amy Schwartz (2005). 'A human rights instrument that works for women: The ICC as a tool for gender justice', in Shamilla Wilson, Anasuva Senjgupta and Kristy Evans (eds), *Defending our Dreams*, London: Zed Books.

Alvarez, Sonia E (1990). *Engendering Democracy in Brazil: Women's Movement in Transition Politics*, Princeton, NJ: Princeton University Press.

—— (2000). 'Translating the global: Effects of transnational organizing on Latin American feminist discourses and practices', *Meridians: A Journal of Feminism, Race, and Transnationalism* 1 (1): 29–67.

Anderson, Bonnie S (2000). *Joyous Greetings: The First International Women's Movement, 1830–1860*, New York: Oxford University Press.

Andrew, Caroline (1995). 'Getting Women's Issues on the municipal agenda: Violence against women', in Judith Garber and Robyne Turner (eds), *Gender in Urban Research*, Thousand Oaks, California: Sage.

—— (1997). 'Les femmes et le local: Les enjeux municipaux à l'ère de la mondialisation', in Manon Tremblay and Caroline Andrew (eds), *Femmes et représentation Politique au Québec et au Canada*, Montréal: Remue-ménage.

—— (2000). 'Resisting boundaries? Using safety audits for women', in Kristine Miranne and Alma Young (eds), *Gendering the City*, Lanham: Rowman and Littlefield.

—— (2003). 'Women in the urban landscape', in Andrea Martinez and Meryn Stuart (eds), *Out of the Ivory Tower*, Toronto: Sumach Press.

—— (2006). 'Où sont les femmes? Where are the women?', Powerpoint Presentation, Montreal October 2006, Conference organised by the City of Montreal, Une ville à la mesure des femmes.

—— (In press). 'Gendering nation states and/or gendering city-states: Debates about the nature of citizenship' in Yasmeen Abu-Laban, *Gendering the Nation-State*, Vancouver: UBC Press.

Annesley, Claire, Francesca Gains and Kirstein Rummery (eds) (2007). *Women and New Labour: Engendering Politics and Policy?* Bristol: Policy Press.

Antrobus, Peggy (2005). *The Global Women's Movement*, London: Zed Books.

Armstrong, Pat, Carol Amaratunga, Jocelyne Bernier, Karen Grant, Ann Pederson and Kay Willson (2002). *Exposing Privatisation*, Ontario: Garamond Press.

Asia-Japan Women's Resource Center (2007). At www.ajwrc.org/English accessed January 2008.

Auckland Women's Centre (2006). 'About us' at www.womenz.org.nz/wc/wcentre.htm accessed 6 June 2006.

Bacchi, Carol (1999). 'Rolling back the state? Feminism, theory and policy', in Linda Hancock (ed.), *Women, Public Policy and the State*, Melbourne: Macmillan Education.

Bagguley, Paul (2002). 'Contemporary British Feminism: A social movement in abeyance?', *Social Movement Studies* 1 (2): 169–185.

Bail, Kathy (1996). *D.I.Y. Feminism*, Sydney: Allen & Unwin.

Banaszak, Lee Ann, Karen Beckwith, and Dieter Rucht (2003). *Women's Movements Facing the Reconfigured State*, New York: Cambridge University Press.

—— (2003). 'When power relocates: Interactive changes in women's movements and states' in Banaszak, Beckwith and Rucht (eds), *Women's Movements Facing the Reconfigured State*, New York: Cambridge University Press.

Barnes, Karen (2006). 'Reform or more of the same? Gender mainstreaming in UN peace operations', paper presented at the Annual Convention of the International Studies Association, San Diego.

Bashevkin, Sylvia (1998). *Women on the Defensive: Living Through Conservative Times*, Toronto: Toronto University Press.

—— (2000). 'From tough times to better times: Feminism, public policy and New Labour politics in Britain', *International Political Science Review* 20 (4): 407–424.

Baynes, Sylvia (1991). 'Waiting for the suffragettes', in Maud Cahill and Christine Dann, *Changing Our Lives: Women Working in the Women's Liberation Movement 1970–1990*, Auckland: Bridget Williams Books.

Beddoe, Deirdre (2000). *Out of the Shadows: A History of Women in Twentieth Century Wales*, Cardiff: University of Wales Press.

Beckwith, Karen (2005). 'The comparative politics of women's movements', *Perspectives on Politics* 3 (3): 583–596.

—— (2000). 'Beyond compare? Women's movements in comparative perspective', *European Journal of Political Research* 37: 431–468.

Bergeron, Suzanne (2003). 'The post-Washington consensus and economic representations of women in development at the World Bank', *International Feminist Journal of Politics* 5 (3): 397–419.

Berry, Jeffrey M (1999). *The New Liberalism: The Rising Power of Citizen Groups*. Washington DC: Brookings Institution Press.

Beveridge, Fiona and Sue Nott (2002). 'Mainstreaming: A case for optimism and cynicism', *Feminist Legal Studies* 10 (3): 299–311.

Beveridge, Fiona, Sue Nott and Kylie Stephen (2000). 'Mainstreaming and the engendering of policy-making: A means to an end?' *Journal of European Public Policy* 7 (3): 385–405.

Bielski, Joan (2005). 'Australian feminism 2004: Gains, losses, countervailing forces, some failures and sobering thoughts', *Social Alternatives* 24 (2): 6–10.

Bondi, Liz and Nina Laurie (2005). 'Introduction: Working the Spaces of Neoliberalism', *Antipode* 37(3): 394–401.

Boscoe, Madeline, Gwynne Basen, Ghislaine Alleyne, Barbara Bourrier-Lacroix and Susan White (2004). 'The Women's Health Movement in Canada', *Canadian Women's Studies* 24(1): 7–13.

Bouchard, Pierrette, Isabelle Boily and Marie-Claude Proulx (2003). 'School success by gender: A catalyst for the masculinist discourse', Status of Women Canada (March), at www.swc-cfc.gc.ca/pubs/pubspr/0662882857/index_e.html.

Braidotti, Rosi (1996). 'Cyberfeminism with a Difference' at www.let.uu.nl/womens_studies/rosi/cyberfem.htm.

Brayton, Jennifer (1997). 'Cyberfeminism as New Theory.' At www.unb.ca/web/PAR-L/win/cyberfem.htm.

'Breakfasts celebrate Women's Day' (1995). *Evening Post*, 8 March, p. 3.

Breitenbach, Esther (1989). 'The impact of Thatcherism on women in Scotland', in Alice Brown and David McCrone (eds), *The Scottish Government Yearbook 1989*, Edinburgh: Unit for the Study of Government in Scotland, University of Edinburgh.

—— (2001). 'The Women's Movement in Scotland in the 1990s' in Esther Breitenbach and Fiona Mackay, *Women and Contemporary Scottish Politics: An Anthology*, Edinburgh: Polygon at Edinburgh.

Breitenbach, Esther and Fiona Mackay (2001). 'Keeping gender on the agenda – the role of women's and equal opportunities initiatives in local government in Scotland' in Breitenbach and Mackay *Women and Contemporary Scottish Politics: An Anthology*, Edinburgh: Polygon at Edinburgh.

—— (eds) (2001). *Women and Contemporary Scottish Politics: An Anthology*, Edinburgh: Polygon at Edinburgh.

Breitenbach, Esther, Alice Brown and Fiona Myers (1998). 'Understanding Women in Scotland', *Feminist Review* 58: 44–65.

Breitenbach, Esther, Alice Brown, Fiona Mackay and Janette Webb (eds) (2002). *The Changing Politics of Gender Equality in Britain*, Basingstoke: Palgrave.

Brodie, Janine, Shelley A M Gavigan, and Jane Jenson (1992). *The Politics of Abortion*, Toronto: Oxford University Press.

Broom, Dorothy H (1991). *Damned If We Do*: *Contradictions in Women's Health Care*, North Sydney: Allen & Unwin.

Brown, A (1991). 'Thatcher's legacy for women in Scotland', in *Radical Scotland*, April–May.

—— (2001). 'Deepening democracy: Women and the Scottish parliament' in Esther Breitenbach and Fiona Mackay (eds), *Women and Contemporary Scottish Politics*, Edinburgh: Polygon at Edinburgh.

Brown, Alice, Tahnya Barnett Donaghy, Fiona Mackay, and Elizabeth Meehan (2002). 'Women and constitutional change in Scotland and Northern Ireland', *Parliamentary Affairs* 55(1): 71–84.

Brown, Debra J (no date). *The Challenge of Caring*, Women's Health Bureau, British Columbia Ministry of Health.

Buechler, Steven M (2000). *Social Movements In Advanced Capitalism: The Political Economy and Cultural Construction of Social Activism*, New York: Oxford University Press.

Burgmann, Verity (2003). *Power, Profit and Protest: Australian Social Movements and Globalisation*, Sydney: Allen & Unwin.

Burstein, Paul, Rachel L Einwohner and Jocelyn Holland (1995). 'The Success of Political Movements: A Bargaining Perspective'. In Craig Jenkins and Bert Klandermans (eds), *The Politics of Social Protest: Comparative Perspectives on States and Social Movements*, Minneapolis: University of Minnesota Press.

Byrne, Paul (1996). 'The politics of the Women's Movement', *Parliamentary Affairs* 49 (1): 55–70.

—— (1997). *Social Movements in Britain*, London and New York: Routledge.

Cahill, Maud and Christine Dann (1991). *Changing Our Lives: Women Working in the Women's Liberation Movement 1970–1990*, Auckland: Bridget Williams Books.

—— (1991). 'Introduction', in Maud Cahill and Christine Dann, *Changing Our Lives: Women Working in the Women's Liberation Movement 1970–1990*, Auckland: Bridget Williams Books.

Campo, Natasha (2005). '"Having it all" or "had enough"? Blaming feminism in the *Age* and the *Sydney Morning Herald*, 1980–2004', *Journal of Australian Studies* 84: 63–72, 236–237.

Canadian Research Alliance for Community Innovation and Networking (2005). Submission to Telecommunications Policy Review Panel, 15 August, University of Toronto: CRACIN.

Canadian Women's Health Network (1999). 'Montréal Health Press may have to stop the presses', *Network* 2 (4) at www.cwhn.ca/network-reseau/index.html.

—— (2002). 'Institute of gender and health: A year in review', *Network* 5 (2/3): 15–16.

—— (2004). 'The Women's Health Bureau', *Network* 6/7 (4/1): 26.

—— (2004). *Annual Report 2003–2004* at www.cwhn.ca/PDF/annual-report200304.pdf.

—— (2005). 'First national Women's Health roundtable and reception on Parliament Hill', *Network* 8 (1/2): 24.

—— (2005a). 'Gearing up for a review of Canada's Women's Health Strategy', *Network* 8 (1/2): 23.

—— (2006). 'CIHR institute of gender and health celebrates five-year anniversary', *Network* 8 (3/4): 24.

—— 'Background', Canadian Women's Health Network, at www.cwhn.ca/about.html.

Carpenter, R Charli (2003). '"Women and children first": Gender, norms, and humanitarian evacuation in the Balkans', *International Organization* 57 (4): 661–694.

Carter, Bridget (2003). 'Marchers find hearty support for maternity unit reopening', *New Zealand Herald*, June 6.

Cederman, Sharyn (1972). 'Consciousness raising', *Broadsheet* 2 (August): 5.

CGS Online (2006). 'Overview of the backlash in Japan', Center for Gender Studies, International Christian University, 23 May. Available at olcs.icu.ac.jp/mt/cgs/e.

Chaney, Paul, Fiona Mackay and Laura McAllister (2007). *Women, Politics and Constitutional Change: The First Years of the National Assembly for Wales*, Cardiff: University of Wales Press.

Chappell, Louise (2002). 'Winding back Australian women's rights: Conventions, contradictions and conflicts', *Australian Journal of Political Science* 37 (3): 475–488.

—— (2002a). *Gendering Government: Feminist Engagement with the State in Australia and Canada*, Vancouver: University of British Columbia Press.

—— (2008). 'Gender mainstreaming in international institutions: Developments at the UN ad hoc tribunals and the international criminal court', in Shirin M Rai and Georgina Waylen (eds). *Global Governance: Feminist Perspectives*, Palgrave.

Checkel, Jeffrey T (2001). 'Why comply? Social learning and European identity change', *International Organization* 55 (3): 553–588.

Chen, Mai (2005). Women's Convention Newsletter, April, Janus Women's Convention Trust.

Childs, Sarah (2004). *New Labour's Women MPs: Women Representing Women*, London and New York: Routledge.

Childs, Sarah and Mona Lena Krook (2006). 'Gender and politics: The state of the art', *Politics* 26 (1): 19–28.

Chin, Mikyung (2000). 'Self-governance, political participation, and the Feminist Movement in South Korea', in Rose J Lee and Cal Clark (eds), *Democracy and the Status of Women in Asia*, London: Lynne Rienner Publisher.

—— (2004). 'Reflections on women's empowerment through local representation in South Korea', *Asian Survey* 44 (2): 295–315.

Cho, Soonkyung (2003). 'Consequences of the entry of the representatives of women's movement organizations into political institutions', *Ildaro*, 15 September, www.ildaro.com.

—— (2004). 'Yet unsolved problems: Discussion on the 17th general election and evaluation of the KWAU's response', presented in the seminar of the 17th General Election and the Women's Movement, 25 May (in Korean).

Cohn, Carol (2004). 'Feminist peacemaking', *Women's Review of Books* 21 (5): 8–9.

—— (2008). 'Mainstreaming gender in UN Security Policy: A path to political transformation?' in Shirin M Rai and Georgina Waylen (eds), *Global, Governance: Feminist Perspectives*, New York: Palgrave Macmillan.

Collins, Simon (2003). 'Dairy giant closes doors on mothers' anti-GM group', *New Zealand Herald*, 2 October.

Coney, Sandra (1993). 'Why the Women's Movement ran out of steam', in Sue Kedgley and Mary Varnham (eds), *Heading Nowhere in a Navy Blue Suit and other Tales from the Feminist Revolution*, Wellington: Daphne Brasell.

—— (1994). *Standing in the Sunshine: A History of New Zealand Women since they Won the Vote*, Auckland: Penguin.

Conway, Janet (2004). *Identity, Place, Knowledge: Social Movements Contesting Globalization*, Black Point, Nova Scotia: Fernwood Publishing.

—— (2006). 'Reinventing emancipation: The world social forum as site for movement-based knowledge production', paper presented at Studies in Political Economy Conference, Toronto.

Cosgrove, Katie (2001). 'No man has the right' in Breitenbach and Mackay (eds), *Women and Contemporary Scottish Politics: An Anthology*, Edinburgh: Polygon at Edinburgh.

Cullen, May and Chris Sinding (1996). 'Changing concepts of women's health – advocating for change', paper developed for the Canada-USA Women's Health Forum, 8–10 August, at www.hwc.ca/canusa.

Curthoys, Jean (1997). *Feminist Amnesia: The Wake of Women's Liberation*, London and New York: Routledge.

Dahlerup, Drude (2004). 'Continuity and waves in the feminist movement – a challenge to social movement theory', in Hilda Rømer Christensen, Beatrice Halsaa, Aino Saarinen (eds), *Crossing Borders. Re-mapping Women's Movements at the Turn of the 21st Century*, Odense: University Press of Southern Denmark.

—— (ed.) (2006). *Women, Quotas, and Politics*, London and New York: Routledge.

Daly, Mary (2005). 'Gender mainstreaming in theory and practice', *Social Politics: International Studies in Gender, State and Society* 12 (1): 433–450.

Dann, Christine (1985). *Up from Under: Women and Liberation in New Zealand*, Wellington: Allen & Unwin.

—— (1991). 'The liberation of women is women's work', in Maud Cahill and Christine Dann, *Changing Our Lives: Women Working in the Women's Liberation Movement 1970–1990*, Auckland: Bridget Williams Books.

della Porta, Donatella (1995). *Social Movements, Political Violence, and the State: A Comparative Analysis of Italy and Germany*, Cambridge and New York: Cambridge University Press.

della Porta, Donnatella and M Diani (1988). *Social Movements: An Introduction*, Oxford: Blackwell.

Devere, Heather and Jane Scott (2003). 'The Women's Movement', in Raymond Miller (ed.), *New Zealand Government and Politics*, Melbourne: Oxford University Press.

Diani, Mario (2000). 'The concept of social movement', in Kate Nash (ed.), *Readings in Contemporary Political Sociology*, Boston: Blackwell Publishers.

Dobrowolsky, Alexandra (2003). 'Shifting states: Women's constitutional organising across time and space' in Lee Ann Banaszak, Karen Beckwith and Dieter Rucht (eds), *Women's Movements Facing the Reconfigured State*, New York: Cambridge University Press.

Domett, Tania and Jacqui True (2005). 'Perspectives: The fight continues for gender equality', *New Zealand Herald*, 5 December.

Donner, Lissa (no date). *Producing a Profile of the Health of Manitoba Women*, The Prairie Women's Health Centre of Excellence.

Drakeford, Mark (1997). *Social Movements and their Supporters: The Green Shirts in England*, Basingstoke: Palgrave Macmillan.

Douglas, Roger (1989). *Unfinished business*, Auckland NZ: Random House New Zealand.

Dryzek, John, David Downes, Christian Hunold, David Schlosberg and Hans-Kristian Hernes (2003). *Green States and Social Movements: Environmentalism in the United States, United Kingdom, Germany, and Norway*, Oxford: Oxford University Press.

Du Plessis, Rosemary and Jane Higgins (1997). 'Feminism' in Raymond Miller (ed.), *New Zealand Politics in Transition*, Auckland: Oxford University Press.

Duncan, Grant (2004). *Society and Politics: New Zealand Social Policy*, Auckland: Pearson Education New Zealand.

Edwards, Julia (1995). *Local Government Women's Committees*, Aldershot: Avebury.

Eisenstein, Hester (1996). *Inside Agitators: Australian Femocrats and the State*, Sydney: Allen & Unwin.

Epstein, Barbara (2001). 'What happened to the Women's Movement?', *Monthly Review* 53 (1): 1–14.

Eschle, Catherine (2001). *Global Democracy, Social Movements, and Feminism*, Boulder Colorado: Westview Press.

Eyerman, Ron and Andrew Jamison (1991). *Social Movements: A Cognitive Approach*, Pennsylvania: Pennsylvania State University Press.

Faludi, Susan (1991). *Backlash: The Undeclared War against American Women*, New York: Crown.

Ferree, Myra Marx (1992). 'The political context of rationality: Rational choice theory and resource mobilization', in Aldon D Morris and Carol McClurg Mueller (eds), *Frontiers in Social Movement Theory*, New Haven: Yale University Press.

Ferree, Myra Marx and Beth Hess (1994). *Controversy and Coalition: The New Feminist Movement across Three Decades of Change*, New York: Maxwell Macmillan International.

Ferree, Myra Marx and Carol McClurg Mueller (2004). 'Feminism and the Women's Movement: A global perspective', in David A Snow, Sarah A Soule and Hanspeter Kriesi (eds), *The Blackwell Companion to Social Movements*, Oxford: Blackwell.

Fitzsimons, Fleur (2005). Janus Women's Convention Newsletter 4 (February): 4.

Franzway, Suzanne, Diane Court, and Robert W Connell (1989). *Staking a Claim: Feminism, Bureaucracy and the State*, Sydney: Allen & Unwin.

Fraser, Nancy (1989). *Unruly Practices: Power, Discourse and Gender in Contemporary Social Theory*, Oxford: Polity.

Freeman, Jo [Joreen] (1972). 'The tyranny of structurelessness', reprinted from *The Second Wave* 2 (1), Glebe, NSW: Words for Women.

Friday, Nancy (1996). *The Power of Beauty*, Harper Collins.

Galligan, Yvonne (2006). 'Women in Northern Ireland's politics: Feminising the armed patriarchy' in Marian Sawer, Manon Tremblay and Linda Trimble (eds), *Representing Women in Parliament: A Comparative Study*, London and New York: Routledge.

Galloway, Alex (1997). 'A report on cyberfeminism', *Switch – Electronic Gender: Art and the Interstic* 9. At switch.sjsu.edu/web/v4n1/alex.html.

Gee, Tony (2002). 'Marchers protest and surgery cuts', *New Zealand Herald*, 5 June.

Gelb, Joyce (1986). 'Feminism in Britain: Politics without power?' in Drude Dahlerup (ed.), *The New Women's Movement: Feminism and Political Power in Europe and the USA*, London: Sage.

—— (1989). *Feminism and Politics: A Comparative Perspective*, Berkeley: University of California Press.

—— (2003). *Gender Policies in Japan and the United States: Comparing Women's Movements, Rights, and Politics*, New York: Palgrave Macmillan.

Gelb, Joyce and Vivien Hart (1999). 'Feminist politics in a hostile environment: Obstacles and opportunities', in Marco Guigni, Doug McAdam, and Charles Tilly (eds), *How Social Movements Matter*, Minneapolis: University of Minnesota Press.

Gillan, Evelyn and Elaine Samson (2000). 'The zero tolerance campaign' in Jalna Hanmer and Catherine Itzin (eds), *Home Truths about Domestic Violence: Feminist Influences on Policy and Practice – A Reader*, London: Routledge.

Glendining, Dana (1996). Women's Studies Association Newsletter 17 (1), Winter.

Goetz, Anne-Marie (ed.) (1995). *Getting Institutions Right for Women*. IDS Bulletin 26, (3), Sussex: IDS.

Goetz, Anne-Marie and Shireen Hassim (eds) (2003). *No Shortcuts to Power: African Women in Politics and Policy Making*, New York: Zed Books.

Goetz, Anne-Marie and Joanne Sandler (2006). 'Should we swap gender'? Paper presented at the Annual Convention of the International Studies Association, San Diego.

Goffman, Erving (1975). *Frame Analysis: An Essay on Organization of Experience*, Harmondsworth: Penguin Books.

Golic, Jelena (2003). 'Aboriginal women and the Internet report', in Jo Sutton and Scarlett Pollock (eds), *E-Quality for Women*, Womenspace. Ottowa: Womenspace.

Goodwin, Jeff and James M Jasper (1999). 'Caught in a winding, snarling vine: The structural bias of political process theory', *Sociological Forum: Mini-symposium on Social Movements*, 14 (1): 27–54.

Goodwin, Jeff, James M Jasper, and Francesca Polletta (eds) (2001). *Passionate Politics: Emotions and Social Movements*, Chicago: University of Chicago Press.

Gray, Gwendolyn (1991). *Federalism and Health Policy*, Toronto: University of Toronto Press.

—— (1998). 'How Australia came to have a National Women's Health Policy', *International Journal of Health Services* 28 (1): 107–125.

—— (1999). 'Women's Health in a Restructuring State' in Linda Hancock (ed.), *Women, Public Policy and the State*, South Yarra: Macmillan.

Griffin, Gabriele (ed.) (1995). *Feminist Activism in the 1990s*, London: Taylor and Francis.

Haller, Vera (2001). 'Anti feminist ad campaign launched on campus', *Women's E News*, 31 May.

Hamel, Pierre (2000). 'The fragmentation of social movements and social justice', in Pierre Hamel, Henri Lustiger-Thaler and Margit Mayer, *Urban Movements in a Globalising World*, London and New York: Routledge.

Hamel, Pierre, Henri Lustiger-Thaler and Margit Mayer (2000). *Urban Movements in a Globalising World*, London and New York: Routledge.

Hankivsky, Olena (2005). *Women's Health in Canada: Beijing and Beyond*, revised edition, Canadian Women's Health Network, at www.cwhn.ca.

Hannan-Andersson, Carolyn (1995). 'Moving positions forward: Strategies for gender and development cooperation', in Eve Friedlander (ed.) *Look at the World Through Women's Eyes: Plenary Speeches from the NGO Forum, Beijing '95, NGO Forum on Women, Beijing '95*, New York: United Nations.

Hara, Hiroko (2005). 'Challenges of women for women, against women in Japan', paper from *Women's Worlds 2005: The 9th International Interdisciplinary Congress on Women*, 24 June, Seoul: Ewha Woman's University.

Hart, Vivien (2003). 'Redesigning the polity: Europe, women and constitutional politics in the UK', in Alexandra Dobrowolsky and Vivien Hart (eds), *Women Making Constitutions*, Basingstoke: Palgrave.

Hassim, Shireen (2003). 'The gender pact and democratic consolidation: Institutionalizing gender equality in the South African State', *Feminist Studies* 29 (3): 504–528.

Health Canada (1999). *Health Canada's Women's Health Strategy*, Minister of Public Works and Government Services Canada.

Hill, Felicity, Mikele Aboitiz, and Sara Poehlman-Doumbouya (2003). 'Nongovernmental organizations' role in the buildup and implementation of Security Council Resolution 1325', *Signs* 28: 1255–1269.

Hobson, Barbara (1999). 'Women's collective agency, power resources, and the framing of citizenship rights', in Michael P Hanagan and Charles Tilly, *Extending Citizenship, Reconfiguring States*, Lanham MD: Rowman & Littlefield Publishers Inc.

Holston, James (2001). 'Urban citizenship and globalization', in A Scott (ed.), *Global City-Regions*, Oxford: Oxford University Press.

Hooks, bell (1986). 'All quiet on the feminist front: Backlash against feminism', *Art Forum International*, December.

Hughes, Donna (2002). 'The use of new communication and information technologies for sexual exploitation of women and children', *Hastings Women's Law Journal* 13 (1): 129–148.

Hyman, Prue (1994). 'New Zealand since 1984: Economic restructuring – feminist responses, activity and theory', *Hecate* 20 (2): 9–36.

—— (2000). 'Hui Raranga Wahine/New Zealand Women's Studies Association Conference', in *Women's Studies Association (NZ) Newsletter* 20 (3): 6–8.

Inglehart, Ronald and Pippa Norris (2003). *Rising Tide: Gender Equality and Cultural Change Around the World*, Cambridge: Cambridge University Press.

James, Colin (2000). 'Breaking glass?'. *Far Eastern Economic Review*, 28 Sept.

Janus Trust (2006), 'Annual Report of the Janus Looking Back. Moving Forward Trust'. Presented by the Chairperson, Hon Margaret Shields, Wellington.

Janus Women's Convention (2005). *Newsletter*, February, New Zealand.

Jasper, James (1997). *The Art of Moral Protest: Culture, Biography and Creativity in Social Movements*, Chicago: University of Chicago Press.

Jennett, Christine and Randall Stewart (eds) (1989). *Politics of the Future: The Role of Social Movements*, Sydney: Macmillan.

Joachim, Jutta (2003). 'Framing issues and seizing opportunities: The UN, NGOs, and Women's Rights', *International Studies Quarterly* 47 (2): 247–274.

Jones, Nicola Anne (2003). *Mainstreaming Gender: South Korean Women's Civic Alliances and Institutional Strategies, 1987–2002*, PhD Thesis, University of North Carolina at Chapel Hill.

Julian, Rae (1991). 'Blinding revelation or dawning awareness?', in Maud Cahill and Christine Dann, *Changing Our Lives: Women Working in the Women's Liberation Movement 1970–1990*, Auckland: Bridget Williams Books.

Jung, Kyungja (2002). *Constitution and Maintenance of Feminist Practice: A Comparative Study on Sexual Assault Centres in Korea and Australia*, PhD Thesis, University of New South Wales.

—— (2004). 'The institutionalization of the Women's Movement: The case of Australia', paper to Korean Women's Institute, Ewha Woman's University, 13 Jan (in Korean).

Kapiti Women's Centre (2005). Newsletter, June, at www.kapitiwomenscentre.org.nz.

Kaplan, Gisela (1996). *The Meagre Harvest: The Australian Women's Movement 1950s–1990s*, St Leonards: Allen & Unwin.

Katzenstein, Mary Fainsod (1987). 'Comparing Women's Movements of the United States and Western Europe: An Overview', in M Katzenstein and C Mueller (eds), *The Women's Movements of the United States and Western Europe: Consciousness, Political Opportunities and Public Policy*, Philadelphia: Temple University Press.

—— (1998). *Faithful and Fearless: Moving Feminism into the Church and the Military*, Princeton: Princeton University Press.

Katzenstein, Mary Fainsod and Carol McClurg Mueller (1987). *The Women's Movements of the United States and Western Europe*, Philadelphia: Temple University Press.

—— (1990). 'Feminism within American institutions: Unobtrusive mobilisation in the 1980s', *Signs: Journal of Women in Culture and Society* 16: 27–54.

Keating, Michael (2005). *The Government of Scotland*, Edinburgh: Edinburgh University Press.

Keck, Margaret E and Kathryn Sikkink (1998). *Activists Beyond Borders: Advocacy Networks in International Politics*, Ithaca: Cornell University Press.

Kelly, Andrew (2005). 'Rural women battle on home front', *Dominion Post*, 3 December, p. 2.

Kenway, J (1992). 'Feminist Theories of the State: To be or not to be?' in Michael Muetzelfeldt (ed.), *Society, State and Politics*, Leichhardt, New South Wales: Pluto.

Keohane, Robert O (2003). 'Global governance and democratic accountability', in David Held and Daniela Archibugi (eds), *Taming Globalization: Frontiers of Governance*, London: Polity.

Kim, Kyonghee (2002). 'A frame analysis of women's policies of Korean government and women's movement in the 1980s and 1990s', *Korea Journal* 42 (2): 5–36.

Kim, Yanghee, Young-Ock Kim, Yeong-Ran Park and Eun-Hee Kim (2002). *A Feasibility Study for Building Korean Gender Management System*, Seoul: KWDI & UNDP.

Klodawsky, Fran and Caroline Andrew (2006). 'A city for all women initiatives', paper presented at the Studies in Political Economy Conference, Toronto.

Korean Women's Association United (1999). *Workshop for Evaluation of Women's Policy in the Kim Dae Jung Government and Policy Suggestion*, Seoul: Korean Association United (in Korean).

Kriesi, Hanspeter (1996). 'The organizational structure of new social movements in a political context', in D McAdam, J D McCarthy and M N Zald (eds), *Comparative Perspectives on Social Movements*, New York: Cambridge University Press.

Kriesi, Hanspeter, Ruud Koopmans, Jan Willem Duyvendak and Marco G Giugni (1995). *New Social Movements in Western Europe: A Comparative Analysis*, Minneapolis: University of Minnesota Press.

Kronsell, Annica (2006). 'Studying silences on gender in institutions of hegemonic masculinity', in Brooke Ackerly, Maria Stern and Jacqui True (eds), *Feminist Methodologies for International Relations*, Cambridge: Cambridge University Press.

Krook, Mona Lena (2004). 'Gender quotas as a global phenomenon: Actors and strategies in quota adoption', *European Political Science* 3 (3): 59–65.

—— (2005). *Politicizing Representation: Campaigns for Gender Quotas Worldwide*, PhD Dissertation, Columbia University, New York.

—— (2006). 'Reforming representation: The diffusion of candidate gender quotas worldwide', *Politics & Gender* 2 (3): 303–327.

—— (2007). 'Candidate gender quotas: A framework for analysis', *European Journal of Political Research* 46 (3): 367–394.

Lake, Marilyn (1999). *Getting Equal: The History of Australian Feminism*, Sydney: Allen & Unwin.

Lang, Sabine (1997). 'The NGOization of feminism', in Joan W Scott, Cora Kaplan and Deborah Keates (eds), *Transitions, Environments, Translations: Feminisms in International Politics*, London and New York: Routledge.

—— (2005). 'Framing the Beast? Transnational women's networks and gender mainstreaming in the European Union', paper presented at the Annual Meeting of the International Studies Association, Honolulu.

Larana, Enrique, Hank Johnston, and Joseph R Gusfield (eds). (1994). *New Social Movements: From Ideology to Identity*. Philadelphia: Temple University Press.

Larner, Wendy and David Craig (2005). 'After Neoliberalism? Community activism and local partnerships in Aotearoa New Zealand', *Antipode* 37 (3): 402–424.

Larner, Wendy and Richard Le Heron (2002). 'The spaces and subjects of a globalising economy: Towards a situated method', *Environment and Planning D: Society and Space* 20 (6): 753–774.

Lawrence, Elizabeth and Nicholas Turner (1999). 'Social movements and equal opportunities work', in Paul Bagguley and Jeff Hearn (eds), *Transforming Politics: Power and Resistance*, London: Macmillan.

Legget, Chris (2005). 'Out of the kitchen and into the fire', *Salient* 21, Victoria University of Wellington Student Association.

Legro, Jeffrey W (1997). 'Which norms matter? Revisiting the "failure" of internationalism', *International Organization* 51 (1): 31–63.

Levy, Ariel (2006). *Female Chauvinist Pigs: Women and the Rise of Raunch Culture*, Pocket Books.

Lister, Ruth (2003). *Citizenship: Feminist Perspectives*, Basingstoke: Palgrave, 2nd Edn.

Lovenduski, Joni (1995). 'An emerging advocate: The Equal Opportunities Commission in Great Britain', in Dorothy McBride Stetson and Amy G Mazur (eds), *Comparative State Feminism*, Thousand Oaks CA: Sage.

—— (2005). *Feminizing Politics*, Cambridge: Polity.

—— (ed.) (2005). *State Feminism and Political Representation*, Cambridge: Cambridge University Press.

Lovenduski, Joni and Vicky Randall (1993). *Contemporary Feminist Politics*, Oxford: Oxford University Press.

McAdam, Doug and Dieter Rucht (1993). 'The cross-national diffusion of movement ideas', *Annals of the American Academy of Political and Social Science* 528: 56–74.

McAdam, Doug, John D McCarthy, Meyer N Zald (eds) (1996). *Comparative Perspectives on Social Movements: Political Opportunities, Mobilizing Structures, and Cultural Framings*. Cambridge/New York/Melbourne: Cambridge University Press.

McAdam, Doug, Robert J Sampson, Simon Weffer, and Heather MacIndoe (2005). ' "There will be fighting in the streets": The distorting lens of social movement theory', *Mobilization* 10(1): 1–18.

McCarthy, John D (1996). 'Constraints and Opportunities in Adopting, Adapting, and Inventing', in Doug McAdam, John D. McCarthy and Mayer N. Zald (eds), *Comparative Perspectives on Social Movements: Political Opportunities, Mobilizing Structures, and Cultural Framings*, New York: Cambridge University Press.

Mackay, Fiona (2001). 'The case of zero tolerance: Women's politics in action?' in Breitenbach, Esther and Fiona Mackay (eds), *Women and Contemporary Scottish Politics: An Anthology*, Edinburgh: Polygon at Edinburgh.

—— (2006). 'The impact of devolution on women's citizenship in Scotland', paper presented at the 20th Congress of the International Political Science Association, Fukuoka.

Mackay, Fiona and Bilton, K (2000/2003). *Learning from Experience: Lessons in Mainstreaming Equal Opportunities*, Edinburgh: Governance of Scotland Forum, University of Edinburgh. (Scottish executive website publication 2003 www.scotland.gov.uk/Publications/2003/05/17105/21750).

Mackay, Fiona, Fiona Myers and Alice Brown (2003). 'Towards a new politics? Women and the constitutional change in Scotland' in Alexandra Dobrowolsky and Vivien Hart (eds), *Women Making Constitutions*, New York: Palgrave Macmillan.

McVeigh, Rory and David Sikkink (2001). 'God, politics, and protest: Religious beliefs and the legitimation of contentious tactics', *Social Forces* 79 (4): 1425–1458.

Maddison, Sarah (2004). '"A part of living feminism": Intergenerational feminism in a working class area', *Journal of Interdisciplinary Gender Studies*, special issue on 'Feminist and Women's Organisations and Networks', 8 (1&2).

—— (2004). 'Young women in the Australian women's movement: Collective identity and discursive politics', *International Feminist Journal of Politics*, 6 (2): 234–256.

—— (2007). 'Feminist perspectives on social movement research', in Sharlene Nagy Hesse-Biber (ed.), *Handbook of Feminist Research: Theory and Praxis*, Thousand Oaks, CA: Sage Publications.

Maddison, Sarah and Richard Denniss (2005). 'Democratic constraint and embrace: Implications for progressive non-government advocacy organisations in Australia', *Australian Journal of Political Science* 40 (3): 373–389.

Magarey, Susan (2004). 'The Sex Discrimination Act 1984', *Australian Feminist Law Journal*, 20 (June): 127–134.

Mann, Patricia (1997). 'Musing as a feminist in a postfeminist era' in Jodi Dean (ed.), *Feminism and the New Democracy*, London: Sage.

Mansbridge, Jane (1995). 'What is the Feminist Movement', in Myra Marx Ferree and Patricia Y Martin (eds), *Feminist Organisations: Harvest of the New Women's Movements*, Philadelphia: Temple University Press.

—— (1999). 'Should Blacks represent Blacks and women represent women? A contingent yes', *Journal of Politics* 6 (3): 628–657.

—— (forthcoming). *Everyday Feminism*, Chicago University Press: Chicago.

Marsh, Ian (2002). 'Interest groups', in John Summers, Dennis Woodward and Andrew Parkin (eds), *Government, Politics, Power and Policy in Australia*, 7th edition NSW: Pearson Education Australia.

Massey, Doreen (1994). *Space, Place, and Gender*, Minneapolis: University of Minnesota Press.

Masson, Dominique (1992). 'Language, power and politics: Revisiting the symbolic power of movements', in William K Carroll (ed.), *Organizing Dissent: Contemporary Social Movements in Theory and Practice*, Toronto: Grammond Press.

—— (2006). 'Engaging with the politics of downward rescaling: Representing women in regional development policymaking in Quebec (Canada)' *GeoJournal* 65 (4): 301–313.

Meehan, Elizabeth and Evelyn Collins (1996). 'Women, The European Union and Britain', *Parliamentary Affairs* 49 (1): 221–234.

Melucci, Alberto (1985). 'The symbolic challenge of contemporary movements', *Social Research* 52 (4): 789–816.

—— (1989). *Nomads of the Present: Social Movements and Individual Needs in Contemporary Society*, London: Hutchinson Radius.

—— (1996). *Challenging Codes: Collective Action in the Information Age*, Cambridge: Cambridge University Press.

Mercier, Edith (1991). 'Self-Help Liberation: The Dunedin Collective for Women', in Maud Cahill and Christine Dann, *Changing Our Lives: Women Working in the Women's Liberation Movement 1970–1990*, Auckland: Bridget Williams Books.

Mercier, Fern (1991). 'An Odyssey', in Maud Cahill and Christine Dann, *Changing Our Lives: Women Working in the Women's Liberation Movement 1970–1990*, Auckland: Bridget Williams Books.

Meyer, David S (2004). 'Protest and political opportunities', *Annual Review of Sociology* 30: 125–145.

Meyer, David S and Suzanne Staggenborg (1996). 'Movements, countermovements, and the structure of political opportunity', *American Journal of Sociology* 101 (6): 1628–1660.

Meyer, David S and Sidney Tarrow (eds) (1998). *The Social Movement Society*, Rowman and Littlefield.

Michaud, Anne (2002). *Women's Safety: From Dependence to Autonomy*, Comité d'Action Femmes et Securité Urbaine.

Mintrom, Michael and Jacqui True (2004). *Framework for the Future: Equal Opportunities in New Zealand*, Wellington: Human Rights Commission.

Morris, Barbara (1973). 'True confessions: Why I joined Auckland women's liberation' *Broadsheet* 11 (July): 9.

Munro, Isobel (2002). 'More reflections', *Women's Studies Association (NZ) Newsletter* 23(2): 8.

NARAL Pro-Choice America Profile, at profile.myspace.com/index.cfm?fuseaction=user. viewprofile&friendid=92607334 accessed January 2008.

Nash, Kate (2002). 'A movement moves … is there a women's movement in England today?', *The European Journal of Women's Studies* 9 (3): 311–328.

National Council of Women (2006) 'What we do' at www.newnz.co.nz accessed 19 June 2006.

National Women's Law Center (2004). *Slip Sliding Away: The Erosion of Hard-Won Gains for Women Under the Bush Administration and an Agenda for Moving Forward*, Washington DC.

New Zealand Press Association (1999). 'Beef hurled in catwalk protest', *Press*, 4 October, p. 9.

O'Connor, Teresa (2003). 'Women's movement still needed', *Nelson Mail*, 20 May.

Onishi, Norimitsu (2007). 'Abe rejects Japan's files on war sex', *New York Times*, 2 March.

O'Regan, Mary (1991). 'Radicalised by the system', in Maud Cahill and Christine Dann, *Changing Our Lives: Women Working in the Women's Liberation Movement 1970–1990*, Auckland: Bridget Williams Books.

O'Regan, Mary with Mary Varnham (1992). 'Daring or deluded: a case study in feminist management', in Rosemary Du Plessis with Phillida Bunkle, Kathy Irwin, Alison Laurie and Sue Middleton (eds), *Feminist Voices: Women's Studies Texts for Aotearoa/New Zealand*, Auckland: University of Auckland Press.

Offe, Claus (1990). 'Reflections on the institutional self-transformation of movement politics: A tentative stage model', in Russell J Dalton and Manfred Kuechler (eds). *Challenging the Political Order: New Social Movements in Western Democracies*, Cambridge: Polity.

Oliver, Pamela E, Jorge Cadena-Roa and Kelley D Strawn (2002). 'Emerging trends in the study of protest and social movements', in Betty A Dobratz, Timothy Buzzell, and Lisa K Waldner (eds), *Research in Political Sociology*, Volume 11, JAI Press, Inc.

Phillips, Anne (1999). *Which Equalities Matter?* Malden: Polity Press.

Pigeon, Nicole (2003). 'Francophone women's groups in minority situations', in Jo Sutton and Scarlett Pollock (eds), *E-Quality for Women*, Ottawa: Womenspace. Available at www.womenspace.ca/equality_book/EnglishEqualityBook.htm.

Pollack, Mark A and Emilie Hafner-Burton (2002). 'Mainstreaming gender in global governance', *European Journal of International Relations* 8 (3): 339–373.

Polletta, Francesca and Edwin Amenta (2001). 'Second that emotion? Lessons from once-novel concepts in social movement research', in Jeff Goodwin, James M Jasper, and Francesca Polletta (eds), *Passionate Politics: Emotions and Social Movements*, Chicago: The University of Chicago Press.

Pollitt, Katha (2001). 'Feminism and women', *Nation*, 25 June.

Pollock, Scarlett (2003). 'Web strategies for equality', in *E-quality for Women*, Womenspace, at womynsvoices.ca/en/node/323.

Pollock, Scarlett and Jo Sutton (2003). *'Women and the Internet: Participation, Impact, Empowerment and Strategies*, Womenspace Consultation Report, Ottawa: Womenspace.

Preddey, Elspeth (2003). *The WEL Herstory*, Wellington: WEL New Zealand and Fraser Books.

Pringle, Judith with Heather Carpenter, Tina Fitchett, Angela Heising, Megan Somerville, Margaret Turnball, and Sharon Collins (1997). 'Women-run organisations: Doing it our way', *Broadsheet*, Issue 213, Autumn 1997.

Prugl, Elisabeth (2007). 'Gender and EU Politics', in K E Jorgenson, Mark A Pollack, and Ben Rosamund, *The Handbook of European Union Politics*, Oxford: Oxford University Press.

—— (2008). 'From equal rights to gender mainstreaming: Feminist politics in German agriculture', in Shirin M Rai and Georgina Waylen (eds), *Global Governance: Feminist Perspectives*, Houndsmill, Basingstoke: Palgrave Macmillan.

Prugl, Elisabeth and Audrey Lustgarten (2006). 'The institutional road towards equality: Mainstreaming gender in international organisations', in Jane Jaquette and Gayle Summerfield (eds), *Women and Gender Equity in Development Theory and Practice: Institutions, Resources, and Mobilization*, Chapel Hill: Duke University Press.

Purkarthhofer, Petra (2006). 'Gender and gender mainstreaming in international peace-building', paper presented at the Annual Convention of the International Studies Association, San Diego, March.

Rahmani, Lagan (2005). *Gender Mainstreaming in the United Nations Human Rights Treaty Bodies*. PhD Thesis, University of Sydney.

Rai, Shirin M (ed.) (2003). *Mainstreaming Gender, Democratizing the State? Institutional Mechanisms for the Advancement of Women*. Manchester: Manchester University Press.

Rankin, L Pauline and Jill Vickers (2001). *Women's Movements and State Feminism: Integrating Diversity in the Public Policy*, Status of Women Canada at www.swc-cfc.gc.ca.

Ray, Raka (1999). *Fields of Protest: Women's Movements in India*, Minneapolis: University of Minnesota Press.

Rees, Teresa (1998). *Mainstreaming Equality in the European Union*, London and New York: Routledge.

Reger, Jo (ed.) (2005). *Different Wavelengths: Studies of the Contemporary Women's Movement*, London and New York: Routledge.

Reger, Jo and Verta Taylor (2002). 'Women's movement research and social movement theory: A symbiotic relationship', in Betty Dobratz, Timothy Buzzell and Lisa Waldner (eds), *Sociological Views on Political Participation in the 21st-Century*, 10: 85–121.

Rehn, Elizabeth and Ellen Johnson-Sirleaf (2002). *Women, War, Peace: The Independent Experts' Assessment on the Impact of Armed Conflict on Women and Women's Role in Peace-building*, New York: UNIFEM.

Reid, Elizabeth (1987). 'The child of our movement: A movement of women', in Jocelynne Scutt (ed.), *Different Lives: Reflections on the Women's Movement and Visions of its Future*, Ringwood, Vic: Penguin.

Richards, Amy and Marianne Schnall (2003). 'Cyberfeminism: Networking on the Net', in Robin Morgan (ed.), *Sisterhood is Forever: The Women's Anthology for a New Millenium*, Washington: Washington Square Press. Also at www.feminist.com/resources/artspeech/genwom/cyberfeminism.html.

Rincker, Margaret Eileen (2006). *Women's Access to the Decentralized State*, Ph.D. Thesis, Washington University in St Louis.

Roseneil, Sasha (1995). *Disarming Patriarchy: Feminism and Political Action at Greenham Common*, Milton Keynes: Open University Press.

Rowbotham, Sheila (1989). *The Past is Before Us: Feminist Politics in Action since the 1960s*, London: Pandora.

Rowe, CJ (2003). 'Digital voyeurism: A new age for peeping toms', Ottawa: Womenspace.

—— (2006). 'Stalking meets the Internet', Ottawa: Womenspace.

—— (2006). 'Father's rights groups & the backlash against feminists in the online world', Ottawa: Womenspace.

Rowland, Robyn (ed.) (1984). *Women Who Do and Women Who Don't Join the Women's Movement*, London/Boston/Melbourne/Henley: Routledge and Kegan Paul.

Rucht, Dieter (2003). 'Interactions between social movements and state in comparative perspective', in Lee Ann Banaszak, Karen Beckwith and Dieter Rucht (eds), *Women's Movements Facing the Reconfigured State*, New York: Cambridge University Press.

Rupp, Leila J (1997). *Worlds of Women: The Making of an International Women's Movement*, Princeton, NJ: Princeton University Press.

Rupp, Leila J and Verta Taylor (1987). *Survival in the Doldrums: The American Women's Rights Movement, 1945 to the 1960s*, Oxford: Oxford University Press.

Rural Women (2006). 'About RWNZ' at www.ruralwomen.org/ accessed 6 June, 2006.

Russell, Meg (2005). *Building New Labour: The Politics of Party Organization*, New York: Palgrave.

Russell, Meg, Fiona Mackay and Laura McAllister (2002). 'Women's representation in the Scottish Parliament and the National Assembly for Wales: Party dynamics for achieving critical mass', *Journal of Legislative Studies* 8 (2): 49–76.

Ryan, Susan (1999). *Catching the Waves: Life In and Out of Politics*, Sydney: Harper Collins.

Samson, Alan (1995). 'French ban women's protest', *Dominion Post*, 5 October, p. 2.

Sandercock, Leonie (2003). *Cosmopolis II: Mongrel Cities of the 21st Century*, New York: Continuum Books.

Sawer, Marian (1990). *Sisters in Suits: Women and Public Policy in Australia*, Sydney: Allen & Unwin.

—— (1993). 'Feminism and the state', in *Refracting Voices: Feminist perspectives from Refractory Girl, 44–45*. Sydney: Southwood Press.

—— (1996). *Femocrats and Ecorats: Women's Policy Machinery in Australia, Canada and New Zealand*, Occasional Paper No. 6. Geneva: United Nations Research Institute for Social Development.

—— (2003). *The Ethical State? Social Liberalism in Australia*, Melbourne: Melbourne University Press.

—— (2006). 'From women's interests to special interests: Reframing equality claims', in Louise Chappell and Lisa Hill (eds), *The Politics of Women's Interests*, London and New York: Routledge.

—— (2007). 'Australia: The fall of the femocrat', in Joyce Outshoorn and Johanna Kantola (eds), *Changing State Feminism*, Houndmills, UK: Palgrave Macmillan.

—— (2007). 'Wearing your politics on your sleeve: The role of colours in social movements', *Social Movement Studies* 6 (1): 39–56.

—— (2008). *Making Women Count: A History of Women's Electoral Lobby*, Sydney: University of New South Wales Press.

Sawyers, Traci and David Meyer (1999). 'Missed opportunities: Social movement abeyance and public policy', *Social Problems* 46 (2): 187–206.

Scalmer, Sean (2002). *Dissent Events: Protest, The Media and the Political Gimmick in Australia*, Sydney: University of New South Wales Press.

Scottish Partnership on Domestic Abuse (2000). *National Strategy to Address Domestic Abuse in Scotland*, Edinburgh: Scottish Executive.

Segal, Lynne (1999). *Why Feminism? Gender, Psychology, Politics*. Cambridge: Polity Press.

Sen, Gita (2005). *Neolibs, Neocons and Gender Justice: Lessons from Global Negotiations*, Occasional Paper 9, Geneva: United Nations Research Institute for Social Development.

Shannon, Elizabeth (1997). *The Influence of Feminism on Public Policy: Abortion and Equal Pay in Australia and the Republic of Ireland*. PhD Thesis, Hobart, University of Tasmania.

Smith, Jackie (1997). 'Characteristics of the modern transnational social movement sector', in Jackie Smith, Charles Chatfield, and Ron Pagnucco (eds), *Transnational Social Movements and Global Politics: Solidarity Beyond the State*, Syracuse: Syracuse University Press.

Somerville, Jennifer (1997). 'Social movement theory, women and the question of interests', *Sociology* 31: 73–95.

Spees, Pamela (2003). 'Women's advocacy in the creation of the International Criminal Court: Changing landscapes of justice and power', *Signs: Journal of Women and Culture* 28 (4): 1233–1256.

Squires, Judith and Mark Wickham-Jones (2004). 'New Labour, gender mainstreaming and the women and equality unit', *British Journal of Politics and International Relations* 6 (1): 81–98.

Stafford, Dorothy (1986) 'Speech at the Inauguration of the Centre for Women's Studies', Christchurch.

Staggenborg, Suzanne (2001). 'Beyond culture versus politics', *Gender & Society* 15 (4): 507–530.

Staggenborg, Suzanne and Verta Taylor (2005). 'Whatever Happened to the Women's Movement?', *Mobilization* 10 (1): 37–52.

Stanley, Liz and Sue Wise (1990). 'Method, methodology and epistemology in feminist research processes', in Liz Stanley (ed.), *Feminist Praxis: Research, Theory and Epistemology in Feminist Sociology*, London and New York: Routledge.

Stevens, Joyce (1995). *Healing Women – A History of Leichhardt Women's Health Centre*, Newtown, NSW: First Ten Years History Project.

Stokes, Wendy (2003). 'The UK Women's National Commission' in Shirin Rai (ed.), *Mainstreaming Gender, Democratizing the State*, Manchester: Manchester University Press.

Strang, David and John W Meyer (1993). 'Institutional conditions for diffusion', *Theory and Society* 22 (4): 487–511.

Stratigaki, Maria (2005) 'Gender mainstreaming vs positive action: An ongoing conflict in EU gender equality policy', *European Journal of Women's Studies* 12(2): 165–186.

Summers, Anne (1993). 'Letter to the next generation', in *Refracting Voices: Feminist perspectives from Refractory Girl*, Sydney: Southwood Press.

—— (1999). *Ducks on the Pond*, Ringwood, Vic: Penguin.

—— (2003). *The End of Equality: Work, Babies and Women's Choices in 21st Century Australia*, Sydney: Random House.

Tarrow, Sidney (1995). 'Cycles of collective action: Between moments of madness and the repertoire of contention', in Mark Traugott (ed.), *Repertoires and Cycles of Collective Action*, Durham & London: Duke University Press.

—— (1996). *Power in Movement: Social Movements, Collective Action and Politics*, Cambridge: Cambridge University Press.

—— (1999). 'Paradigm warriors: Regress and progress in the study of contentious politics', *Sociological Forum* 14 (1): 71–77.

Taylor, Verta (1989). 'Sources of continuity in social movement: The Women's Movement in abeyance', *American Sociological Review* 54 (5): 761–775.

—— (1997). 'Social movement continuity: The Women's Movement in abeyance' in Doug McAdam and David A Snow (eds), *Social Movements: Readings on their Emergence, Mobilization and Dynamics*, Los Angeles: Roxbury.

—— (2000). 'Mobilizing for change in a social movement society', *Contemporary Sociology* 29 (1): 219–231.

Taylor, Verta and Nancy Whittier (1995). 'Analytical approaches to social movement culture: The US Women's Movement' in Hank Johnston and Bert Klandermans (eds), *Social Movements and Culture*, Minneapolis: University of Minnesota Press.

—— (1997). 'The new feminist movement' in Laurel Richardson, Verta Taylor and Nancy Whittier (eds), *Feminist Frontiers IV*, New York: Mcgraw Hill.

Teghtsoonian, Katherine (2004). 'Neoliberalism and gender analysis mainstreaming in Aotearoa/New Zealand', *Australian Journal of Political Science* 39 (2): 267–284.

Tilly, Charles (1978). *From Mobilization to Revolution*, Reading, MA: Addison-Wesley Publishing Co.

—— (1984). *Big Structures, Large Processes, Huge Comparisons*, New York: Russell Sage Foundation.

Towns, Ann E (2004). *Norms and Equality in International Society: Global Politics of Women and the State*, PhD Thesis, University of Minnesota.

Tripp, Aili Mari (2004). 'Transnational feminism and political representation in Africa', paper presented at the American Political Science Association Annual Meeting, Chicago.

True, Jacqui (2003). 'Mainstreaming gender in global public policy', *International Feminist Journal of Politics* 5 (3): 368–396.

—— (2007). 'Gender mainstreaming and regional trade governance in Asia-Pacific Economic Cooperation (APEC)', in Shirin Rai and Georgina Waylen (eds), *Gender, Governance and Globalisation*, New York: Palgrave.

True, Jacqui and Michael Mintrom (2001). 'Transnational networks and policy diffusion: The case of gender mainstreaming', *International Studies Quarterly* 45 (1): 27–57.

United Nations Department of Peacekeeping Operations (DPKO) (2005). Gender Mainstreaming in Peacekeeping Operations Progress Report. New York: United Nations.

United Nations Secretary-General (2002). *Women, Peace and Security*, Study Submitted by Secretary-General pursuant to the Security Council Resolution 1325 (2000). New York: United Nations.

Van Dyke, Nella, Sarah A Soule and Verta Taylor (2004). 'The targets of social movements: Beyond a focus on the state', *Research in Social Movements, Conflicts and Change*, 25:27–51.

Vancouver Women's Health Collective (2004). 'Outreach and activism' at www.womenshealthcollective.ca/whats_new.htm.

Verloo, Mieke (2005). 'Displacement and empowerment: Reflections on the concept and practice of the Council of Europe approach to gender mainstreaming and gender equality', *Social Politics: International Studies in Gender, State and Society* 12 (1): 344–365.

Vézina, Ghislaine (2005). *Initiatives Municipales Prenant en Considération les Interets Particuliers des Femmes*, Gouvernement du Québec, Ministère des Affaires Municiples et Régions.

Walby, Sylvia (1997). *Gender Transformations*, London and New York: Routledge.

—— (1999). 'The new regulatory state: The social powers of the European Union', *British Journal of Sociology* 50 (1): 118–140.

—— (2002). 'Feminism in a global era', *Economy and Society* 31 (4): 533–557.

Walter, Natasha (1998). *The New Feminism*, London: Little Brown.

Wandor, Michelle (ed.) (1990). *Once A Feminist*, London: Virago.

Warrington, Molly (2003). 'Fleeing from fear: The changing role of refuges in meeting the needs of women leaving violent partners', *Capital and Class* 80: 123–150.

Warwick, Alex and Rosemary Auchmuty (1995). 'Women's studies as feminist activism', in Gabriele Griffin (ed.), *Feminist Activism in the 1990s*, London: Taylor & Francis.

Weldon, Laurel (2002). *Protest, Policy and the Problem of Violence against Women: A Cross-national Comparison*, Pittsburgh: University of Pittsburgh Press.

—— (2002a). 'Beyond bodies: Institutional sources of representation for women in democratic policymaking', *Journal of Politics* 64 (4): 1153–1174.

—— (2006). 'Inclusion, solidarity, and social movements: The global movement against gender violence', *Perspectives on Politics* 4 (1): 55–74.

Whittier, Nancy (1995). *Feminist Generations: The Persistence of the Radical Women's Movement*, Philadelphia: Temple University Press.

Whitzman, Carolyn (2002). 'The "voice of women" in Canadian local government', in Caroline Andrew, Katherine Graham and Susan Phillips (eds), *Urban Affairs: Back on the Policy Agenda*, Montreal and Kingston: Queens University Press.

—— (2006). 'Women and community safety', *Women & Environments International Magazine*, 70/71: 24–27.

Whitzman, Carolyn and Marie-Dominique Lahaise (1990). 'London inspires Montreal which inspires Toronto which inspires London…', *Women and the Built Environment* 15/16: 22–23.

Wilding, Faith (no date). 'Where is feminism in cyberfeminism?'. At www.obn.org/ cfundef/faith_def.html.

Wilson, Elizabeth (2004). 'Feminism today', *Hecate* 30 (1): 212–222.

Winnipeg Consultation Organising Committee (1994). *The Strength of Links: Building the Canadian Women's Health Network*, Report of the Canada-Wide Consultation Meeting Held in Winnipeg, Manitoba, May 21–24, and including a 1994 Network Update. Typescript.

Women's Action Centre against Violence (Ottawa-Carleton) (1995). *Safety Audit Tools and Housing: The State of the Art and Implications for CMHC*, Report prepared for Central Mortgage and Housing Corporation.

Women in Cities International (2007). *Building Community-based Partnerships for Local Action on Women's Safety*, at www.femmesetvilles.org.

Women's Health Victoria (2006). *Womenshealthmatters: From Policy to Practice, 10 Point Plan for Victorian Women's Health, 2006–2010*. Typescript.

Women's Studies Association NZ (1995). Women's Studies Association Newsletter 15 (3), Autumn.

—— (1997). Women's Studies Association Newsletter 18 (1), Spring.

—— (1997a). Women's Studies Association Newsletter 18 (2), Summer.

Working Together for Women's Health: A Framework for the Development of Policies and Programs (1990). Prepared by the Canadian Federal/Provincial/Territorial Working Group on Women's Health, with assistance from Anne Rochon Ford.

Yeatman, Anna (1990). *Bureaucrats, Technocrats, Femocrats: Essays on the Contemporary Australian State*, Sydney: Allen & Unwin.

Yoon, Jung Sook (2004). 'Exploring changes in progressive women's movement' *Chang-Jak-Kwa Bi-Pyung* 125: 55–69 (in Korean).

Young, Stacey (1997). *Changing the Wor(l)d: Discourse, Politics and the Feminist Movement*, London and New York: Routledge.

Young Women's Caucus (2005). Janus Women's Convention, 6 June Wellington Town Hall, New Zealand.

Zald, Mayer N and Bert Useem (1987). 'Movement and countermovement interaction: Mobilization, tactics, and state involvement', in Mayer N Zald and John D McCarthy (eds), *Social Movements in an Organizational Society*, New Brunswick, NJ: Transaction Books.

Index

Abdela, Lesley 101
Abe, Shinzo 85
Abe, Toshiko 84, 86, 88n20
abeyance xii–xvi, 2, 5, 9–10, 12, 17–18, 23, 29, 35, 49, 52, 55, 60–1, 65, 75, 121–3, 128
abortion 53–4, 57, 80–2, 87, 146–7, 149
Action Network on Japanese Military Comfort Women 86
Advisory Council on Women's Health, Canada 59
alliances *see* coalition(s)
Amnesty International (Scotland) 154
Annan, Kofi 101
anti-feminist *see* backlash
anti-nuclear movement 21, 70, 154–5, 157n8
anti-state orientation *see* contentious politics
anti-Vietnam War movement 4
Ashcroft, John 80
Asia-Pacific Economic Cooperation (APEC) 91, 98–9, 103; Budget and Management Committee 98–9; Women Leader's Network 99
Auckland Women's Centre (New Zealand) 68, 131

backlash ii, 10, 36, 65, 74, 79, 80–2, 85–7, 152; anti-feminist(s) 81–4, 130; conservative 2, 7, 8, 84–5; countermovements 11, 79, 80, 87, 128; religious 80, 87; right-wing 81–5
Bagguley, Paul 23, 29, 31n36
Banaszak, Lee Ann 29
Bashevkin, Sylvia 20
Basic Law for Gender Equality (Japan) 84
Basic Plan on Women's Development (Korea) 40

battered women's shelters *see* service provision: refuges
Beckwith, Karen 5, 9, 13n31
Beijing: Fourth World Conference on Women 20, 41, 44, 92, 96; Platform for Action 20, 59, 96, 108, 132
Bielski, Joan 38
Boscoe, Madeline 50
British Columbia Rural Women's Network (Canada) 132
Broadsheet (New Zealand) 71
Broom, Dorothy 62
Brown, Alice 26
Bush, George W 80, 81, 87

Cahill, Maud 67, 77n4
Campaign for Nuclear Disarmament 21
Campbell, Kim 149
Canadian Feminists Alliance for International Action 131
Canadian Women's Health Network 51, 58, 60–1
Canberra Women's Health Centre 53
Chappell, Louise 100, 104n41
childcare 20, 27, 94, 154
citizenship 117, 119–22, 148
civic organisations *see* community
civil rights movement xv
claims-making 10–11, 73, 150; comfort women (Japan) 84, 86; equal opportunities in employment 20, 27; equal pay 8, 19, 130–1, 154; family law 40; health 50–1; human potential 148; human rights 91, 96; poverty 25, 44; reproductive rights xii, 50, 52; RU-486 54; sexism 70, 129; sexual violence 152–3; social change xv, 35–7, 50, 51, 62, 67, 79, 127, 130, 156, 157; violence 22, 25, 28, 50, 122, 155

For Product Safety Concerns and Information please contact our EU
representative GPSR@taylorandfrancis.com
Taylor & Francis Verlag GmbH, Kaufingerstraße 24, 80331 München, Germany

www.ingramcontent.com/pod-product-compliance
Lightning Source LLC
Chambersburg PA
CBHW050709280326
41926CB00088B/2888